CW01431052

Central Banking
for Emerging
Market Economies

Dr. A Vasudevan, currently Honorary Advisor in the Reserve Bank of India, was Executive Director of the Reserve Bank between May 1996 and end-August 2000. As the Executive Director, he was in-charge of research, statistics, monetary policy and information technology departments. He has had vast international experience — Advisor to Executive Director for India at the International Monetary Fund (IMF) between 1984 and 1989; Member of the Indian Delegations to semi-annual IMF/World Bank and G-24 meetings between 1984 and 1989 and again between 1993 and 2000; represented India at the UNDP Conference on financing of sustainable development at Santiago, Chile; Central Bank Deputy at the Group of Two Deputies' meetings; and Member of the Task Force on Implementation of Standards and the Follow-up Group on the Implementation of Standards, appointed by the Financial Stability Forum.

Among the several Committees on which he served, the important ones were: Expert Group on Saving and Capital Formation in India, Government of India, 1996 (Member), the Working Group on Money Supply, Reserve Bank, 1998 (Vice-Chairman), and the Committee on Technology Upgradation in Banking Sector, Reserve Bank of India, 1999 (Chairman).

Apart from the present volume (published: 2003, reprinted: 2003), Dr. Vasudevan has edited the newly published book *Money and Banking : Select Research Papers by the Economists of Reserve Bank of India* (Academic Foundation, 2003). Having authored/edited a few other books earlier, Dr. Vasudevan has numerous scholarly writings of his own in various professional journals, both Indian and foreign. He also taught M.A. students at the University of Bombay between 1966-69 on the theories of money and economic development and central banking.

Currently Dr. Vasudevan is engaged in writing the history of Reserve Bank of India — a task he has been entrusted with by a committee of the central bank, chaired by Dr. C. Rangarajan.

Central Banking for Emerging Market Economies

A. Vasudevan

AF

ACADEMIC FOUNDATION

NEW DELHI

Reprint: 2003

First Published in 2003 by
ACADEMIC FOUNDATION
4772-73 / 23 Bharat Ram Road,
(23 Ansari Road), Darya Ganj,
New Delhi - 110 002.

Phones : 23245001, 02, 03, 04.
Fax : 011-23245005
e-mail : academic@vsnl.com
www : academicfoundation.com

Copyright : Academic Foundation. © 2003.

All rights reserved. No part of this book shall be reproduced, stored in a retrieval system, or transmitted by any means, electronic, mechanical, photocopying, recording, or otherwise, without written permission from the publishers.

Central Banking for Emerging Market Economies
by A. Vasudevan
ISBN 81-7188-281-1

Laser-Typeset at AF's DTP Division.
Printed at Jeetendra Art Press, Delhi.

$\mathcal{T}_o$

All those who shaped my life
and in particular to

The memory of late Professor Amiya Kumar Dasgupta and late Professor Anand S Raturi and to the scholarly Professor P.R. Brahmananda for nurturing my interest in economics;

My senior colleagues at the Reserve Bank, Messrs V.G. Pendharkar, late V.B. Kadam, and K.L. Deshpande for setting examples of precision in writing and thoroughness in recounting details for younger colleagues like me to follow;

My younger colleagues at the Reserve Bank, Messrs Narendra Jadhav, K. Kanagasabapathy, Deepak Mohanty, Madhusudan Mohanty, Michael Debabrata Patra, Partha Ray, Ranjit Pattnaik, Sitikantha Pattanaik, and Mridul Saggar for the help given in promoting my professional work and for challenging my ways of thinking; and

My wife, Parvathi Vasudevan for quiet encouragement and her understanding of what it takes to be an analytic among policy-makers and a policy-oriented professional among the academics.

Contents

Foreword *11*

Preface *15*

Section I   The Rationale of Central Banking

1. Introduction *21*

- Why Do We Need a Central Bank ?
- The Recent Upsurge of Interest in Central Banking
  — the Reasons For
- The Context of Open/Semi-open Economies
- Why Central Banking for Emerging Market Economies ?
- The Indian Context
- Is the Indian Context Unique?

Box 1 : Central Banks by the End of the Twentieth Century

Section II   The Nuts and Bolts of
Central Banking --- Reorientations

2. Currency and Payment System *41*

- Issue and Distribution of Currency
- Printing and Issuance of Notes only by the Central Banks?
- A Service Provider to Issue and Distribute Currency

...Contd....

...Contd....

• Principles of Currency Issue — Any Fiduciary Rules?
• Could there be a Currency Board Instead of Central Bank?
• Payment System Services
• Electronic Money

Box 2 : Real Time Gross Settlement (RTGS) Systems

3. Banker to Government **61**
• Maintenance of Accounts
• Domestic Debt Management
• Conflict of Interests — Debt Management and Monetary Policy
• Sovereign Bond Issues Abroad
• Should There Be a Separate Debt Management Agency ?

Box 3 : Types of Auctioning
Box 4 : On the 'Crowding Out'
Box 5 : Ad hoc Treasury Bills: The Indian Experience

4. Banker to Banks **85**
• The Essential Tasks and the LoLR Function
• Bank Restructuring
• The Areas Where Commercial Banks Could be of Help

Box 6 : Theoretical Perspectives on Adverse Selection

Section III **The Shining Star of Central Banking**

5. Monetary Policy Making in Open/Semi-open Economies **101**
• Objectives of Policy
• Reconciling Dual Objectives through a Policy Rule
• The Taylor Rule

...Contd....

- The Case for Rules As Against Discretion
- The Case for Discretion
- Indicators of Policy
- Lags in Policy
- Instruments of Policy
- Transmission Mechanism of Policy
- An Evaluation of the Channels in the Context of EMEs
- Uncertainties Due to Lags
- Transparency of Policies and Practices

Box 7 : *Liquidity Adjustment Facility in India*

Box 8 : *Bank Reserves, Reserve Money, Money Supply, and Money Multiplier*

Box 9 : *Payments Systems and Monetary Policy*

Section IV The New Concerns

6. Financial Stability *155*

- Financial Stability in the context of Financial Development
- The Early Warning Signals and Hedging Mechanisms
- Liquidity Forecasts
- Prudential Regulation and Supervision of Banks
- The International Initiatives in Evolving Standards and Codes
- Prudent Supervision by Central Banks and Other Agencies or by a Superbody?
- International Dimensions of Financial Stability Issues

Box 10 : *Early Warning Signals of Crisis*

Box 11 : *Risk Management in Banks*

Box 12 : *The Basle Principles for Effective Banking Supervision*

Box 13 : *Key International Standards and Codes*

Box 14 : *The Indian Initiatives in Respect of International Standards and Codes*

...Contd....

7. Autonomy and Organizational Issues *211*

• Issues in Autonomy and Independence of
  Central Banks

• Should Decision Making Processes be
  Left Out of Central Banks?

• Independence, Accountability and
  Central Bank Governance

• Independence in the Context of Implementation of
  International Standards / Codes

8. Conclusions *229*

Attachment :

The Asian Economic Crisis of the 1990s *237*

Select References   *249*

Index   *263*

Foreword

O NE of the great pleasures of my term at the International Monetary Fund in the early eighties was working with — and learning from — Dr. Asuri Vasudevan, our economic adviser from India's Reserve Bank. He displayed a profound knowledge of economics, a remarkable clarity of thinking and a lucid writing style. Having spent his lifetime at the Bank in research on central banking, it is laudable indeed that he has now undertaken to share his vast knowledge with posterity.

Naturally, he writes from the viewpoint of "emerging economies" — those that have unshackled themselves from heavy regulation and are adopting market oriented policies. The central banks in these economies are moving away from the traditional passive role of issuers of money, financiers of government and overlookers of the banking scene and have taken on the new challenges of more transparent domestic policies and of opening to the outside world, which Vasudevan refers to as "internationalisation". Although bankers in the past as financiers of world trade were always linked to each other closely, the new world which we see today is getting so closely integrated, that one wonders how long one could talk of uniquely 'national' policies. Given this global integration, one is never sure of the final impact of policies framed in the national context. We need a deep knowledge of the sweeping assumptions underlying our theoretical constructs, as well as how the markets react, in order to understand and estimate the outcomes of such national policy initiatives. Moreover, markets are considered paramount, necessitating informing the public of the intentions of policy makers, so that markets can function better. Also, central banks are held to be accountable to the public for the achievement of well defined objectives. This "brave new world" is a far cry from the days when central banks emerged out of the chaos that was caused by powerful princess engaging in costly wars of conquest.

In this context, Vasudevan's tantalising voyage through the theory and practice of central banking is a path-breaking and salutary effort. It deserves to be a manual for the modern central banker and those outside who wish to unravel the traditional mystique of monetary or economic policies.

This book is undoubtedly a work of encyclopaedic proportions, which only a master of the subject will dare to undertake. We central bankers owe a deep debt of gratitude for Vasudevan's efforts. Virtually no important aspect of central banking is left out, and there is detailed coverage of recent developments in inflation targeting in monetary policy, management of exchange rates and foreign reserves in volatile foreign currency regimes, handling of external and internal financial crises, adopting more transparent accountancy and reporting standards for governments and financial entities, assessment of soundness of the financial sector, as a whole and as individual institutions, and the enormous responsibilities involved in adopting speedy "real time" payment and settlement systems. The international dimensions of these developments, now that banking has ceased to be a predominantly national enterprise, are well examined, including the nexus with international institutions such as the International Monetary Fund, the World Bank and the Bank for International Settlements. Of course, this is an area of continuous evolution of novel insights and initiatives and the readers will enjoy a good briefing on the emerging issues.

In his preoccupation with the micro and macro economic aspects of finance, Vasudevan touches peripherally on the so-called "development" aspects of central banking, in which India was a pioneer among emerging markets. Whether central banks devote time on developing the financial system, say into rural areas which are thinly banked, has become a matter of debate and those who follow the practice in developed financial markets in concentrating on price stability objective, tend to underplay the significance of the objective of deepening of markets. The tendency for extraneous non-economic factors to influence decisions in development banking has created some disenchantment on this subject even in emerging economies. This matter deserves the incisive analytical skills of Vasudevan in a future edition of this work.

On the whole, Vasudevan's treatise is a delightful read for all who are seriously interested in central banking. I enjoyed the book immensely, as much as I have enjoyed the intellectual prowess of the writer.

A.S. Jayawardena
GOVERNOR
Central Bank of Sri Lanka
Colombo

September 30, 2002.

$\mathcal{P}$*reface*

THIS book has been conceived essentially as a reference book to prepare advanced students of colleges/universities to face policy matters, as well as the officer-staff of central banks and leading commercial bank managements to address the new developments in the analytics of the operational aspects of central banking. These developments have been prominent since about the beginning of the 1970s. But they have altered the face of central banks and the views about the role of central banking in an environment that is marked increasingly by market driven processes and international integration of economies. To understand the developments in true perspective, the readers of this book would need to have sufficient background in economics, in particular monetary economics, and in international finance.

The new waves of thinking were first seen most vividly in the working of central banks in industrial economies. But when winter comes, will spring be far behind ? Central banks in emerging market economies could not afford to lag behind : they in fact have found it necessary to adapt themselves to the changing economic environment, reorient their traditional tasks, and ready themselves to face new challenges and growing economic uncertainties.

The book is not so much about the practices and procedures per se as about the analytical aspects of the issues that confront central bankers in emerging market economies on almost a day-to-day basis. The notion that central bankers make a living by printing notes is old-fashioned and is no longer valid. Nor do central bankers depend solely on their ability to lend to governments or to banks for their upkeep. No doubt they have to take care of payments system and act as bankers to governments and banks. But they do more — much more. They are there to prevent financial failures, and have to be accountable for their actions. This is what democratic societies expect of them.

An explanation about the title of this book is required. The expression, 'emerging market economies' is of recent origin. The traditional classification of countries into 'industrial' and 'developing' economies has been found to be *not* useful for gaining insights about the efforts of the governments and the impulses that drive economic activities in economies that do not fall under the category of industrial economies. Many such economies have in recent years undertaken economic reforms wherein the markets are allowed to play their part for purposes of gaining allocative efficiency. In the process, the economies are exposed to a degree of uncertainty hitherto *not* experienced by them. Central banking *for* such economies has to be dynamic and interactive. It is this thought that prompted me to write this book.

The book has many references to the Indian experience essentially because many of the financial sector reforms in India announced and implemented since about 1992 are a part of the overall strategy of economic liberalization. India is as much an emerging market economy as some of the emerging market economies of East Asia. Now that India has been recognized as a 'systemically important' country by the international financial community and is a member of the Group of Twenty (G-20), its case as an emerging market economy has become

strong. The references to India are in the nature of examples
and clarifications to the arguments advanced in the narrative.
Research workers in other countries and in central banks of
other emerging market economies may find these references
useful for purposes of comparing the Indian experience with
their own. But to make the narrative more general and analytical, I avoided giving too many details about the organizational and other reform issues relating to India.

It is my luck that I could pursue my academic interests while
serving the Reserve Bank of India. This was facilitated by the
fact that I was associated with the economic research department right from the day of my joining the Reserve Bank. It was
also my luck that I spent good many years at academic institutions in India before joining the Reserve Bank, and at the
International Monetary Fund on secondment from the Reserve
Bank. This helped me to hone up my analytical tools and
presentational skills. But it was the years of my association with
the Reserve Bank of India and the International Monetary Fund
that helped me to appreciate the fact that the distinction
between pure theory and operational aspects of central banking is an oversimplified one. In any case, the distinction
cannot be maintained. For, events occur so rapidly that policy
makers at the central banks are hard pressed for time to work
out policy strategies that are theoretically sound. Often they
seek policies that would be perceived to be credible. This is
especially true in countries where markets are growing and in
transition to integration. Markets do not wait endlessly for
central bank actions. Central banks have to therefore act, act
in the living present. The interactive processes that take place
in such a frame are fascinating and are of great educative value.
At least it has been so for me. In these processes with which
I was involved in some capacity or the other between 1991 to
2000, I came across a number of persons within the Reserve
Bank of India and elsewhere from whom I learnt a great deal,
sometimes willingly and sometimes unknowingly, about the
great many dimensions of the problems on hand and the

possible courses that one could take to address them. It has become, therefore, difficult for me to single out my debts to any one person or a group of persons within the Reserve Bank of India in the *writing* of this book. Implicitly, I alone am responsible for the views expressed and for whatever errors that may remain in this book.

I am highly obliged to Mr. A.S. Jayawardena, Governor, Central Bank of Sri Lanka for writing the 'foreword' to this book. Governor Jayawardena's support and friendship over the years have been a rich source of strength for my family and me.

Finally, I sincerely thank the publishers for bringing out the book in quick time and for extending to me the best of courtesies.

A. Vasudevan

Mumbai
October 31, 2002.

Section I

The Rationale of Central Banking

1. Introduction *21*

- Why Do We Need a Central Bank ?
- The Recent Upsurge of Interest in Central Banking — the Reasons For
- The Context of Open/Semi-open Economies
- Why Central Banking for Emerging Market Economies ?
- The Indian Context
- Is the Indian Context Unique?

Box 1 : Central Banks by the End of the Twentieth Century

1

Introduction

Why Do We Need a Central Bank ?

Central banks have been there since the second half of the 17th century and over the years have developed into organizations that are central to not only monetary policy making but also to development and regulation of financial structure. Most modern societies find it difficult to function in an orderly and stable manner without the presence of central banks (or monetary authorities as they are sometimes called) (See **Box 1** at the end of this chapter for the number of such institutions at the end of the 20th century). However, there have been a number of strands of thought that indicate that the need for central banks was not regarded as necessary. There was, for instance, the free banking school during the 19th century which favored banking freed from the presence of a central bank. The main point of the free banking school was shaped by the practical question as to whether "the issue of bank-notes should be monopolized by a 'central bank'", as Sayers argued, and whether banking should be viewed as different from free trade and free competition which are considered as beneficial. The free banking school considered a single bank of issue, often obliged to the government for the privileges it enjoys, to be susceptible to the pressure of short-sighted governments, whereas a number of competing banks of issue would be somewhat elusive and would most likely pursue commercial prudence in the matter of note issues. In other words, discretion on the part of a single bank of issue could be dangerous. Walter Bagehot too favored the refrain of the free banking school, although he did not favor the abandonment of the one-reserve system that was represented by the Bank of England. He argued that credit in business is like 'loyalty in government' and wanted to reform and improve the Bank of England rather than eliminate its supreme position. In his view, the Bank of England was established as the central bank not because it served any useful commercial purpose, but because it was so legislated in reward for its role in 1694 and thereafter, in providing government finance in needy times at favorable terms.

The controversies about central banking versus free banking were most clearly brought out by Vera Smith in the book, *The Rationale of Central Banking*. In more recent years, the writings of Milton Friedman and von Hayek advocated definite rules for central banks that had considerable influence. The essence of their argument is that central banks may not have a role to play if discretion has to play a part. While Friedman thought of a rule for expansion of currency, Hayek went as far as to propose the radical step of allowing and encouraging private note issuers to compete, almost akin to the Bagehot proposal. In this proposal, there would be no central bank and no central reservoir of reserves.

The emergence of the rational expectations school in the 1970s provided a case for central banks to intervene. More recently, writings on central banking have pointed to the need for incentive-oriented contracts and regulation of banks as primordial for achieving the postulated objectives. In this context, the decision-processes in central banks have come under scrutiny and it was felt that in the light of the recent experiences of financial instability and crisis-situations, currency board arrangements could function as alternative to central banking.

At the same time, the European Central Bank model has shown that while monetary policy decision-making processes could be centralized, the operating procedures and mechanisms could be decentralized. But in emerging economies, where the legal structures relating to banking and financial sector are not likely to be robust, the need for a central bank is very substantial, given the strong compulsions for undertaking reform measures to diversify, and develop financial sector and to integrate its different segments.

The Recent Upsurge of Interest in Central Banking — the Reasons for

There has been in recent years, at any rate since the early 1980s, an enormous upsurge of interest in central banking for more than one reason in industrialized as well as developing economies. The factors contributing to the heightened interest are several. They are :

... the growing professionalism of central banks as against the political colors of finance ministries;

... the inability of the financial sector to grow without central bank support;

... the need for financial sector development for fostering growth, one of the objectives of central banks;

... the internationalization of financial markets, making it necessary for an organizational apparatus like the central bank to oversee and take regulatory measures to ensure that the processes of market development are set in place in an efficient manner;

... the flows of funds across borders almost on real time basis, and as payment services are often provided by central banks themselves, such flows would not be possible without central banks not knowing about it;

... the growth of financial innovations having implications

for both liquidity position and rate changes, the two aspects which form the essence of monetary policy; and

... the high growth of trade in goods and services due to opening up, necessitating the use of funds for settlement through the central banks.

These factors however do not necessarily suggest that monetary policy is superior to other areas of economic policy but they do imply the critical position that monetary policy and central banks have come to occupy in modern times, notwithstanding the uncertainties introduced by the operation of several of these factors.

The Context of Open/Semi-open Economies

In the 1940s and 1950s, countries were generally categorized into developed and underdeveloped/less developed economies. By about the end of the 1950s, the expression, 'underdeveloped'/'less developed' was considered as connoting 'static' state of the economies and not reflective of the policy efforts made to improve the economic performance. By the early 1960s, the word 'developing' replaced the 'underdeveloped'/'less developed'. The 'developed' economies were referred to as 'industrialized' economies by international financial institutions in particular the International Monetary Fund (IMF) since about the middle of the 1970s. The number of industrialized economies (IEs) was placed at 20-25 while the rest of the countries of the world, numbering over 150 was considered as 'developing'.

Within the broad group of developing economies, there are many which carry distinct features and are more developed than the rest. Such economies featured as showcases for high economic performance and were quickly labeled (by the late 1980s) as 'emerging market economies' (EMEs). The word, market in the above label was given emphasis for the preference of the identified countries to be market-oriented in their policy pursuit. They are distinguished from the 'transition' economies that emerged in the early 1990s from the shadows of totalitarian/communist policy regimes in East Europe and the erstwhile Soviet Union, even though the transition economies have also shown their preference for market orientation in their policies. EMEs thus should be treated as a subset of the developing economies but are rarely recognized as such. Some of the earliest ones to be known as EMEs were: Argentina, Brazil, Chile, and Mexico in Latin America, Hong Kong, Indonesia, Korea, Malaysia, the Philippines, Singapore and Thailand in Asia. China was recognized as an EME by the early 1990s.

No one EME has one homogenous economic structure. In fact, they have more than one economic structure: one modern, dynamic and growing rapidly, and the other traditional with remote and old-fashioned technologies. The financial markets can be classified into informal and organized. The latter however is more dominant. The institutions in the organized financial sector are fashioned generally along the lines of those that exist in industrialized countries.They compete for the growing intermediation role in the domestic markets. In many cases, they compete for such a role in foreign markets as well. The informal markets in EMEs would over time shrink in relation to the growing share of the organized markets. What marks the EMEs is their market orientation and their commitment to and pursuit of measures that bring about structural changes in their economies. They tend to be 'open' and exposed to competitiveness. In most EMEs, the real growth rates have been high mainly because of the robust performance of their services sector. The domestic saving rates in EMEs have also been found to be relatively high. As openness is more or less assured, EMEs attract notable amounts of foreign investments.

Why Central Banking for Emerging Market Economies ?

One is tempted to ask as to why one should focus on modern day central banking in and for EMEs. Could this be different from central banking in developing economies ? Prima facie, there is difference. Central banks in EMEs have been closely replicating the practices of central banks of industrialized economies, partly because the financial markets of EMEs are not only growing but also increasingly integrating. The relationship between the financial and real sectors in EMEs has, from most empirical exercises, been very close with the result the central banks in these countries are hard pressed to ensure that the financial sector develops and diversifies rapidly but without undue volatility. Financial sector development would not be possible unless there is a direct intervention of central banks. Here incentives as much as institutional mechanisms have a role to play. This would imply that as in industrialized economies, risk-return profiles assume critical importance in the decision-making processes of investors and market participants in EMEs as well. The central banks in EMEs therefore will have to undertake actions that lead to price discovery of financial assets that investors prefer to hold in their portfolios in substantial amounts. In general, the central banks act through the government securities markets as much as through the credit and money markets to influence the liquidity in the economy and thereby influence the rates of return on different assets. The risk part of the portfolio choice will have to be undertaken through a variety of actions including appropriate supervisory and monitoring processes. For influencing the liquidity, central banks in EMEs act not only through that official rate of interest that is the best representative of the whole spectrum of interest rates in the economy but also through open market operations and other indirect instruments of policy. The central banks in EMEs tend to eschew direct allocative mechanisms. In developing economies, on the other hand, such direct controls abound. Again in developing economies, the interest rates are generally less flexible and open market operations are very narrow because of the limited depth and variety of the financial markets and extremely fragile financial integration. As market innovations are likely to be near absent, the central banks in developing economies would tend to focus more on determining the appropriate stock of money that the economy would hold and to accordingly provide for the supply of money. Whereas in EMEs, the quantities are not the only desideratum: they will have to be taken into account so long as there is stability in the demand for money. EMEs have to also closely track the rate variables since they provide considerable insights about the investors' behavior.

The Indian Context

In this book, we regarded India as an emerging market economy on the basis of the general considerations that we have laid down above under the sub-head, the context of open/semi-open economies. Although the IMF and the World Bank have not officially proclaimed India as an emerging market economy, there is a general recognition that India is a candidate for such a mention. The fact that India is a part of the G-20 (Group of Twenty Countries about which reference will be made later in the book) along with other recognized EMEs shows that India is de facto an emerging market economy. The central bank of the country, namely the Reserve Bank of India (RBI) has played a major role in bringing about a shift in the policy regime ever since the middle of 1991. The Reserve Bank is headquartered in what was known as Bombay, now renamed as Mumbai (India). It has been established by legislation in 1934 through the Reserve Bank of India Act, 1934. The Reserve Bank started functioning effective April 01, 1935. The first paragraph (a part of the Preamble) of the Act states that "Whereas it is expedient to constitute a Reserve Bank for India to regulate the issue of Bank notes and the keeping of reserve with a view to securing monetary stability in India and generally to operate the currency and credit system of the country to its advantage..." This provides the essential tasks that the Reserve Bank (to be alternately used as the Bank, the capital letter B in the word, bank, emphasizing the reference in the rest of this book) is expected to perform. The two important points that need to be noted here are: (a) to secure monetary stability within the country; and (b) to operate the currency and credit system to the advantage of the country. The first of these points is often 'interpreted' as indicative of price stability, while the second is regarded as ensuring adequate credit availability to finance economic activities for the good of the country. In other words, the economic activities funded by credit could be not only for consumption or investment within the country but also for use in productive activities abroad.

The Reserve Bank is obligated and entitled to transact business of the Government of India. It could transact Government business of States (provinces) on the basis of agreements. It has a right to issue bank notes on which there would be no stamp duty. It transacts in foreign exchange and is required to maintain the cash reserves of scheduled banks. The minimum cash reserves (expressed as proportion of the concerned bank's demand and time liabilities) have to be 3 per cent of such liabilities but the Bank could raise the ratio to as much as 25 per cent. The Bank could appoint any bank as its agent. It also has powers to collect credit information from banking companies. The RBI Act also empowers the Bank to regulate non-banking institutions receiving deposits and other financial institutions.

The RBI Act would need to be viewed along with the Banking Regulation Act (BR Act), 1949 which provides powers to the Reserve Bank of India to issue directions to banking companies generally or to any banking company in particular when the Bank is satisfied that it is in the public interest to do so or in the interest of banking policy or to protect the interests of the depositors or to secure better management of the banking company.

The working of the Reserve Bank since its inception and more particularly since India's Independence has been somewhat more broad-based than traditional central banks in that it had to act to promote financial and economic development without jeopardizing monetary stability. It helped to set up a number of financial institutions to provide development finance as well as to promote and foster financial markets. The establishment of the Industrial Development Bank of India, the National Bank for Agriculture and Rural Development, the Industrial Reconstruction Bank of India, the Unit Trust of India, and the Discount and Finance House of India are best examples of the active initiative and capital involvement of the Reserve Bank of India. These institutions have been hived off from the parent body over time but the relationships fostered among them provide considerable understanding of the dynamics of financial development. Since 1991-92, with the shift in the economic policy regime, the Bank had to play an activist role of a different variety. It was required to not only pursue monetary policies to the advantage of the country but also promote financial sector reforms for realizing enduring and sustainable economic growth and stability.

Is the Indian Context Unique?

The obvious answer to this question is in the negative. Many countries outside the category of IEs are more or less in the same position as India. A number of countries in Asia have been adopting economic policies that would promote strong and sustainable growth along with price and financial stability. For instance, the economy of Sri Lanka has been adopting structural adjustment measures under series of arrangements with the International Monetary Fund (IMF) ever since the end of the 1980s. It has also a dual economic structure. Its population is relatively small but its per capita real income is higher than that of India. But the improvement of its economic position has been impeded ever since the 1980s by continuous extra-economic disturbances. Assuming that these disturbances are neutralized, it should be possible for this island economy with vast possibilities of free trade and tourism prospects to improve its overall economic performance with the help of financial sector and legal reforms to levels that could be treated as close to some of the emerging economies of East Asia. The role of the Central Bank of Sri Lanka in such an endeavor will be critical. Similarly, there are a number of countries that are undertaking comprehensive reforms both in the macroeconomic and structural areas, ensuring that markets have a role to play in the growth process. Such countries, and not merely those labeled as EMEs by the International Monetary Fund (IMF) and World Bank (WB), should come under the description of emerging market economies, so long as the reforms undertaken by the countries are not halted and are being pursued continuously for years. It is this perspective that informs this book.

References :

Bagehot, Walter (1873); Friedman, Milton (1959); Goodhart, Charles (1988); Hayek, F A (1978); Kareken, J H and Wallace N (1978); King, R G (1983); Klein B (1974); Reserve Bank of India (1992-93 to 2000-2001); Sayers, R S (1957); Smith, Vera C (1936); White L H (1984).

Box 1

Central Banks by the End of the Twentieth Century

1. **Afghanistan** : Da Afghanistan Bank, Kabul, estd. in 1939 as the Central Bank of Afghanistan.

2. **Albania** : Bank of Albania, Tirana, estd. in 1922.

3. **Algeria** : Banque d'Algerie, Algiers, estd. 1962.

4. **Angola** : National Bank of Angola, Luanda, estd. in 1976.

5. **Argentina** : Banco Central de la Republica Argentina, Buenos Aires, estd. in 1935.

6. **Armenia** : Central Bank of the Republic of Armenia, Yerevan, estd. in 1993.

7. **Aruba** : Central Bank van Aruba, Oranjestad, Operational since 1986.

8. **Australia** : Reserve Bank of Australia, Sydney, estd. formally in 1945, and legislated under the present name in 1959.

9. **Austria** : Oesterreichische Nationalbank, Vienna, estd. in 1816.

10. **Azerbaijan** : National Bank of Azerbaijan, Baku, estd. in 1992.

11. **Bahamas** : Central Bank of the Bahamas, Nassau, estd. in 1974, with its predecessor the Bahamas Monetary Authority created in 1968.

12. **Bahrain** : Bahrain Monetary Agency, Manama, estd. 1973.

13. **Bangladesh** : The Bangladesh Bank, Dhaka, estd. in 1971.

14. **Barbados** : Central Bank of Barbados, Bridgetown, estd. in 1972.

15. **Belarus** : National Bank of the Republic of Belarus, Minsk, estd. in 1990.

16. **Belgium** : Banque Nationale de Belgique S.A., Brussels, estd. in 1850.

17. **Belize** : Central Bank of Belize, Belize City, estd. 1982, taking over operations of Monetary Authority of Belize set up in 1976.

18. **Bermuda** : The Bermuda Monetary Authority, Hamilton, estd. in 1969.

19. **Bhutan** : Royal Monetary Authority of Bhutan, Thimphu, estd. in 1982.

20. **Bolivia** : Banco Central de Bolivia, La Paz, founded in 1928.

21. **Bosnia and Herzegovina** : Central Banka Bosne I Herzegovine, Sarajevo, started operations on Aug 11, 1997.

22. **Botswana** : Bank of Botswana, Gaborone, estd. in 1975.

23. **Brazil** : Banco Central do Brasil, Brasilia, estd. in 1965.

24. **Brunei** : Brunei Currency Board, Brunei Darussalam, estd. in 1967.

Contd...

(...BOX - 1 CONTD...)

25. **Bulgaria** : Bulgarska Narodna Banka, Sofia, estd. in 1879, reorganized in 1989.

26. **Burundi** : Banque de la Republique du Burundi, Bujumbuna, estd. in 1964.

27. **Cambodia** : National Bank of Cambodia, Phnom Penh, estd. in 1954.

28. **Canada** : Bank of Canada, Ottawa, estd. in 1934.

29. **Cape Verde Islands** : Banco de Cabo Verde, Santiago, Cape Verde Islands, estd. in 1976.

30. **Caribbean, Eastern** : Eastern Caribbean Central Bank, St Kitts, estd. in 1983.

31. **Cayman Islands** : Cayman Islands Monetary Authority, Grand Cayman, estd. in 1996.

32. **Central African States** : Banque des Etats de l'Afrique Centrale, Yaounde, estd. in 1972.

33. **Chile** : Central Bank of Chile (Banco Central de Chile), Santiago, Founded in 1925.

34. **China** : The People's Bank of China, Beijing, estd. in 1948 but formally began to function as the central bank in September 1983.

35. **Colombia** : Banco de la Republica, Colombia, Santafe de Bogota, estd. in 1923.

36. **Comoros** : Banque Centrale des Comores, Moroni

37. **Congo** (Democratic Republic) : Banque Nationale du Congo, Kinshasa-Gombe, estd. in 1964.

38. **Costa Rica** : Banco Central de Costa Rica, San Jose, estd. in 1950

39. **Croatia** : Hrvatska Narodna Banka, Zagreb, estd. in 1991.

40. **Cuba** : Banco Central de Cuba, Havana, estd. in 1950, now named the Central Bank of Cuba.

41. **Cyprus** : Central Bank of Cyprus, Nicosia, estd. in 1963.

42. **Czech Republic** : Czech National Bank (Ceska narodni banka), Prague, estd. in 1993.

43. **Denmark** : National Bank of Denmark (Danmarks Nationalbank), Copenhagen, estd. in 1818, renamed as in the bracketed portion in 1936.

44. **Djibouti** : Banque Nationale de Djibouti, Djibouti, estd. in 1977.

45. **Dominican Republic** : Banco Central de la Republica Dominicana, Santo Domingo, estd. in 1947.

46. **Ecuador** : Banco Central del Ecuador, Quito, estd. in 1927.

47. **Egypt** : Central Bank of Egypt, Cairo, estd. in 1961.

Contd...

(...BOX - 1 CONTD...)

48. **El Salvador** : Banco Central de Reserva de El Salvador, San Salvador, estd in 1934.

49. **Eritrea** : National Bank of Eritrea, Asmara, estd. in 1993.

50. **Estonia** : Bank of Estonia (Eesti Pank), Tallinn, estd. in 1919 and re-established in 1990.

51. **Ethiopia** : National Bank of Ethiopia, Addis Ababa, estd. in 1964.

52. **European Union** : European Central Bank, Frankfurt, estd. in 1998 but took over responsibility from January 01, 1999.

53. **Fiji** : Reserve Bank of Fiji, Suva, estd. in 1973 as the Central Monetary Authority of Fiji and in 1984, took over as the Central Bank.

54. **Finland** : Bank of Finland, Helsinki, estd. in 1811.

55. **France** : Banque de France, Paris, estd. in 1800, monetary policy since January 1999 resides with the Eurosystem. .

56. **Gambia, The** : Central Bank of the Gambia, Banjul, estd. in 1971.

57. **Georgia** : National Bank of Georgia, Tbilisi, estd. in 1990.

58. **Germany** : Deutsche Bundesbank, Frankfurt, estd. in 1948, monetary policy since January 1999 resides with the Eurosystem. .

59. **Ghana** : Bank of Ghana, Accra, estd. in 1957.

60. **Greece** : Bank of Greece, Athens, estd. in 1927.

61. **Guatemala** : Banco de Guatemala, Guatemala City, estd. in 1946.

62. **Guinea Republic** : Banque Centrale de la Republique de Guinee, Conakry, estd. in 1960.

63. **Guyana** : Bank of Guyana, Georgetown, estd. in 1965

64. **Haiti** : Bank of Haiti, Port-au-Prince, estd. in 1979.

65. **Honduras** : Banco Central de Honduras, Tegucigalpa, estd. in 1950.

66. **Hong Kong** : Hong Kong Monetary Authority, Hong Kong, estd. in 1993.

67. **Hungary** : National Bank of Hungary (Magyar Nemetzi Bank), Budapest, estd. in 1924.

68. **Iceland** : Central Bank of Iceland (Sedlabanki Islands), Reykjavik, estd. in 1961.

69. **India** : Reserve Bank of India, Mumbai, estd. in 1935.

70. **Indonesia** : Bank Indonesia, Jakarta, estd. in 1828.

71. **Islamic Republic of Iran** : Bank Markazi Jomhouri Islami Iran, Tehran, estd. in 1960 as Central Bank of Iran, the present name is in vogue since 1983.

72. **Iraq** : Central Bank of Iraq, Baghdad, estd. in 1947.

Contd...

(...BOX - 1 CONTD...)

73. **Ireland** : Central Bank of Ireland (Banc Ceannais Na hEireann), Dublin, estd. in 1943, monetary policy since January 1999 resides with the Eurosystem.

74. **Israel** : Bank of Israel, Jerusalem, estd. in 1954.

75. **Italy** : Banca d'Italia, Roma, estd. in 1893, monetary policy since January 1999 resides with the Eurosystem.

76. **Jamaica** : Bank of Jamaica, Kingston, estd. in 1960.

77. **Japan** : The Bank of Japan, Tokyo, estd. in 1882.

78. **Jordan** : Central Bank of Jordan, Amman, estd. in 1963.

79. **Kazakhstan** : National Bank of Kazakhstan, Almaty, estd. in 1990.

80. **Kenya** : Central Bank of Kenya, Nairobi, estd. in 1966.

81. **Korea, North** : Central Bank of the DPR of Korea, Pyongyang, estd. in 1946.

82. **Korea, South** : The Bank of Korea, Seoul, estd. in 1950.

83. **Kuwait** : Central Bank of Kuwait, Safat, estd. in 1968.

84. **Kyrgyz Republic** : National Bank of the Kyrgyz Republic, Bishkek, estd. in 1990

85. **Laos** : Bank of the Lao, PDR, Vientiane, estd. in 1955

86. **Latvia** : Bank of Latvia (Latvijas Banka), Riga, estd. in 1922, reestablished in 1990.

87. **Lebanon** : Central Bank of the Lebanon (Banque du Liban), Beirut, estd. in 1964.

88. **Lesotho** : Central Bank of Lesotho, Maseru, estd. in 1980 as a monetary authority, it turned into central bank in 1982.

89. **Liberia** : National Bank of Liberia, Monrovia, estd. in 1974.

90. **Libya** : Central Bank of Libya, Tripoli, estd. in 1955.

91. **Lithuania** : Bank of Lithuania (Lietuvos Bankas), Vilnius, founded in 1922, reestablished in 1990.

92. **Luxembourg:** : Banque Centrale du Luxembourg, Luxembourg, estd. in 1945, monetary policy since January 1999 resides with the Eurosystem.

93. **Macau** : Monetary and Foreign Exchange Authority of Macau, Macau, estd. in 1980.

94. **Macedonia** : National Bank of the Republic of Macedonia, Skopje, estd. in 1992.

95. **Madagascar** : Banque Centrale de Madagascar, Antananarivo, estd. in 1973.

96. **Malawi** : Reserve Bank of Malawi, Lilongwe, estd. in 1964.

Contd...

(...BOX - 1 CONTD...)

97. **Malaysia** : Bank Negara Malaysia, Kuala Lumpur, estd. in 1958.

98. **Maldives** : Maldives Monetary Authority, Male, estd. in 1981.

99. **Malta** : Central Bank of Malta, Valletta, estd. in 1968.

100. **Mauritania** : Banque Centrale de Mauritanie, Nouakchott, estd. in 1973.

100. **Mauritius** : Banco de Mexio, Mexico DF, estd. in 1925.

101. **Moldova** : Banca Nacionala a Moldovei, Chisinau, estd. in 1991.

102. **Mongolia** : Bank of Mongolia, Ulaanbaatar, estd. in 1924.

103. **Morocco** : Bank Al-Maghrib, Rabat, estd. in 1959.

104. **Mozambique** : Banco de Mocambique, Maputo, estd. in 1975.

105. **Myanmar** : Central Bank of Myanmar, Yangon, estd. in 1947

106. **Namibia** : Bank of Namibia, Windhoek, estd. in 1990.

107. **Nauru** : Bank of Nauru, Nauru (Central Pacific), estd. in 1976.

108. **Nepal** : Nepal Rastra Bank, Kathmandu, estd. in 1956.

109. **Netherlands** : De Nederlandsche Bank N.V., Amsterdam, estd. in 1814 monetary policy since January 1999 resides with the Eurosystem.

110. **Netherlands Antilles** : Bank van de Nederlandse Antillen, Curacao, estd. in 1828, the present name has been in force since 1962.

111. **New Zealand** : Reserve Bank of New Zealand, Wellington, estd. in 1933.

112. **Nicaragua** : Banco Central de Nicaragua, Managua, estd. in 1961.

113. **Nigeria** : Central Bank of Nigeria, Abuja with a Lagos Office, estd. in 1958.

114. **Norway** : Central Bank of Norway, Oslo, estd. in 1816.

115. **Oman** : Central Bank of Oman, Ruwi, estd. in 1974.

116. **Pakistan** : State Bank of Pakistan, Karachi, estd. in 1948.

117. **Panama** : Banco Nacional de Panama, Panama, estd. in 1904, now operates as a commercial and development bank under a law of 1975.

118. **Papua New Guinea** : Bank of Papua New Guinea, Port Moresby, estd. in 1973.

119. **Paraguay** : Banco Central del Paraguay, Asuncion, estd. in 1952.

120. **Peru** : Banco Central de Reserva del Peru, Lima, estd. in 1922.

121. **Philippines** : Central Bank of the Philippines (Bangko Sentral ng Pilipinas), Manila, estd. in 1949, reestablished under the name given in brackets in 1993.

122. **Poland** : National Bank of Poland (Narodowy Bank Polski), Warsaw, estd. in 1945.

Contd...

(...BOX - 1 CONTD...)

123. **Portugal** : Bank of Portugal, Lisbon, estd. in 1846, monetary policy since January 1999 resides with the Eurosystem.

124. **Qatar** : Qatar Central Bank, Doha, estd. in 1993.

125. **Romania** : Banque Nationale de Roumanie, estd. in 1880, reverted to central bank in 1990 after a brief time of being a foreign department.

126. **Russian Federation** : Central Bank of the Russian Federation, Moscow, estd. in 1990.

127. **Rwanda** : Banque Nationale du Rwanda, Kigali, estd. in 1964.

128. **Samoa** : Central Bank of Samoa, Apia, estd. in 1984.

129. **San Marino** : Istituto di Credito Sanmarinese, San Marino, Republic of San Marino, estd. in 1986.

130. **Sao Tome e Principe** : Banco Central de Sao Tome e Principe, Sao Tome Islands, South Atlantic, estd. in 1992.

131. **Saudi Arabia** : Saudi Arabian Monetary Agency, Riyadh, estd. in 1952.

132. **Seychelles** : Central Bank of Seychelles, Mahe, estd. in 1978.

133. **Sierra Leone** : Bank of Sierra Leone, Freetown, estd. in 1963.

134. **Singapore** : The Monetary Authority of Singapore, Singapore, estd. in 1970.

135. **Slovakia** : National Bank of Slovakia, Bratislava, estd. in 1993.

136. **Slovenia** : Bank of Slovenia, Ljubljana, estd. in 1991.

137. **Solomon Islands** : Central Bank of Solomon Islands, Honiara, estd. in 1983.

138. **Somalia** : Central Bank of Somalia, estd. in 1960.

139. **South Africa** : South African Reserve Bank, Pretoria, estd. in 1920.

140. **Spain** : Banco de Espana, Madrid, estd.in 1829, monetary policy since January 1999 resides with the Eurosystem.

141. **Sri Lanka** : Central Bank of Sri Lanka, Colombo, estd. in 1949.

142. **Sudan** : Bank of Sudan, Khartoum, estd. in 1960.

143. **Suriname** : Centrale Bank van Suriname, Paramaribo, estd. in 1957.

144. **Swaziland** : Central Bank of Swaziland, Mbabane, estd. in 1974 initially as a monetary authority, became central bank in 1979.

145. **Sweden** : Sveriges Riksbank, Stockholm, estd. in 1656.

146. **Switzerland** : Swiss National Bank, Zurich, estd in 1907.

147. **Syrian Arab Republic** : Central Bank of Syria, Damascus, estd. in 1956.

Contd...

(...BOX - 1 CONTD...)

148. **Taiwan** : The Central Bank of China, Taipei, estd. in 1928.

149. **Tajikistan** : National Bank of the Republic of Tajikistan, Dushanbe, estd. in 1991.

150. **Tanzania** : Bank of Tanzania, Dar es Salaam, estd. in 1966.

151. **Thailand** : Bank of Thailand, Bangkok, estd. in 1942.

152. **Tonga** : National Reserve Bank of Tonga, Nuku' Alofa, estd. in 1989.

153. **Trinidad and Tobago** : Central Bank of Trinidad and Tobago, Port of Spain, Trinidad, estd. in 1964.

154. **Tunisia** : Banque Centrale de Tunisie, Tunis, estd. in 1958.

155. **Turkey** : Central Bank of the Republic of Turkey, Ankara, estd. in 1931.

156. **Turkmenistan** : Central Bank of Turkmenistan, Ashgabat, estd. in 1992.

157. **Uganda** : Bank of Uganda, Kampala, estd. in 1966.

158. **Ukraine** : National Bank of Ukraine, Kyiv, estd. in 1991.

159. **UAE** : Central Bank of the UAE, Abu Dhabi, estd. in 1973 originally as currency board became a central bank in 1980.

160. **United Kingdom** : Bank of England, London, estd. in 1694.

161. **United States** : Federal Reserve System, Washington DC estd. in 1914.

162. **Uruguay** : Banco Central del Uruguay, Montevideo, estd. in 1966.

163. **Uzbekistan** : Central Bank of Uzbekistan, Tashkent, estd. in 1991.

164. **Vanuatu** : Reserve Bank of Vanuatu, Port Vila, estd. in 1980.

165. **Venezuela**: Banco Central de Venezuela, Caracas, estd. in 1940.

166. **Vietnam** : State Bank of Vietnam, Hanoi, estd. in 1951.

167. **West African States** : Central Bank of West African States, Dakar, estd. in 1962.

168. **Yemen** : Central Bank of Yemen, Sana'a, estd. in 1971, merged with the Bank of Yemen after the unification of the two sectors of Yemen in 1990.

169. **Yugoslavia** (Federal Republic of Serbia and Montenegro): National Bank of Yugoslavia, Belgrade, estd. in 1883 (renamed as above since 1963).

170. **Zambia** : Bank of Zambia, Lusaka, estd. in 1964.

171. **Zimbabwe** : Reserve Bank of Zimbabwe, Harare, estd. in 1964.

Source : Central Bank Directory, 2000, Morgan Stanley Dean Witter, London, 1999).
[The dates of establishment and of operation may not coincide]

Section II

The Nuts and Bolts of Central Banking
--- Reorientations

2. Currency and Payment System 41

- Issue and Distribution of Currency
- Printing and Issuance of Notes only by the Central Banks?
- A Service Provider to Issue and Distribute Currency
- Principles of Currency Issue — Any Fiduciary Rules?
- Could there be a Currency Board Instead of Central Bank?
- Payment System Services
- Electronic Money

Box 2 : Real Time Gross Settlement (RTGS) Systems

3. Banker to Government 61

- Maintenance of Accounts
- Domestic Debt Management
- Conflict of Interests — Debt Management and Monetary Policy
- Sovereign Bond Issues Abroad
- Should There Be a Separate Debt Management Agency ?

Box 3 : Types of Auctioning

Box 4 : On the 'Crowding Out'

Box 5 : Ad hoc Treasury Bills: The Indian Experience

4. Banker to Banks 85

- The Essential Tasks and the LoLR Function
- Bank Restructuring
- The Areas Where Commercial Banks Could be of Help

Box 6 : Theoretical Perspectives on Adverse Selection

2

Currency and
Payment System

Issue and Distribution of Currency

Central banks supply currency in quantities that are supposed to be in accordance with the demands of economic units for hard cash. But it is difficult to estimate with any robust degree of confidence the demand for currency, although there are some studies to suggest the factors that normally have influence over the demand for currency. Phillip Cagan's study of 1958 was one of the early ones of this kind. The issue of currency, it is pointed out, is generally on account of the increase in real income, and decline in the short-term rate of interest. But as Cagan had argued, it could also be because of rise in tourism, and the periodicity of cash payments to employees (i.e., whether salaries are paid weekly as in some of the Western economies or monthly as in most developing economies). In the context of developing or emerging market economies, one could add a few more factors — cash leakages arising from large mobilization of cash deposits rendered possible by expansion of bank branches, sharp accretion of foreign exchange reserves, and cash payments by the governments on account of such special operations as procurement of agricultural commodities and food-for-work programs that seem to be relevant in the agriculture-dominated economies such as India. While all these factors appear plausible as contributing to a realistic estimation of demand for currency, it is not clear whether they can be all reckoned in EMEs (as for example India) where the data on each of the factors are not easily available on a time-series basis. One may have to therefore resort to use of prox-ies on the basis of some intuitive reasoning. Assuming the proxies to be robust, the estimated demand for currency would be indicative of the requirements of currency for transaction purposes, provided there is no sharp shift in the financial regime. For, liberalization of the financial sector would often imply shift away from currency holdings to other financial assets like deposits, equity shares, bonds, and other instruments of saving, to name a few.

In reality, the central banks supply currencies on the basis of what has been absorbed by the economy in the past, with an 'add on' that would represent the increased requirement of cash to meet the enhanced nominal value of transactions on account of the rise in output and prices. In large countries such as India, and reasonably large island economies (such as Sri Lanka), the distribution of currency poses many problems because of differences in regional development, and in the banking facilities in different regions. Essentially the indents from different offices of the central bank of the country for currency notes would be collated and added on to get at the country's requirement of currency. The figure so arrived at would be compared with the amount of currency absorption of the past one or two years and the existing stocks of currency notes in the currency chests located in different regions of the country. Distribution of currency, on the other hand, is essen-tially an operational exercise and has to be region-centric. The higher the volume of transactions (i.e., the higher the devel-opment of the region), the higher the need for cash, assuming that the ratio of currency to deposits or to other assets does not alter in the short term. But it must be noted that such ratios are not available for regions and in fact can hardly be constructed since currency cannot be held and accounted for within a region of the country. The ratios valid for the country as a whole would have to be, therefore, assumed as valid for regions as well. However, in the medium to long term as financial sector develops and is diversified, currency holdings would have to be lower relative to the holdings of deposits and/ or other financial assets. This would be particularly so as electronic payment modes are increasingly used both in wholesale and retail transaction segments. As such, it would be prudent to economize cash balances by assuming the ratios to drift downward in a gradual, measured way.

This point is illustrated in **Table 1** attached to this chapter. The table gives an idea of the movements in currency with the public (Cp) in India since 1970-71 and in relation to money supply and deposits. Cp is statistically measured by deducting the cash held in the vaults of the banks from currency in circulation. The table shows that while the year to year growth in Cp varied considerably, the secular rate of growth was much lower than that in money·supply defined here as M3 (broad money consisting of Cp and aggregate deposits with banks and 'other deposits' with RBI). (Broad money in the literature is referred to as M2 not as M3 but in India this is referred to as M3). The ratio of Cp to M3 as a result showed a secular decline. There was also a secular decline in the ratio of Cp to aggregate deposits with banks. The secular trends seen in the case of India is in line with the trends noticed in respect of industrialized economies as well as some of the other EMEs in East Asia and Latin America.

Printing and Issuance of Notes Only by the Central Banks ?

Most central banks derive the advantage of seignorage while undertaking the task of printing of notes. Seignorage is the social saving that arises from the use of paper currency instead of say gold that was used for minting coins. It arises in other words from the fact that the intrinsic value of the currency note is lower than its face value. The central bank as a result gains in terms of profit, since the assets that support the note issue are nominally valued at the face value of the total notes issued whereas the expenses incurred would be much less than the reported face value. But this is not the real reason why the central banks print notes. The public would be more comfortable with the central bank printing and distributing currency rather than the government, since governments are known to be notoriously extravagant in their expenditures and would therefore take the easy recourse of printing notes whenever they need money to meet their expenditure needs. If the power of printing were to be vested with the government, it is often pointed out, there would be encouragement to incur unproductive expenditures, which would give rise to inflationary pressures. Central banks being separate entities and established generally under distinct statutes, would lay down for themselves certain rules for printing of currency. Even when they help Governments with credit, they do so generally in what may be described as the market place. This is in contrast to the situation in which Walter Bagehot, a British economist of the 19th century and is often regarded as the authority on central banking issues of the said century, found it necessary to be critical of the role of the Bank of England in extending such credit liberally in the early 19th century. Central banks rarely provide hard cash or an open loan facility without the Treasuries lodging government securities. Central bank credit to the government takes place whenever the bank buys government securities. The buying and selling of government securities is a regular exercise in which the central banks participate. These transactions get recorded and would be known to market participants since they affect the yield structure and security prices. There are very few countries in the world wherein government securities are issued freely at will (without limits) and currency created. Such an automatic monetization is rare these days and the practice of issuing perpetual securities such as the ad hocs (ad hoc treasury bills at a relatively low fixed interest rate that existed in the Indian context till end March 1997) cannot coexist with financial liberalization. It is only in dirigiste regimes and in regimes where central banks function as subservient to the Treasury that automatic monetization is likely to be prevalent.

The seignorage that arises in the process of printing notes would doubtless help strengthen the central banks' balance sheets and would in most cases contribute to enhancement of central banks' profits. Often times, profits are passed on to Governments after netting the expenditures of central banks from the total of the central banks' receipts. This is a transparent way of transfering resources (rather profits) to Government and would be more transparent than the method of Government printing notes to meet their expenditure requirements.

A Service Provider to Issue and Distribute Currency ?

Theoretically it is possible to dispense with the central bank and have a service provider instead to issue and distribute currency. But this cannot be done in EMEs since the public has to have confidence in the currency that is issued. Such confidence may not be forthcoming if the service provider is a private individual not accountable to the nation at large. Central banks therefore would have to retain this function. It is not that central banks do not like to lose out on seignorage but they may not like to be burdened with supervision and monitoring of the operations of the service providers, and with legal issues that may arise in the event of complaints of fraud and irregularities in issuing and distributing currency. Moreover, the service charges of service providers could be high and could well be exorbitant and may well exceed the costs that central banks would incur for discharging the same function. Again, there is the question of providing police protection and security for private service providers in discharging the task of issuing and distributing currency.

Central banks, however, need not own printing presses. In fact in many EMEs, Governments own printing presses. Where governments do not own printing presses or where the production capacity of government printing presses is insufficient to meet the demands, central banks could at a price get currency notes of approved sizes and designs printed by well-known private service providers abroad under agreed security arrangements. This is not unknown in the case of many EMEs. The printing costs in such cases could still be sufficiently low enough to permit seignorage benefits to arise.

Principles of Currency Issue — Any Fiduciary Rules ?

One of the fundamental principles of currency issue by central banks is that there has to be some fiduciary rule that needs to be widely known to the general public. The rule would specify the amount and the form of backing for the currency essentially to provide confidence in the currency that is issued to the public. Historically, the backing was in the form of gold. Over time, foreign exchange reserves and government securities have come to be regarded as good financial assets for backing purposes. Government securities are supposed to be as good as gold since it is presumed that sovereign governments do not default on their debt and are therefore gilt-edged. The backing in terms of foreign currencies that could be used for international trade purposes is as good as gold in that they are widely accepted across the countries. But the 100 per cent backing of currency by foreign exchange reserves alone or by gold alone or by any other eligible security is rarely in vogue in countries where central banks exist. More often than not, the backing is in terms of a mix of assets — gold, foreign currencies and government securities, and in some cases highly rated private securities. But no one asset or even the total amount of backing needs to be expressed in terms of a certain proportion of the currency issued. Such a proportional reserve system is hardly in evidence in recent years. What countries generally do is to declare the currency as legal tender and support it with a defined requisite in the form of a minimum amount of backing. The Indian position is in line with this practice. Section 33(2) of the Reserve Bank of India Act, 1934 states: "The aggregate value of the gold coin, gold bullion and foreign securities held as assets and the aggregate value of the gold coin and gold bullion so held shall not at any time be less than two hundred crores of rupees and one hundred fifteen crores of rupees, respectively". Gold coin and gold bullion, however, would have to be valued, as per the RBI Act at a price equivalent to or lower than the international price for the periods in reckoning. Many EMEs have adopted the international market price as the basis for valuation of gold held as backing for note issue. For purposes of ease of measurement, international market prices of gold are taken either as at the end of a period (month) or as an average of daily quoted rates for a period (month or 2/3 months).

Could There Be a Currency Board Instead of a Central Bank ?

One of the interesting questions often posed is whether it is possible to have, in place of central banks, currency boards. Currency boards, by definition, issue currency only when there is 100 per cent backing of foreign currency reserves. The argument placed in favor of this proposal is that for many countries, acquiring gold in the face of limited gold supplies and holding of government securities in support of the high fiscal deficit and high debt to GDP ratios would act as a severe constraint, and the backing for currency should therefore be only in terms of 'usable' foreign currencies. In other words, currency would be issued only when foreign currency reserves increase. While this is the essence of the currency board arrangement, it would also imply that when foreign exchange reserves decline for some reason, an equivalent amount of currency would have to be withdrawn from circulation. Reducing currency in such a situation is easier said than done. Often currency boards will find it impractical to handle the problem.

Yet currency board arrangements seem to have worked fairly satisfactorily in small, open economies, especially city-States and small islands. The economic literature shows that currency boards were considered unsuitable for diversified and large economies where sophisticated skills in monetary management are very much required. For this reason, currency board arrangements existed hardly in 9 countries at the end of the 1980s. The situation, however, changed in the 1990s. Two major features characterized the 1990s. One relates to the emergence of East European countries and of what have come to be known as 'transition' economies carved out of the erstwhile USSR and are increasingly market-oriented, requiring the currency issue to be backed by gold and foreign exchange reserves rather than government securities, since the government securities are not traded owing to weak public finances. Secondly, the eruption of currency and financial crises in the 1990s in some parts of Latin America, and East Asia and in Russia that saw capital outflows meant that monetary systems have to be sound and stable through accumulation of adequate foreign exchange reserves so that the confidence of the investors is restored. These two features ignited interest in the currency board arrangement as a way out to resolving currency problems and monetary instability.

A typical currency board would also have a number of features. Of these, three are most frequently mentioned. These are: an exchange rate that is fixed to a reserve currency — the 'anchor' currency; automatic full convertibility; and a long-term commitment to the system (i.e., a rule-bound, not discretionary, monetary policy). These features are regarded as essential rules that cannot be disobeyed if one were to have currency board arrangement. On the other hand, a central bank can opt for either a pegged or a floating exchange rate regime. A central bank can also choose to have limited convertibility. Since central banks often prefer to have flexibility and fine-tuning capacities, they opt for a measure of discretion in the conduct of monetary policy. A typical currency board, as pointed out by Steve Hanke (1999), cannot create credit: it cannot lend to the government or act as a lender of last resort, whereas most central banks could create credit. Currency boards run on 'automatic pilot' as Hanke argues, with changes in base money (reserve money or monetary base) wholly determined by changes in the demand for such money arising out of variations in the balance of payments. In other words, the currency boards cannot theoretically create inflation and finance government spending. And they earn seignorage only from interest whereas the central banks earn it also from inflation.

It is the powerful anti-inflationary bias of the currency board that often seemed to weigh in decisions to have currency board arrangements. This argument was most effectively used by some economists especially those identified with the monetarist school of thought as the best defense for advocating currency boards in EMEs. The argument is often stretched to point out that price stability is necessary to improve growth performance as well as financial intermediation. The superiority of currency boards over central banks was also subject to empirical tests in recent years. For instance, Ghosh, Gulde and Wolf (1998) used extensive data set of all Fund-member countries covering over 25 years, regardless of specific country characteristics. It found that currency board arrangements have done better than even other fixed exchange rate regimes. They also did not find any negative effects on growth. Hanke using data for 98 developing countries for the period 1950-93 found that currency boards with fixed exchange rates performed better than countries with pegged rates in terms of annual GDP growth rates, annual inflation rates and budget deficits in relation to GDP. However, the recent experience (2002) with Argentina's experiment with the currency board arrangement proved to be a great mistake because of the fixed exchange rate in the face of high and growing external liabilities. When the liabilities have been found to be unsustainable, the demand for the US dollar increased sharply, thereby forcing the abandonment of the fixed exchange rate system and the ban on withdrawal of local currency deposits. The experience shows that the discipline required for installing an effective currency board arrangement has to be rigorous and in place on an enduring basis.

A currency board arrangement can, however, be a part of a well-defined financial relationship-structure wherein the central bank could still have a place. For instance, it is possible to work out the relationship between the central bank and the government with regard to the maintenance of Government deposits and extension of credit to Government. But such a structure could make the arrangement less transparent. For there is no reason why central banks alone should maintain Government deposits and accounts. Commercial banks in fact could handle Government accounts (as was the case in Hong Kong) but where banks are not sufficiently strong, there is no other option but to have central banks to handle Government transactions (as was the case in many transition economies). Again, in defense of central bank, it could be said that it is needed to perform the public debt management function. In reality, this function is often performed by many central banks. In any case, this function has to be outside the purview of the currency board. But it is often argued that this function could well be entrusted to a separate agency under the Treasury as was attempted in New Zealand. We shall deal with this question in some more detail in one of the subsequent chapters. For the present, it could be said that this issue has not been finally settled. There is yet another issue where central banking seems to have an edge over the currency board arrangements. As many EMEs do not have enough foreign exchange reserves, reserve management poses a problem especially when reserves do not cover the currency issued for the currency board. The central banks can handle this function better because they are not bound by the rule of the 100 per cent backing of foreign exchange reserves for currency issue. Where currency boards are permitted to exist along with the central banks, reserve management would still have to be undertaken by central banks even though the earnings from foreign exchange holdings would form the major source of income for the currency board. Moreover, currency boards do not perform bank supervision and other prudential tasks. Central banks have traditionally undertaken such tasks but it is possible that supervision could be entrusted to a separate agency. Where such a separate agency cannot be established, it would be necessary to ensure that the support that central banks provide to banks that are in difficulties would not be inconsistent with the currency board arrangement rules.

It should also be recognized that even though there are some advantages in setting up currency boards to face currency crisis situations, the legal and other institutional arrangements that need to be set in place for a board to work could be time consuming and intractable. Besides, it is not as yet well established that currency board arrangements would succeed in large economies as in respect of small economies. Central banks thus are the ideal institutions to perform the task of issuing and distributing currency within reasonable costs.

Payment System Services

Most central banks provide payment system services but this function has not been given due recognition till almost the 1980s. The Bank of England has in fact included this function as a part of the mission statement adopted in the second half of the 1990s. The Federal Reserve Bank of New York regarded payment system as one of the three important functions, the other two being bank supervision and monetary policy.

The reasons for the outburst of active interest in the provision of payment services are many. Banking transactions have grown in both volume and diversity and financial markets have shown evidence of growing integration in all the EMEs. Large strides in technologies in recent years have enabled movement of funds from one corner of the world to another at almost the click of a button in an integrated computerized environment. As a result of the large technology strides, risks, especially the credit, liquidity, legal and security risks have increased for all the participants in the payment systems including the central banks. Financial crises need not be confined to national borders: they could well be across the national borders. As Maxwell Fry (1999) has pointed out, the payment system in the financial sector can be likened to what 'nuclear power is to the energy sector'.

In developing countries, and in many EMEs, settlements of transactions are still done to a significant extent through the medium of cash while non-cash transactions are generally settled by means of cheques or drafts drawn on banks by individuals, business entities or banks themselves. It is only in very recent years, in EMEs in particular, electronic fund transfers and payments by credit, debit and smart cards are being used as payment medium. Transactions by paper instruments and electronic means are growing rapidly and continuously in EMEs. The growing use of non-cash payment modes is because they provide evidence of payment made for settlement of a transaction by the drawer/authoriser of the paper instrument/ electronic payment. If the transaction is large valued, the paper-based and electronic payments would be safe, certain and in some cases, economical and quick. In respect of small-valued and retail transactions, payment by cards (in particular the credit cards) is increasingly becoming popular especially in urban areas where the extent of computerization and technology adaptations by the financial and other business entities have been found to be sufficiently high.

Central banks have been actively involved in creating and operating payment systems for reducing risks and for making the conduct of monetary policy effective. It is also said that an efficient payment system is often a key determinant of a country's economic growth. For these reasons, as Maxwell Fry et al (1999) have reported, central bank ownership of payment systems in transitional and other developing countries has assumed critical importance. In these countries, this characteristic is clearly visible, much more than in the industrialized countries partly because commercial banks or private service providers are not in a position to provide payment services as in industrialized countries and partly because the technological and business strengths and legal provisions relating to payment systems are often perceived to be less than equitable and robust. There is also a high capital cost involved in setting up modern payment and settlement systems. Such high costs may not be borne by private sector partly because the costs cannot possibly be passed on to consumers for the payment services rendered. Central banks therefore have to set up and maintain modern payments and settlement systems in EMEs till such time that the private sector is in a position to bear the incremental costs over the initial capital cost base. In other words, central banks in EMEs should exercise the option of divesting the payment and settlement systems at some point of time in future.

Central banks seek to promote efficiency in payment systems not only through operational involvement but also through supervision. Most central banks in EMEs tend to develop and run modern high-speed cheque processing and large value electronic payment systems. Small value electronic payment systems such as cards are, however, left to banks or other service providers. This is not only because of operational convenience but also because of the need to undertake payment oversight on transactions that carry potential risks or are likely to be not legal.

The two payment systems that are widely in vogue are the deferred net settlement (DNS) and the real time gross settlement (RTGS) (For details, see **Box 2** for RTGS system). Most industrial economies have RTGS systems. A large number of emerging economies have DNS systems even for large value transfer of funds. Some of these economies have been attempting to put in place RTGS systems for large value fund transfers/transactions. Emerging economies tend to opt for a combination of DNS and RTGS systems for reasons of the unique institutional arrangements in place. The RTGS systems, however, carry much lower order of risks than the DNS systems. However, to be effective, RTGS systems will have to be supported by robust laws as also payment policies that relate to provision of intra-day liquidity and denial of overnight carryovers, besides appropriate technology designs/topology, institutional infrastructure and strong surveillance mechanism (See CPSS, BIS (2000), and Maxwell Fry et al (1999)). These pre-conditions should be met, as otherwise the setting up of RTGS systems would not give the desired benefits.

Development of a robust payment system is essential for lubricating monetary policy and for enabling the conduct of monetary policy to be effective. As financial diversification takes place, households and other economic units including banks will tend to hold less of hard cash and hold interest-yielding assets. The higher the rate of interest, the lower the demand for cash. An efficient payment system by improving the turnover of money affects the demand for cash holding. The implications of such a situation for monetary policy needs to be carefully understood since banks like other economic units would economize cash and generate assets that provide returns on the assets in which they invest. Such investments would be the source of money supply. Central banks will have to be watchful of banks' asset-generating behavior because of their commitment to price stability as an objective. While this issue is being discussed in greater detail in Chapter 5, it is important to note that it is not the currency issue and distribution that is as vital in EMEs as provision of efficient payment services wherein the need to ensure that sufficient cash is placed in the economy is secured.

Electronic Money

Electronic money is a commonly used expression in many of the journals of banking and technology. It must be clearly understood that it is not the same as the electronic fund transfers (EFT). For, when EFT occurs, the money underlying such transfers, namely, the bank deposits do not change. EFT normally takes place when large amounts are involved—the so-called wholesale route. On the other hand, in the retail mode, electronic money, or e-money, or e-cash has been in existence in many industrialized economies since about the early 1990s. E-money can exist outside the bank deposits. It could be generated through the computers and issued by banks as well as by others (non-banks). It has no physical attributes like cash. Its value is stored in a computer chip or in a hard disk. The chip could be embedded in a card such as the smart card. Such a card is truly a stored value card or an electronic wallet and could be used in settling comparatively small value transactions. Unlike the hard cash that is recognized as the legal tender, e-money is not. It is enveloped by a number of technology forms, digital manner of its issue as well as encryptions for purposes of security.

Assume that a bank issues an e-cash card (smart card) to its customer. The bank does so by downloading money on to the memory chip on the card from the customer's account with the bank. When the cardholder does not use the card, i.e., does not spend money, the bank would have funds downloaded on the card as a 'float'. When the card is used, the money passes from card to card or from card to a vending machine of a merchant which has the capability to read the card. The card can also be 'charged up' whenever needed.

When the bank issues e-cash card, the liabilities of the bank change: its deposits would fall while the 'special' e-cash liability will correspondingly increase. The conventional deposits thus are replaced by e-cash liabilities. When the card is used, and the merchant who gets the proceeds deposits the e-cash into his bank account, the traditional deposits get replenished at the system level (For, the merchant may have a bank account at a bank other than the one which issued the e-cash card). But if the merchant decides to pay her suppliers with the value received from the e-money payments of her customers, funds will be circulating outside the banking system. If a large amount of money moves in the cyberspace, the central bank's ability to exactly gauge where e-money is stored or in existence would weaken. If instead of banks, the cards are issued by well known non-bank companies, and funds move around the internet, central banks will find it difficult to know how much of float is outside the banking system.

Fortunately, the world as it is today has come to recognize the potential of e-money misusage to the extent the theoretical possibilities suggest. It is also possible that given the immense possibilities of overissue of e-money by banks as well as by non-banks, there can be valid enough doubts about the public having full confidence in the money that would fast erode in value. After all, the public's confidence rests in the value that is stored in money and its convertibility into real assets. It is therefore not certain that there will ever be a complete replacement of cash even where digitalized signatures and other security features are widely prevalent and are known to be robust. However, limited use of electronic money is possible and is in fact in evidence in a few industrialized economies having sophisticated technologies. But there is as yet no definitive evidence of electronic money being *widely* used even in IEs. But it may over time become more popular in IEs and spread to EMEs to some extent. Such a development however would not imply that the fundamentals of monetary management should be very different from the one where considerations of quantities and rates are regarded as critical.

The implications of the emergence of electronic forms of payment and the growing use of paper-based instruments in EMEs are several. First and foremost, the importance of reserve money in monetary management is likely to wane and the reserve money-money supply relationship as expressed through the money multiplier mechanism about which detailed reference has been made in the subsequent chapter on monetary policy would not hold good. Secondly, the demand for printing of hard cash would be on the decline and the ratio of currency to deposits or to GDP is likely to show a sharp secular decline. Thirdly, the central banks would have to in the interim period spend their energies on equating the social and private costs of payments based on modern technologies and on economizing cash.

Box 2 follows...

Box 2
Real Time Gross Settlement (RTGS) Systems

Settlement of payment transactions can be either on a net or on a gross basis. The timing of the settlement can be of two kinds: immediate which is described as being in 'real' time or on the same day, either in batches at predetermined (or discrete) intervals or at the end of the day (often referred to as 'deferred'). A payment system which operates as a gross settlement system in which both processing and final settlement of funds transfer instructions take place continuously (or in real time) is widely known as the Real Time Gross Settlement System.

One of the crucial elements of an RTGS system is the queuing of transaction messages. All participants of the system send messages to an identified central system. These messages are placed in a queue and the transactions are settled in a certain order, with option for the sender to change priorities of her transactions.

The RTGS settlement enables the resolution of bottlenecks or what has come to be referred to as 'gridlock', which may arise when a series of interdependent payments are stalled due to insufficient funds to settle the original or primary transaction. For example, a debit to a bank may not be made for want of sufficient balance in the bank's account even as the bank awaits a credit that may be in a queue. This would lead to a bottleneck that cannot be resolved until the first debit entry is effected. This is a typical gridlock in an RTGS system and it therefore becomes necessary to provide intra-day liquidity to the participants. Since each transaction has to be settled individually, the liquidity needs under an RTGS system would be sharply higher than that under the netted system. The provision of intra-day liquidity could be free of charge or could be at a nominal cost. The participants would have to ensure that there is no debit balance in their account at the end of the day.

RTGS system is adopted as a part of the risk control strategy. For, the risks inherent in a net settlement system, viz., settlement risk, principal credit risk and systemic risk are such that default by one bank would have a 'domino' effect on the payment system as a whole. This has been the main driving force behind the growing interest in adopting RTGS system among many developing countries. Many EMEs have already set in place RTGS systems. India has decided to set up RTGS system. Sri Lanka is yet another country which is planning to set up RTGS system.

The RTGS system could work alongside DNS system that is in place for certain defined set of transactions. For example, the RTGS system could be operated in respect of transactions in the money and government securities markets and may not operate for stock market transactions. For the latter type of transactions, DNS system could operate and the balances of the banks through which the settlements have to be made could be booked finally at the end of the day in the books of the central banks of the country where banks maintain cash balances for settlement purposes. If as a result of such a netting process, a bank finds that its cash balances at the end of the day would be lower than the balances needed to be maintained under the statutory cash reserve ratio, the system would have to either permit the support of a fund that has to be created for the purpose or allow for rewinding of the transaction entries. The latter is in practice not easy to implement, and it is only the creation of a special fund of a substantial amount that could help the system to run smoothly.

Sources: Bank for International Settlements (1997), *Real Time Gross Settlement Systems*, Report prepared by the Committee on Payment and Settlement Systems, Basle, March; Reserve Bank of India (1999), *Annual Report, 1998-99*, Mumbai).

Table 1

**Trends in Currency with the Public in India,
1970-71 through 1999-2000**

(Amounts in Rupees crores)

Years	Currency with public (Cp)	M3	Aggregate Deposits (AD)	Cp/M3	Cp/AD
1970-71	4371	11020	6589	0.40	0.66
71-72	4801	12693	7812	0.38	0.61
72-73	5438	15013	9517	0.36	0.57
73-74	6321	17624	11250	0.36	0.56
74-75	6347	19549	13127	0.32	0.48
75-76	6705	22480	15698	0.30	0.43
76-77	7873	27781	19787	0.28	0.40
77-78	8631	32906	24205	0.26	0.36
78-79	10231	40112	29715	0.26	0.34
79-80	11654	47226	35181	0.25	0.33
80-81	13426	55774	41937	0.24	0.32
81-82	14474	62752	48110	0.23	0.30
82-83	16659	73184	56339	0.23	0.30
83-84	19603	86525	66631	0.23	0.29
84-85	22672	102933	79666	0.22	0.28
85-86	25059	119394	94046	0.21	0.27
86-87	28382	141632	112941	0.20	0.25
87-88	33559	164275	130319	0.20	0.26
88-89	38329	193493	154470	0.20	0.25
89-90	46300	230950	184052	0.20	0.25
90-91	53048	265828	212106	0.20	0.25
91-92	61098	317049	255066	0.19	0.24
92-93	68273	364016	294430	0.18	0.23
93-94	82301	431084	346258	0.19	0.24
94-95	100681	527596	423531	0.19	0.24
95-96	118258	599191	477589	0.20	0.25
96-97	132087	696012	560731	0.19	0.24
97-98	145579	821332	672213	0.18	0.22
98-99	168944	980960	808280	0.17	0.21
1999-2000	189082	1124174	932059	0.17	0.20

Note: M3 in India is nothing but broad money (M1 plus time deposits with banks).

3

Banker to Government

Maintenance of Accounts

Central banks in most countries are required either by statutes or by agreements to act as bankers to Governments and accordingly they maintain the Governments' domestic currency and foreign currency accounts. But as central banks would be located only in a few places in the country, it would be essential for central banks to appoint and authorize commercial banks or/and other financial entities to function as their agents to undertake the requisite tasks as bankers to Government. The receipts and payments in and payments out of the domestic and foreign currency accounts of the agents, however, are accounted for on a daily basis, and entered into the central-ized account of the Government, department-wise/ministry-wise, maintained at the central bank of the country. Fortunately, modern electronic technologies enable the banks to achieve a high degree of efficiency needed for maintenance of government accounts. Such a system helps Governments to monitor their fiscal position on a more regular basis than would be possible with outmoded technologies.

Central banks in EMEs normally do not charge the governments for the services they render as their bankers. On the other hand, they pay to commercial banks fees for rendering the agency

function. Most central banks in EMEs provide payment services to all the participants in the financial system including
the governments. Governments issue cheques and receive
cheques and posting these entries (debits and credits in the
Government books of accounts) after clearance in the payments
system can turn out to be costly for central banks. It may,
therefore, become necessary for central banks in these countries to charge their governments the costs associated with
cheque and electronic clearing. This recommendation is not
without precedent. The Federal Reserve Banks in the United
States, for instance, charge for clearing the cheques issued by
the US Government. The central banks also incur other types
of costs associated with the function of being bankers to governments. The services the central banks provide in the form
of information gathering and information setting in the formats
required by Governments are often numerous and would be
of highly specialized genre. The costs in this regard could
therefore turn out to be high and should be considered for
recovery from the governments. Imposition of charges for such
services would be considered essentially as a transparent practice. It would no doubt raise incomes of central banks but as
the profits of central banks in EMEs are generally transferred
to their governments, the governments should not object to
such a transparency practice from being adopted.

Domestic Debt Management

As bankers to Government, central banks are often required
to manage the sovereign domestic debt. Governments borrow
from the public and from financial and non-financial institutions when they find receipts from taxes and fees and other
charges fall short of their expenditures or commitments to
expenditures. The deficits that arise as a result would have to
be financed either by domestic or by foreign borrowings. But
it is just not enough for governments merely to indicate their
deficits and borrowing needs. They need to take into account
the willingness on the part of the participants in the domestic

and foreign markets to lend to the governments. Let us first consider the major issues in domestic borrowing and domestic debt management. They are cited to be the following: the timing of the issue of government paper, the maturity profile, the yield structure on government securities, the open market operations, the type of securities to be issued, the amount of devolvement on the central bank in case the outcomes of security auctions are widely different from the original expectations, and the private placement of securities with the central bank.

Most central banks in EMEs reveal their preference to borrow through auctioning of government securities rather than through other direct means such as the statutory liquidity requirements on financial entities, in particular, commercial banks. While statutory liquidity requirements may exist for purposes of protecting the banks' interests (as a prudential measure), most EMEs would prefer to keep such requirements at the minimum. The minimum is dictated mainly by prudential considerations although it could also reflect the fact that in many economies, the public finance position is not sufficiently robust enough to result either in fiscal balance or fiscal surplus. The auctioning of government securities would help the financial entities including banks to secure effective yield rates that would be comparable to the yield rates on other similar instruments, assuming the investment portfolio managers (often referred to as treasury managers) to be relatively efficient. Statutory liquidity requirements as a result would be less burdensome than would be the case when the yield rates are fixed. The central banks can use different ways of auctioning in order to find out what the markets can bear but there is no standard auctioning system that one could commend to EMEs (See **Box 3** at the end of this chapter for different auctioning systems that are prevalent in the world). Participation in the auctions will be high if auctioning methods and practices are transparent and are made widely known to the public at large.

The central banks act as advisors to governments on the question of the absorptive capacity of the public with respect to the public borrowings that governments seek. They generally tender advice to the governments on the total value of debt paper to be issued in a year at the time of the preparation of the budget. They also work out some understandings with the governments on the strategies that would be adopted during the year for raising the required resources and for successful debt management.

The actual size of borrowing from the market by the Government is determined essentially by the Treasury on the basis of considerations such as the size of the accumulated debt, the discharge obligations during the year ahead, the expected revenue position vis-à-vis the budgeted expenditure levels, and the relative attractiveness of the government paper to the individual and corporate and institutional investors. There are in general limits up to which the Government could incur debt and while borrowing is often set with reference to the above considerations, they are led also by the method that is employed to finance the fiscal deficit. But it is the size of the debt that ultimately matters because it is related to the question as to whether it is sustainable.

The debt sustainability should be estimated by the governments in a credible manner. For, that is important for the success of public borrowing programs. This idea is not a mere abstraction and can be understood in terms of a simple formula. The economic literature often points out that it could be realized if the real rate of growth of the economy is sufficiently high enough to provide the ability to service the debt (both redemptions or principal repayments and interest payments). This simple rule would need to be translated into simpler terms of estimating not only the rate of growth of the economy but also the anticipated real rate of return. In this context, it is important to recognize that most central banks provide indications that help one to appreciate the significance of the principle of debt sustainability. There are many central banks that furnish to the wider public their expectations of the medium term paths of interest rates and consumer prices. This will help gain an idea of the real rate of interest which, going by the rule about debt sustainability, should be lower than the real output growth rate (Bispham (1987), Hamilton & Flavin (1986), Mason (1985), Spaventa (1987)). Real interest rate is worked out by adjusting the expected inflation rate against the current nominal interest rate. If the nominal interest rate is 10 per cent and the expected inflation rate is 8 per cent, then the real interest rate would turn out to be 2 per cent. If the real output growth is 5 per cent, then the country would still be able to borrow, since the real rate of interest is placed at only 2 per cent. The theoretical reasoning behind the principle is that if the interest rate and prices are kept under check, the present value of both liabilities and assets could be more reliably worked out and the net worth of the government would be more easily ascertainable. But often times, it is not possible to work out net worth in a comprehensive way, since it entails having complete information on contingent liabilities and assets from various tiers of government and public sector undertakings and major private corporate entities. Therefore, it is difficult to know as to whether the Government is solvent even if the real rate of interest is lower than the real growth rate under conditions of rising debt. In view of this problem, the simple rule should be treated as a kind of a reference indicator rather than as a policy guide.

Many EMEs, therefore, prefer to also monitor the solvency condition of the government. The condition requires that primary surplus (revenue position minus interest payments) is generated. This would imply that the fiscal situation has to be strong with expected revenue exceeding current expenditure. But even such an exercise may not be relevant except for the short run. In the medium term, however, the solvency condition has to hold but for it to be credible, there has to be sound fiscal policy in place, a policy that should take into account the real performance of the economy, and the extent of compliance with the policy. Assuming that the compliance to policy is reasonably good, fiscal policy even when it is accompanied by a moderately accommodating monetary policy would work best mainly when the private sector investments are buoyant and revenue receipts keep growing. In this context, improvement in the tax base has to be strong since it is more critical than merely raising tax rates. For, high tax rates often would give incentives for tax evasion or non-compliance, and could lead to rent-seeking and corruption among public servants. This does not mean that tax rates have to be sharply cut and rendered low, because there is no sound empirical justification for the theoretical argument advanced by Professor Laffer in the context of the US economy that low tax rates will lead to better economic performance. Even in the US economy, there is no definite evidence of the validity of the theoretical argument that low tax rates had led to higher investment, lower prices, higher output, and therefore higher government revenues. There is much less justification for sharp reductions in tax rates in EMEs where the tax base and tax compliance are known to be relatively low. There is now a further complication developing as the structures of EMEs are increasingly shifting from the commodity-producing activities to services-producing activities that are not easily amenable to appropriate assessments of income. Sound fiscal policy would also require that the expenditure policies too be guided by self-imposed limits on the number and diversity of activities that the State needs to pursue. It is here that most EMEs would find it hard to lay down rules and follow them. In some cases, they find it hard to even work out politically feasible solutions. Parliamentarians rarely like to limit their discretion in the matter of State spending. But sooner or later, excess spending will impose high social and economic costs. Where tax buoyancy is not significantly evident, and where the public sector is large, diversified, and loss-making, it is best the State considers divestment or selling off its shares from its public sector undertakings to the wider public and other corporate entities.

With reference to the economic reforms that are being carried out since about the middle of 1991 in India, one of the arguments widely debated was the question of fiscal debt sustainability. Fiscal deficits in relation to GDP after showing some downward drift in the first few years have remained doggedly at relatively high levels. Thus in respect of the Central Government, the gross fiscal deficit to GDP which was 7.9 per cent in 1990-91 moved down to 4.9 per cent in 1996-97 and then moved up to 5.7 percent in 2000-01. This ratio seemed to have not shown any decline in the two subsequent years. Tax-GDP ratio too moved downward by 100 basis points from little over 10 per cent in 1990-91. It is against this background, it was argued by Mihir Rakshit (2000) that the Domar rule about the sustainability of public debt as obtained when the interest rate on government borrowing is less than the GDP growth rate would not be valid because the applicability of the rule is conditional upon a number of factors such as the scale of government borrowing, proportion of consumption and investment in the aggregate expenditure on goods and services by the government, the return on the government's capital expenditure, the extent of monetised deficit, and the patterns of government borrowing from the public. Rakshit argued that the rule is not as relevant as the proportion of public expenditure that would be incurred on accumulation of assets, for when the investment rate goes up, the growth rate of the economy would itself go up. In his view, the fiscal program should also be subject to the constraint of placing limits on the net Reserve Bank's credit to government, and on borrowing from the banks through the statutory liquidity ratios. Besides, he advocated some long-term measures aimed at reduction of pre-tax-transfer income inequality and poverty. Objecting to the advocacy of higher investment per se, and pointing out the need for making several adjustments to the data, Saumitra Chaudhuri (2000) noted that one should not lose sight of the importance of the institutional issues that are key to efficient capital allocation and to more rapid economic growth. Growth, in his view, under an unreconstructed institutional structure would remain sub-optimal and would be vulnerable to external competition. In essence, what Chaudhuri pointed out was that while monetisation and inflation tax could be used to provide growth for some time, it can not be used as a sustainable mechanism.

The debate in India, however, does not add to the analytical content of our discussion. In fact, it is conducted mainly with reference to the fiscal deficit of the Central Government and not with reference to the entire public sector. If one were to construct such an estimate, it would be approximately 10 per cent of GDP at the end of the 20th century, nearly the same as in 1990-91. Such a large fiscal deficit position would not be sustainable because of the fact that it leads to crowding out of private investment via the high interest rates and possibly to exchange rate depreciation as well. We shall discuss the issue of crowding out in the following part of this chapter and again in Box 4 at the end of this chapter.

Conflict of Interests —
Debt Management and Monetary Policy

Central banks in developing and emerging economies have to take active interest in the fiscal position because the size of the deficit and the mode of financing influence interest rates and prices, the two variables that all central banks most assiduously track. We shall be dealing with the content and operational aspects of monetary policy in Chapter 5 of this book, but at this juncture, it would be useful to briefly touch upon the essence of the arguments for the application of monetary policy. Monetary policy has to do with money and central banks generate money supply. But in doing so, they would, without exception, seek to ensure that the general price stability is not jeopardized. In fact price stability is always regarded as an important goal of monetary policy. Many central banks also seek to influence employment/output position as a central task of their functioning. They hope to realize this objective through either creating credit and thereby money supply or through changes in the interest rates. The output/ employment expansion, it is said, would occur if producers have enough funds to invest. Bank credit would help producers to fund their investment and inventory plans but the central banks would have to ensure that bank credit expansion is not excessive because it could lead to price increases and endanger price stability. Producers, on the other hand, would seek credit in larger quantities if the cost of credit is relatively low or attractive and if there are no significant restrictions on the availability of credit. Lower interest rates are often viewed as keeping the costs of investment under check and so long as the rates of return on investment are higher, the demand for credit would be considerable. Acquiescence to such a credit demand would lead to increase in money supply in turn leading to increase in prices.

Interestingly enough, lowering the interest rate in order to stimulate investment could redistribute resources differently from what the governments would seek. The redistribution would be in favor of producers and generally richer sections of people. However, this may not be necessarily anti-growth if the investments arising out of such resource redistribution fructify within the technologically-feasible period of time. But more often than not, fiscal deficits lead to higher interest rates that discourage investment and could favor the consumers and creditors, the outcomes that are not viewed favorably by most policy makers.

Public debt accumulates as fiscal deficits occur continuously and add on to the accumulated debt more than the redemption payments. Fiscal deficits have to be financed by governments by borrowing from the public, or from the central bank or from commercial banks and other financial and corporate bodies or from external sources. Foreign financing of deficits has been found to be limited in EMEs partly because bilateral official aid is restricted and partly because the government papers issued by the governments of EMEs are not much traded. Hence the dependence on domestic financing of fiscal deficits. In case the borrowing is limited only to the central bank, it virtually means an open access for the Government to the printing press. Such monetised deficit, as Rangarajan et al (1989) have argued, would result in a vicious cycle of monetisation leading to larger deficits which in turn would further push up monetary financing, ending eventually in a build-up of inflation. If government borrowing is perceived to be large and cannot be monetised through central bank support, domestic financial markets will have to come to the rescue of the governments. Market borrowing through the issuance of treasury bills and bonds of a wide variety of maturities in the presence of normal levels of liquidity in the economy could imply crowding out of the private sector. The crowding out occurs due to the competing demands of the government for the same amount of funds available in the markets and when the government offers higher market interest rates or fiscal incentives on purchases of government securities, the private sector finds itself positioned in a liquidity bind. This has particularly harsh implications for the economy in buoyancy or on the upturn of the economic cycle or when the private sector exhibits dynamism (See **Box 4** at the end of this chapter for an analytical exposition of the concept of 'crowding out').

From the point of view of the central bank which normally holds bonds not only for providing backing to currency but also for conducting open market operations, the rise in interest rates owing to large public sector borrowing would reduce the prices of government securities and the value of the investment portfolios. They also push up the loan rates and raise the cost of investment, which unless absorbed by cutting down the profits, would have to be passed on to the consumers. Where the income levels are low and the demand for goods is less elastic, the possibility of increased interest cost of investment being passed on to the consumers would be imminent. If this were to be the case, the rise in interest rate would trigger expectations of price increases and make it difficult for the central bank to pursue one of its main goals, namely, price stability.

In case the market does not absorb the offered bonds even at higher yield rates, the central bank, by virtue of the fact that it is a debt manager, would have to ensure that the announced amounts of borrowing are realized by absorbing the bonds and thereby extending credit to the government (which represents a variant of what may be called devolvement when the auction system is in vogue) or by agreeing to private placement of Government securities for subsequent offloading by the central bank on the market. Devolvement occurs when central banks do not properly gauge the liquidity in the economy or the portfolio behavior of financial institutions. Direct monetization by absorbing the securities, be they bonds or treasury bills, offered by the governments at a certain interest rate is rarely preferred by central banks. But direct monetization should not be ruled out in all EMEs. If one were to go by the experience in India, direct monetization through the issue of what had come to be known as the ad hoc treasury bills existed till the end of March 1997 from the mid-1950s (See **Box 5**). Private placements of government securities with the central banks, on the other hand, are of recent origin in India: they have been in vogue only since the second half of the 1990s. Private placement, theoretically speaking, is a form of monetization in that the securities are first absorbed by the central bank on a voluntary basis even though it provides in the process credit to government and increases money supply. Private placement is justified often on the ground that it is a temporary device to support government's financing needs. It, however, implies that the central bank monitors market conditions and times the sales of government securities in not too distant a future. To illustrate, a central bank could agree to private placement of government securities on day 1 and as liquidity conditions improve would offload those securities in the market say on day 25. Central banks, however, would involve in such operations only if they are sure that such offloading would be possible within a foreseeable future, which could be a month, or a quarter, or a half of a year or a year. But private placement cannot be used in an unlimited way. It will not, for instance, succeed if the Government issues securities on sale continuously at frequent intervals or if the liquidity in the markets is somewhat constrained.

It is not that private placements of government securities with central banks are always voluntary: it could well be thrust on central banks that are not assertive enough. Once the central bank agrees to have private placement, it has to face certain implications. For example, commodity prices could increase on the expectation that the private placement would fuel up aggregate demand in the short run. Central banks in EMEs should therefore be very cautious in agreeing to private placement. It is not that the central banks cannot correct the problems that arise from private placement. Some of the measures that central banks could undertake are worth mentioning here. Central banks could do what they are best capable of, namely, injecting liquidity into the economy. They do so by letting the banks to be liquid just before announcing the government security auctions of the securities held as part of private placement, say through liberal refinancing at competitive interest rates, or through absorption of foreign exchange from the market or through what in India has come to be known as 'reverse' repo operations. The consequent increase in market liquidity would help the central banks to reduce the possibility of its accepting private placement or to offload the privately placed securities on to the credit markets. But all these measures still would lead to increase in aggregate demand and rise in prices. Expecting to off-load privately placed securities at a later date, however, may not always succeed for, banks could refuse to absorb government securities in periods of economic buoyancy and if the expected yield rates on bonds are not as attractive as the rates that would be obtained from lending.

The unwillingness of banks to invest in government securities under the above conditions can be particularly justified if the secondary market trading in government securities is not sufficiently large and deep enough. In many EMEs, the secondary markets for government securities are not in fact well developed and therefore the banks will be reluctant to face liquidity risks by holding government securities that would be far in excess of the statutory liquidity requirements. But if the liquidity conditions are not influenced by central bank interventions, and the level of real activity is normal, the banks would still prefer to expand their loan portfolio rather than the investment portfolio partly because of their professional competence in lending and partly because they often face high demand for credit in most EMEs. Besides, a number of bank borrowers would be willing to pay higher interest rates than the government and would in general pose a challenge to the working of the crowding out phenomenon. But in choosing their borrowers, banks require good information systems on their credit-worthiness, and robust risk management strategies. Where the information systems and risk management are weak, banks would be subject to the illusion of making profits by selecting borrowers who are willing to pay high interest rates and not seriously worry about the recovery of loans. Such cases are said to be present in all the economies, but in a more significant way typically in EMEs. Such a phenomenon has come to be known as 'adverse selection' (See **Box 6** at the end of the next chapter as to what it means and how it works). Adverse selection is essentially a by-product of information asymmetries. Central banks will have address the problem of adverse selection not so much because it leads to inflation expectations but because it renders the banking sector very fragile.

Let us consider yet another possibility. Central banks in EMEs where monetary policy has to promote output / employment expansion along with price stability will still be faced with the dilemma of managing large borrowing requirements of the government if the economy is in the downturn and public expenditures are largely unproductive. Banks could theoretically be compelled to invest in government securities with their resources by manipulating the statutory requirements about the holding of government securities. In case the monetary authorities are also persuaded, if not required, to ensure at the same time to keep the interest servicing costs of government low, the only option that the central bank could exercise in the circumstances would be to sharply increase liquidity in the system either through special refinancing schemes, or liquidity-providing repo operations/open market operations. Such a strategy will succeed in the short run but it would eventually lead to increase in prices since the economy will be subject to 'too much money chasing too few goods'. Aggregate demand would accelerate if in addition to domestic liquidity-injecting measures, the central banks in EMEs were to be compelled to purchase foreign securities at artificially depreciated rates from the foreign exchange market because of the large-scale capital inflows.

The concerted monetary-fiscal action for accommodating the fiscal need of lowering the interest servicing costs as mentioned above will water down the monetary discipline and harm the overall economic performance in the medium term. More importantly, the central banks will be disabled to influence market expectations because they will not be in a position to defend the already-positioned medium term paths of interest rates and prices or to set in place such medium term paths.

Sovereign Bond Issues Abroad

The above cases illustrate the dilemmas that central banks face in donning the dual role of being the domestic debt manager of governments as well as a monetary policy-maker. The dilemmas cannot be resolved even if the government borrows from abroad through issue of medium-term bonds instead of relying on the domestic markets. For, external borrowing can be costly and would be subjected to the volatility of exchange rates. It can also impact on the external credit ratings of the country. Besides, the sovereign bond issues would compete with the permitted corporate bond issues abroad and raise the costs of borrowing in foreign currencies. In case external borrowing leads, as it often would, to depreciation in the exchange rate of the domestic currency vis-à-vis the foreign currency, there would be implications for inflation expectations especially for those EMEs that have considerable import propensities. In such an event, the domestic currency component of debt servicing requirements will go up, generating pressure on the fisc.

Sovereign bond issues abroad can be undertaken only if the countries have robust fiscal position, a relatively low and sustainable debt-GDP ratio, and flexible exchange rate arrangements. They could, however, be undertaken on a limited scale in normal times when the economic fundamentals are perceived to be sufficiently strong in order to find out the creditworthiness of the country in the international financial markets and to signal to markets of the authorities' commitment to adopting transparency practices.

Should there be a Separate Debt Management Agency?

It is against this background of conflict of interests, a proposal has been mooted in recent years for assigning the debt management function to a separate entity that would coordinate its actions with the central bank of the country for purposes of timing and economizing on the costs of borrowing. The philosophical underpinning of the proposal is that the government would fully fund its deficit by borrowing from the public at market rates and completely avoid the central bank. The government would in the process (a) enable the central bank to pursue its central task of monetary policy conduct without getting diverted into issues of debt management, and (b) work out strategies to minimize borrowing costs the way the manufacturing firms would do. The objective of minimization of costs would imply that the decisions would be taken on (i) the size of the issue, (ii) the proportions of the issue in terms of bonds, treasury bills and different variants such as indexed bonds, (iii) the proportions of the issue in terms of home currency and in terms of denominated foreign currencies where foreign currency borrowing is permitted, (iv) the timing of issues, as well as the maturity patterns of issues, and the amount of coupons that may have to be issued in the case of government bonds. These decisions would essentially rest with the governments and not with the central banks even when there is no separate debt management entity within the government. A separate entity would not mean that it would never consult with the market participants, including the central bank. In fact, consultation with the central bank would be crucial. As one which tracks liquidity in the economy on a daily basis, the central bank would be in a unique position to give advice to the separate debt management entity on the size and timing of the issues. As a banker to the government, the central bank, however, would conduct the processing of tenders for bonds and bills, and have the registry. In most cases, the central bank would also provide the clearance and settlement services in respect of the government securities.

New Zealand established a separate government office to manage government debt in the late 1980s and is credited to have achieved considerable success in ensuring that the Reserve Bank of New Zealand has autonomy in monetary policy making. Ireland, Sweden, Australia and the United Kingdom have also separate sovereign debt management units. There are other countries such as Austria, Belgium, Canada, Denmark, Finland, Hungary, Netherlands, Portugal, Spain, and the United States that have evolved sophisticated debt units responsible for public debt management.

Apart from the conflict of interest between debt management and monetary policy considerations, two other reasons for transfer of debt management to a separate debt management office have been adduced. There is, for instance a need to avoid utilizing 'inside' information, particularly in favor of monetary policy for influencing debt management policy. Even if separate entities are not created for debt management, it is essential to create a clearer allocation of the responsibilities for debt management and monetary policy so that accountability for respective actions would be clear. EMEs could follow these examples by working out suitable legislations and institutional mechanisms relating to the autonomy of their central banks and sound fiscal responsibility.

References :

Bean, Charles R and W H Buiter (1987), *The Plain Man's Guide to Fiscal and Financial Policy*, London, Employment Institute, October.

Bispham J A (1987), "Rising Public Sector Indebtedness: Some More Unpleasant Arithmetic", in Boskin, Michael, et al, eds., *Private Savings and Public Debt*, Basil Blackwell, USA.

Buiter, W H (1985), "A Guide to Public Sector Debt and Deficits", *Economic Policy*.

Chaudhuri, Saumitra (2000), "Fiscal Management: An Alternative View of the Circumstances", *Money & Finance*, Vol.2, No.2, July-September.

Hamilton, J D and M A Flavin (1986), "On the Limitations of Government Borrowing: A Framework for Empirical Testing", AER, Vol 76, No 4.

Mason, P R (1985), "The Sustainability of Fiscal Deficits", *IMF Staff Papers*, Vol 32, No 4 December.

Rakshit, Mihir (2000), "On Correcting Fiscal Imbalances in the Indian Economy: Some Perspectives", *Money & Finance*, Vol.2, No.2, Jul.-Sept.

Rangarajan, C, Anupam Basu and Narendra Jadhav (1989), "Dynamics of Interaction Between Government Deficit and Domestic Debt in India", *RBI Occasional Papers*, Vol 10, No 3, September.

Spaventa, Lugi (1987), "The Growth of Public Debt: Sustainability, Fiscal Rules and Monetary Rules", *IMF Staff Papers*,

Box 3

Types of Auctioning

There are essentially four basic types of auctions which are widely used and analyzed in the economic literature. These are :

1. The Ascending-bid Auction

This is also called the open, oral or English auction. The price is successively raised until only one bidder remains, and that bidder wins the object at the final price. This auction can be run by having the seller announce prices, or by having the bidders call out prices themselves, or by having bids submitted electronically with the best current bid posted. In the model that is most commonly used by auction theorists (sometimes called the Japanese auction), the prices rise continuously while bidders gradually quit the auction. Bidders observe when their competitors quit, and once some one quits, she is not allowed to return or come back into bidding. There is no possibility for one bidder to preempt the process by making a large 'jump bid'.

2. The Descending-bid Auction

This works almost the opposite way to the ascending-bid auction. This auction was supposedly used in the sale of flowers in the Netherlands and has come to be known as the Dutch auction. In this auction, the auctioneer starts at a very high price, and then lowers the price continuously. The first bidder who calls out that she will accept the current bid price wins the object at that price.

3. *The First-price Sealed-bid Auction*

In this type of auction, each bidder submits independently a single bid, without seeing others' bids, and the object is sold to the bidder who makes the highest bid. The winner pays her bid (i.e., the price is the highest or 'first' price bid).

4. *The Second-price Sealed-bid Auction*

It is also known as Vickrey auction. Here too, each bidder independently submits a single bid, without seeing others' bids, and the object is sold to the bidder who makes the highest bid. However the price she pays is the second-highest bidder's bid or 'second price'. The Vickrey auction takes the name from the article that Professor W Vickrey wrote in 1991 (See Vickrey, W, "Counterspeculation, Auctions, and Competitive Sealed Tenders", *Journal of Finance*, 16, 1961, pp.8-37).

Sources: Paul Klemperer, "Auction Theory: A Guide to the Literature", *Journal of Economic Surveys*, Vol. 13, No. 3, 1999. Paul Klemperer has edited two volumes entitled, *The Economic Theory of Auctions*, Edward Elgar, Cheltanham, UK and Northampton, Mass, USA, 2000, in which a number of good articles in which the above articles of Klemperer and Vickrey figured.

Box 4

'Crowding Out'

The phenomenon of 'crowding out' of private spending by increasing government borrowing essentially for purposes of augmenting output is widely discussed in the literature on public finance. Essentially it points to the rise in interest rates due to government borrowing having an effect on the investment plans of the private sector. To the extent the private spending moves down, there will be no significant change in the overall spending that occurs due to government spending through borrowing. In other words, there will be no change in the level of output. This is particularly valid at full employment.

Under less than full employment, however, fiscal expansion through government borrowing could increase aggregate demand (spending) and output. This is in line with the Keynesian analysis and the development strategies adopted by a number of developing countries. The increase in output resulting from large government spending in turn increases the demand for money and bidding up of the interest rates. If, however, private spending were to be highly interest elastic, then the multiplier effects of fiscal expansion would be small. In other words, fiscal expansion would crowd out the interest sensitive components of private spending.

Assume that there is capital mobility, and the exchange rates are flexible. Also assume that market expectations are allowed to play their part. Then the effects of the policy of fiscal expansion through government borrowing would be uncertain and could be complex. Nonetheless, crowding out cannot be ruled out. For the fiscal deficits may be considered permanent, not transitory, and such anticipated deficits would lead to expectations of higher interest rates especially in the long end of the market, and to exchange rate appreciation.

But there is one strand of thought that questions the validity of the argument that fiscal expansion would affect overall spending in the economy. This line of thinking is associated with David Ricardo and more recently with Robert Barro. As per this line of thinking, government deficits do not matter at all. For, private individuals would anticipate the fact that government borrowing now would have to be repaid at a certain future date and therefore would increase their savings (and thus consume less) so that there would be enough money when the government debts had to be repaid. The government could well have taxed people instead of borrowing the money and in essence this meant that there is 'equivalence' between taxes and bonds. This Ricardian equivalence, as it has come to be known as, would be valid in inter-temporal context as well since the current generation would save more when governments incur deficits and bequeath the wealth to the succeeding generation which would pay taxes to enable the government to pay back the debt. The succeeding generation gets back in debt repayments what it has paid as additional or increased taxes.

The Ricardian equivalence argument has not been settled empirically in the case of industrialized economies. The few exercises carried out with the Indian data, however, show the irrelevance of the Ricardian equivalence proposition. It must, however, be recognized that in countries like India, the private sector behavior in relation to the government's fiscal stance could well be short-sighted because of a number of imperfections that had characterized the economies in transition from a regulated regime to a more liberalized regime.

Sources: Haque, Nadeem U (1988), "Fiscal Policy and Private Saving Behaviour in Developing Economies", *IMF Staff Papers*, Vol 35, No 2, June, pp. 316-35; M S Mohanty (1995), "Budget Deficits and Private Saving in India: Evidence on Ricardian Equivalence", *RBI Occasional Papers*, Vol 16, No 1, March, pp. 1-25; Charan Singh (1998), "Ricardian Equivalence and Consumption in India", *RBI Occasional Papers*, Vol 19, No.1, March, pp.39-60.

Box 5

Ad Hoc Treasury Bills :
The Indian Experience

Monetization by the central bank of a country can take different forms. In essence, however, it means the central bank providing credit to governments by absorbing government securities, be they bonds or treasury bills, of different maturity periods. A somewhat unique Indian experience with monetization was in relation to the practice of the Reserve Bank of India in vogue since 1954-55 till the end of the fiscal year (April-March) 1996-97 to provide credit by absorbing ad hoc treasury bills whenever the Government of India fell short of the minimum balance that it has to maintain with the Reserve bank for the smooth conduct of day to day business. It was agreed mutually between the Government of India and the Reserve Bank since the mid-1950s that the Government would hold Rs. 50 crore as balance as on Fridays when the Reserve Bank's weekly books of accounts would be closed for purposes of compilation of weekly statement of affairs of the Bank for submission to the Central Board of Directors or its committee. To adhere to this agreement it had become necessary to ensure that the account of the Government is replenished whenever the actual balances were below Rs. 50 crore level. The ad hoc treasury bills that were created were generally in multiples of Rs. 5 crore. It followed from this arrangement that whenever the account has a surplus, ad hocs would be cancelled in such amounts as necessary so that the balance is at least at the agreed level. Originally, the agreement was to be in the nature of a temporary arrangement but it later become a regular feature till it was dismantled in the 1990s.

Interestingly enough, the arrangement led very quickly to what had come to be known as 'funding'. The outstanding ad hocs were converted into dated securities, a practice that began in July 1958 and lasted till the arrangement of ad hocs existed. Initially the magnitude of such funding was in the range of Rs. 50-100 crore a year. With the very large accumulation of ad hocs with the Reserve Bank and the attendant problems of rolling over large amounts of short term paper, there was not only a spurt in the amount of funding but also a fundamental change in the basic characteristics of conversion. In the earlier years of conversion, the ad hocs were converted into Government dated securities with some specific maturities at varying rates of interest. From 1982, however, the conversions were only into 4.6 per cent special securities with no specific date for redemption and with the funding entirely taken up by the Reserve Bank.

Ad hocs in effect represent the automatic monetization of Government's budget deficit. In September 1994, a supplemental agreement was signed by the Government of India and the Reserve Bank of India to the effect that over a three year period the arrangement of ad hocs would be phased out. Yet another supplemental agreement was signed by the Government and the Bank in March 1997 to the effect that the outstanding ad hoc treasury bills as on March 31, 1997 would be funded into special securities, without any specified maturity at an interest rate of 4.6 per cent and that the Bank shall make ways and means advances to the Government, if so required, at such rates of interest as may be mutually agreed from time to time up to an agreed limit. Once the ways and means advances are utilized, the Bank would trigger fresh floatation of government securities. This arrangement is in vogue since 1997-98.

4

Banker to Banks

The Essential Tasks and the LoLR Function

Traditionally the central banks required commercial banks to keep a certain amount of bank reserves (cash) with them in order to signal that there would no financial panic since the central banks could put to use such reserves effectively when actually the time of panic arrives. Walter Bagehot in his classic book entitled *Lombard Street* (1873) observed that the Bank of England "... must in time of panic do what all other similar banks must do; that in time of panic it must advance freely and vigorously to the public out of the reserve" (p.147). Bagehot further added : "And with the Bank of England, as with other banks in the same case, these advances, if they are to be made at all, should be made so as if possible to obtain the object for which they are made. The end is to stay the panic; and the advances should, if possible, stay the panic. And for this purpose there are two rules : First, that these loans should only be made at a very high rate of interest. This will operate as a heavy fine on unreasonable timidity, and will prevent the greatest number of applications by persons who do not require it. The rate should be raised early in the panic, so that the fine may be paid early; that no one may borrow out of idle precaution without paying well for it; that the banking reserve may be protected as far as possible.

"Secondly, that at this rate these advances should be made on all good banking securities, and as largely as the public ask for them. The reason is plain. The object is to stay alarm, and nothing therefore should be done to cause alarm. But the way to cause alarm is to refuse someone who has good security to offer" (p.147). This classic description had become a kind of a commandment for all those central banks that were established subsequently.

In the language of the post-Bagehot years, the description of Bagehot as cited above is akin to what is often said, viz., that central banks should act as lenders of last resort (LoLR). In other words, LoLR would imply four elements: (a) it would provide liquidity to illiquid but solvent banks; (b) such loans should be at a penalty rate; (c) lending should be against collateral valued at prices prevalent before the panic; and (d) loans should be made available without limit so long as the borrowing commercial bank is solvent and can provide collateral. The four elements are rather like rigid conditions that may not be present in all cases. In any case, they may not be very helpful. For, as Charles Goodhart (1995) pointed out, it is often difficult to distinguish illiquidity from insolvency. This comment of Goodhart has become particularly relevant since the currency and financial crises in Mexico, and many parts of East Asia in the 1990s. In fact, the LoLR function has come to be applied when economies are in crisis or crisis-like situations, although it is well recognized that it would be applied whenever the central banks perceive the need to rescue commercial banks from facing serious liquidity shortages. This is not to say that every central bank loan to a commercial bank is necessarily a reflection of the LoLR function of the central bank. For, the central banks for reasons of monetary policy, may offer liberally refinancing facilities to commercial banks at reasonable or competitive rates of interest. Refinancing is one of the mechanisms through which banks could draw funds from the central bank generally against collateral, often to promote specific purposes (say against credit extended for export purposes beyond a certain limit). General refinancing facilities too are extended against collateral but they are for the general aim of overcoming temporary liquidity shortages of banks. However, refinancing is not seen as an effective tool of liquidity management. As far as possible, this mechanism should be used by central banks as a discretionary one to ensure that banks exercise financial discipline in working out their asset-liability mismatches. Ordinarily, however, it would be difficult to know when LoLR function is performed in normal times, and when it is triggered to fend off panic. It is often taken for granted that central banks would have adequate resources to tide over difficulties but this may not be true in case the financial crisis is very large due to large-scale defaults by corporate entities of the loans extended by commercial banks. In the financial crisis episodes of the 1990s, the asset price crashes, the large short term borrowing from abroad and huge carry-over of liabilities in the domestic credit market by corporate entities and the wrong selection of borrowers by banks due to information asymmetry have come into open as intractable problems. The last mentioned factor, more commonly referred to in the literature on banking as 'adverse selection' is a critical factor where the central banks' role in being a banker to banks would be under test (See **Box 6** at the end of this chapter for a theoretical account of adverse selection). Adverse selection could occur even when banks on their own adopt credit rationing to equilibrate the credit market but they often are faced with asymmetric information about the risks in lending to particular borrowers. The risks in lending could be to some extent assuaged if collaterals are used as a sorting device to differentiate potential borrowers as well as to enable borrowers to choose a specific type of loan contract. But in many EMEs, the banks are not well trained in measurement of risks in lending. Even if one were to assume that this is not a serious constraint, the recovery of loans might not be easy because of lax banking laws and ineffective enforcement mechanisms. Assuming that credit information bureaus exist

and provide an idea of the profile of creditworthiness of
borrowers, there have to be institutional devices to see that
the borrowers too have knowledge of the pattern of behavior
of banks in the use of collaterals as a way of reducing the risks
in lending. The borrowers rarely get such information because
of lack of transparency practices in the lending policies and
procedures. The central banks in EMEs will therefore have to
see that asymmetries in information are eliminated. Otherwise,
they would have to be constantly in readiness to perform LoLR
function whenever a bank is in a liquidity bind. What is
important to note for central banks is that very rarely the credit
market would collapse without the adverse selection in operation. Adverse selection is an ex ante concept in that it would
have taken place well before the defaults occur. Once the
defaults arise, banks become fragile and financial conditions
will become tight with the result the credit worthiness of
borrowers will decline sharply eventually affecting the macroeconomic performance. Addressing such crisis-situations
require large-scale bail-outs which the central banks in the concerned countries may not be able to undertake on their own,
as the financial crisis experiences of the 1990s have demonstrated. To cite an example, when Mexico faced currency crisis at the end of 1994, the cost of the rescue operation was
found to be so considerable that the Bank of Mexico could not
have handled it all on its own. The US loan guarantees to meet
the crisis were said to be of the order of US $ 50 billion. In
addition, other donors pitched in US $ 10 billion. The Inter-
national Monetary Fund provided a facility that permitted
Mexico to draw upto US $ 17.8 billion. Such bail-outs turned
to be not unique: other currency and financial crises in the
1990s had to be also met by international efforts at rescuing
the emerging economies faced with systemic crises. The central banks, however, have to provide comfort as effective lenders of last resort not so much by improving their capital base
as by strengthening their balance sheet positions. More importantly, the central banks would have to undertake pre-emptive

actions that help to avoid getting into situations where they have to be lenders of last resort. Such pre-emptive actions have been identified as falling in the areas of (a) banking regulations based on prudential principles and monitoring and (b) supervision of commercial banks with respect to such regulations — an aspect that would be the center of the discussion in the section dealing with the 'new concerns' in this book.

We have noted that central banks take care of temporary liquidity gaps in the banking system through a variety of general and special refinancing mechanisms in line with the institutional arrangements in place. Where general or specific refinancing is not allowed, there could still be other ways of addressing the temporary liquidity shortages of banks. One for instance relates to the payment system area (please refer to **Box 2**). Central banks could make a provision of intra-day liquidity on either collateralized or clean basis in the context of the real time gross payment system whereby the financial transactions are settled on a gross and real time basis. The intra-day liquidity is generally provided on certain contracted terms and cannot be carried forward to the next day. If carry-overs are at all allowed, they would be in the nature of exceptions only when there is clear evidence that the banks are placed in highly exceptional circumstances. Even in such circumstances, the borrower banks will have to bear high and often exorbitant penalties. But this mechanism, as already noted, is mainly a way of smoothening out the gridlocks in the payment system and should not be strictly speaking considered as influencing the overall liquidity. A more common way and in fact likely to be most effective of exercising the LoLR function is restricted to the use of open market operations (OMO). Central banks did not operate OMO during the days of Bagehot. They are now known to modulate liquidity requirements of the economy through OMO including the repo and reverse repo operations, and if need be through foreign exchange swaps. When central banks buy government securities from banks, they inject liquidity into the system. When they sell government securities to banks, they absorb some amount of liquidity from the system. The repo is a more recent innovation and is a shortened form of repurchase agreements essentially in the form of contracts to sell and subsequently repurchase securities at a specified date and price. The central bank can sell its securities and suck liquidity for the period of the repo and can do what is called in the Indian context, the reverse repo, by buying securities in order to expand liquidity during the period of the maturity of the repo. Such actions form part of the open market operations of the central bank. When central banks buy foreign exchange from the foreign exchange market, they inject liquidity. Contraction of liquidity would occur when they sell foreign exchange. Open market operations help arrive at what is perceived to be the reasonable level of market interest rates. And it is through the interest rates the central banks often like to transmit influences on prices and on investment.

In general the LoLR function is considered as if it is a framework with rigid rules. But central banks rarely accept a situation where there is no flexibility in their operations as bankers' bank. In fact, in the United States, the Fed has always held the view that discounting is only a privilege and not a right. The Reserve Bank of India regards refinancing as a discretionary instrument to modulate the liquidity position.

The evidence on the functioning of the LoLR function was studied by a number of economists. Two studies made by Miron (1986) and Bordo (1990) are worth mentioning here. Miron showed that the Federal Reserve Board's creation in 1914 has helped to reduce bank panics. Between 1915 and 1928, there were no financial panics in the US. But between 1929 and 1933, panics and failures of banks were considerable. However, as argued by Friedman and Schwartz (1963), the series of bank failures during this period were because of the failure of the Fed to prevent decline in money stock. Some consider the Fed as having been lax in putting in place the Bagehot principles. This view has been accepted. Bordo's analysis compares the situation in the United Kingdom and the United States in relation to the existence of the LoLR system. After 1866, the Bank of England adopted the principles of Bagehot and prevented incipient crises at least till the World War I. During the period, 1870-1913, the United States experienced four panics mainly because it did not have a central banking system with LoLR.

It is however difficult to measure the effect of LoLR on banks' behavior. The inter-country comparisons may not be adequate to bring into open such effects. If the banks perceive the central banks' LoLR function as a safeguard of the financial system and indulge in questionable lending practices, there will be a moral hazard. If on the other hand, there is 'free' banking, i.e., banking without a central bank, there could arise unknown risks to the financial system. The modern day central banks consider it their duty to foster financial stability and use the LoLR function with considerable degree of discretion.

As bankers to banks, central banks also provide a number of services, often of technical nature. For instance, payment and settlement services in most developing and emerging economies are provided by central banks often without any levy or at highly subsidized cost. Some central banks also provide their skills either directly through secondment of their personnel or through training, in areas such as risk management, information technology, foreign exchange management, and treasury management (management of investment portfolios). In some emerging countries, they on their own or at times collaborating with commercial banks have created new institutional arrangements for development of money and government securities markets.

Bank Restructuring

Central banks in EMEs also help commercial banks to gain improved viability through such measures as consolidation and mergers of banks, and through appropriate licensing procedures for opening of branch offices. Economies of scale, in this process, are expected to help banks to economize on costs. Indirectly, this process would help improve banking habits and lead to increase in the savings of the household sector. In India, in the 1950s and the early 1960s, some of the small banks were consolidated under the guidance of the Reserve Bank of India. After the nationalization of 14 major commercial banks in 1969, branch licensing was undertaken on a large scale partly to increase the scale and range of lending operations of banks in far-flung areas of the country and partly to help create avenues for households to save in the form of bank deposits.

Central banks can help banks to exploit the economies of scope by expanding the functional coverage of banks. For instance, the nationalized banks in India since 1969 have been allowed to diversify their loans into areas other than export and modern large scale industries. They could increase their loans to agriculture and small scale industries whose share in the nation's GDP was at that time as high as 50 per cent. Banks were permitted to invest in capital markets within some prudential limits. More recently, since about the mid-1990s, banks have been encouraged to provide customer services in a variety of areas such as insurance, investment banking, and other fee-based activities.

The central bank's role in helping commercial banks to exploit the economies of scale and scope, follows to an extent from the central bank's function as a regulator and supervisor of the financial, especially the banking system, and partly from the felt need to improve the effectiveness of monetary policy. But bank restructuring as a subject came to the forefront in recent years mainly because of a number of banking crises, in particular during the 1990s. Banking crises occurred mainly because of high rates of credit growth, higher than the rates of real output growth. Other causes and factors that intensify the crises were identified as the inadequacy of capital base, poor assessment of credit risks by banks, inadequately diversified loan portfolio, lending to connected business units, large mismatches in currency and maturity of securities held, restrictive labor practices in banks, inability to cope with cyclical swings in economic activity, exchange rate volatility, declines in asset prices, exogenous shocks such as the oil price hikes, insufficient competition, credit allocations by Governments or monetary authorities, inadequate legal framework to recover debts, and inadequate regulatory and supervisory regimes (BIS 1999). To address these problems, and to go ahead with bank restructuring, a number of approaches have been advocated. Some of them could be tried in combinations. The approaches are — capital injection preferably by the Governments, institution of asset management corporations by law, if need be or by the regulatory authority of the central banks, domestic bank mergers, and foreign take-over of domestic banks. Deposit insurance could also be helpful in forestalling runs on banks.

Central banks will have to play an active role in bank restructuring in EMEs besides providing general assistance and special accommodation facilities. Often times, central banks will need to coordinate their actions with the Governments since bank restructuring without the support of corporate restructuring would not be effective. Besides, central banks will need to put in place strict guidelines relating to exposure limits in respect of domestic loans, and foreign exchange and maturity limits and insist on banks to adopt transparency practices through disclosures and dissemination of their auditing and accounting policies and practices. Where public sector banks are dominant as in India, it is essential central banks evolve the guidelines in consultation with the Government and widely disseminate the outcomes of such coordination exercises.

The Areas Where Commercial Banks Could be of Help

Commercial banks, working as agents of the central bank in the handling of government accounts, or in the distribution of currency provide welfare-oriented services to the general public. Such services are usually provided at reasonable cost. Had they not been providing such services, the central banks would have been rendered ineffective in the discharge of their functions as bankers to government and as issuers and distributors of currency.

In some industrialized countries, large commercial banks also function as service providers. For instance, cheque processing activity is permitted to be undertaken by commercial banks. In the US, private service providers that could include commercial banks compete with some of the Federal Reserve Banks in processing cheques. In India, cheque processing is presently being done both by the Reserve Bank of India and some designated commercial banks. The Indian and the US models in this regard would be largely followed by other EMEs as well as some of the developing countries. Banks could also issue notes (as in Hong Kong) but this is not a widely favored proposition.

Box 6

Theoretical Perspectives on Adverse Selection

Adverse selection occurs in the credit market when lenders (i.e., banks) provide funds to projects that do not give assured viability, hoping that projects will succeed over time with some assumed or promised actions on the part of borrowers. It could also occur when banks, not fully aware of the different risks that borrowers carry, provide funds at high interest rates in order to improve banks' expected profits. An increase in interest rates, however, decreases the demand for loans. This happens because the viable and less risky borrowers will not seek bank financing. This will mean that banks' expected profits would not improve. An increase in interest rates in fact would bring about adverse or bad consequences for the banks' liquidity position that depends mainly on repayment amounts. Banks, however, could use collaterals such as real estate as screening device to assess the risks of different loans. However, if the values of collaterals collapse, or where recovery from sales of collaterals in the event of default is not enabled because of weak laws, banks' liquidity would be subjected to potential stress. In order to reduce losses from bad loans, banks will have to ration the volume of loans, instead of raising the rate of interest on their loans — a conclusion that was most vividly brought out by Stiglitz and Weiss (1981).

Adverse selection occurs essentially because of asymmetric information. In countries where demand for credit is often in excess of supply of credit, there will be no 'equilibrium' in the classical sense of the term. However, there could still be equilibrium when credit rationing is introduced at a rate of interest beyond which the supply of credit will tend to move downward. The credit rationing could also occur if there is a ceiling on the loan rate of interest. However, as the ceiling rates on loans are not favored in IEs as well as in EMEs, banks become price setters on the credit market with a view to optimizing the twin objectives of maximizing their profits and minimizing their risks. In a competitive situation where there are a large number of banks, banks become quantity setters on the deposit market, while retaining their position as price setters on the credit market. In simple terms, this means that the banks' demand for deposits and nominal interest rates on loans will be determined with a view to maximizing their own profits, taking into account the returns sought by depositors and the loan rates set by competitor banks.

Asymmetric information occurs because one side of the market — borrowers in this case — has better information than the other — banks in this case. The borrower thus knows more than the lender about her creditworthiness. Thus 'private' information could lead to malfunctioning of markets. To protect from the adverse consequences of information asymmetries, guarantees by professional entities could mitigate to some extent the consequences.

Assume for the sake of argument that a borrower, B, of a bank after taking the loan differs from the profile of the project that B supplied to the bank for gaining loan sanction. B would have behaved so in order to make profits by cutting costs through the use of low quality inputs or materials in her products. Sales of B's products may pick up initially but once the markets realize that B's products are inferior in quality compared to those of competitor firms, sales of B's products would decline, causing a sharp dip in B's profits. This could lead to B defaulting on the loans taken from her bank. Such a case is one of moral hazard, since B's action was 'immoral' in relation to the position envisaged while applying for bank loan.

The literature on asymmetric information has grown enormously since the 1970s and it is being applied in numerous areas of economics and finance. The first major contribution on asymmetric information was that of Akerlof (1970). Subsequently, Spence (1973 and 1974) demonstrated how agents in a market could use signaling to counteract the effects of adverse selection. Stiglitz along with Rothschild complemented the insights given by Akerlof and Spence through a seminal article in 1976. In 1981, Stiglitz along with Weiss analyzed credit markets with asymmetric information and pointed to credit rationing to reduce the impact of bad loans.

Section III

The Shining Star of Central Banking

5. Monetary Policy Making in Open/Semi-open Economies *101*

- Objectives of Policy
- Reconciling Dual Objectives through a Policy Rule
- The Taylor Rule
- The Case for Rules As Against Discretion
- The Case for Discretion
- Indicators of Policy
- Lags in Policy
- Instruments of Policy
- Transmission Mechanism of Policy
- An Evaluation of the Channels in the Context of EMEs
- Uncertainties Due to Lags
- Transparency of Policies and Practices

Box 7 : *Liquidity Adjustment Facility in India*

Box 8 : *Bank Reserves, Reserve Money, Money Supply, and Money Multiplier*

Box 9 : *Payments Systems and Monetary Policy*

Monetary Policy Making in Open / Semi-open Economies

MONETARY policy making is at the heart of central bank's functioning. Most central banks make it appear as though it is a simple-looking framework of setting up objectives (or targets), indicators, and instruments and provide rationale for their policy actions. This is deceptively convincing. For, monetary policy is one of the several but critical areas of economic policy. It is important therefore to ensure that the framework is comprehensive and reflective of clarity as EMEs develop markets and openness. The process of such financial development and openness would operate inevitably under the constraint of uncertainties. Comprehensiveness is vital to reduce informational problems that are associated with market development and to be transparent about the objectives, practices, and procedures of policy. Clarity is necessary to provide clear signals to the commodity and financial markets about the stance of monetary policy and to improve expectations formation processes.

The relevant authority of monetary policy is the central bank or the 'monetary authority' (not the currency board) but this does not necessarily mean that the authority is absolute. The potential instruments of policy would include a variety of rate and quantity variables. The rate variables are typically the short term ones, of which one would be officially designated as the main indicator of the stance of policy. The rate variables are: the inter-bank call money rate, the rediscount rate, the bank rate, the refinance rate, the short-dated treasury bill rate, the short period deposit rate, and the repo rate. The quantity variable would generally be one of the following: the reserve money (bank reserves plus currency with the public), or the non-borrowed bank reserves, or the money supply — either the narrow one of transactions money consisting of currency with the public and demand deposits with banks or the broader one of transactions money plus fixed or time deposits with the banking system). It must, however, be noted that money supply is used as an indicator variable as well as a target variable, even though it is not wholly controlled by central banks.

Objectives of Policy

The objectives of monetary policy are often stated in terms of the ultimate ones and the intermediate ones. The latter, *viz.*, the intermediate objectives, however, has lost relevance since there is very little of empirical proof to show that there is a clear-cut channel by which one could transit first to the intermediate objective and then move over to the ultimate objective through the use of some policy instrument or the other, with certainty. The mechanism of such transmission is unclear. However, references exist in the economic literature to money supply targeting as an intermediate target or a center of focus of central banks, especially in EMEs. Nominal income targeting and exchange rate targeting are the other possible candidates for serving as the intermediate objectives (targets). Given the lack of clarity about the channel of transmission from a policy instrument to the ultimate target passing through an intermediate target, it would be appropriate to concentrate only on the ultimate objectives (targets) as goals of policy.

What should be the ideal number of ultimate objectives of monetary policy ? There is no definitive answer to this question. Going by the Tinbergen-type argument, the number of objectives should not be too many, since it is not always possible to have an equal number of policy instruments to realize the objectives. Therefore, it is said that if the number of objectives is 'n' in number, there should at least be 'n' number of instruments of policy. The principle of 'n × n' objective-instrument compatibility is considered as necessary for appropriate identification of the system underlying the policy model.

The ultimate objectives that are often mentioned by a majority of central banks are two. These are: price stability (defined as low and stable increase in the general level of prices or inflation) and full employment or output maximization (sometimes referred to as growth in output). Some central banks (for instance, of New Zealand, Canada, the United Kingdom, Australia, Sweden, Finland and Spain) have specifically adopted price stability as the only objective and have accordingly, specified inflation targets for the year. Such inflation targeting is adopted also by a few EMEs. In the US, both the objectives are pursued but the monetary policy regime has been biased towards inflation targeting within the framework of the duality of objectives.

Inflation control is viewed as vital because it enables countries to pursue the growth objective in an orderly and definitive manner. It is said that for every economy, there would be a threshold rate of inflation at which economic growth is maximized or optimized. Robert Barro working with data for a sample of countries and with a simple statistical method of graphs of trade-offs, showed that high inflation rates of over 10 per cent would be inimical to growth, and that optimal growth is possible only when the inflation rate is below 7 per cent. Some studies on India where inflation is measured in terms of changes in the wholesale price index of 'all commodities' taken as an appropriate proxy for measuring inflation based on consumer prices, showed that at 6-7 per cent threshold rate of inflation, it is possible to optimize growth. (See Barro, Robert J (1995); also Vasudevan A, B K Bhoi and S C Dhal (1999) in Vasudevan, A et al (eds) (1999)). A recent study by Khan and Senhadji (2000) showed that the threshold beyond which inflation would have a negative impact on growth is lower for industrial countries (1-3 per cent) than for developing countries (7-11 per cent) depending on the estimation method.

The studies show that there is a fairly close relationship between inflation and growth but this cannot be an argument for having only one objective for monetary policy. It can at best be used as an argument in favor of having inflation control. Essentially, the single objective pursuit by pure inflation targeters is advocated on the ground that it is transparent and clear, and makes the central bank accountable. The objective, however, is rarely given as a point estimate. It is usually stated as a range and generally specified for the medium term period. Since the central bank generally pursues the inflation target as a matter of course, it often specifies it. But this need not necessarily be the case, for the inflation target could well be given by the government. There could be deviations from the medium term target path but when the deviation is by a certain specified basis point, the central banks are often required to consult the government about the course of policy actions that need to be taken both by the monetary and fiscal authorities to bring the inflation outcome back to the target path. This does not imply that one needs to be a pure 'inflation nutter', as picturesquely described by Mervyn King: it is enough to have inflation targeting in the form of a specified inflation target even where the central bank is required to pursue dual objectives.

Despite the strong academic support for and interest in the advocacy of a single objective, namely the inflation targeting, most central banks (and in any case in most EMEs) pursue more than one objective of monetary policy not merely for complying with the statutory requirements but also because they perform certain functions of micro-economic and strategic nature that are intimately linked with the pursuit of the macro objectives of central banking/monetary policy. This point needs some elaboration. One of the micro-economic functions for instance pertains to prudential regulation and supervision of banks that affects not only the behavior of the market (both borrowers and lenders) but also the reserve money/monetary base. Reserve money is nothing but liquid cash in the economy. It represents, to put it in simple terms, the currency with the banks, the cash held in the vaults of the banks, and the cash reserves held with the central bank of the country. To the extent the reserve money or the cash base provides the basis for lending, the banks would supply credit whereas it is the market behavior that determines the demand for credit. Monetary policy has impact on the supply side of credit but to be credible, it has to ensure that the supply of and demand for credit are equal. In addition to the microeconomic functions, central banks perform strategic functions such as the management of payment and settlement system. This, as we have already seen, is generally in the hands of central banks in EMEs. The payment infrastructure facilitates cash flows in the financial system. This in turn affects the market behavior and impacts on the banks' decisions relating to loan operations. Monetary policy by working through the quantity and rate variables would have to reckon the banks' behavior in regard to lending and therefore will have to consider the strategic functions as well.

Reconciling Dual Objectives through a Policy Rule

As central banks often pursue two objectives, they will have to reconcile them to avoid problems of inconsistency in policy making. For this purpose, it would be necessary to quantify the objectives. However, very rarely do the central banks show an inclination to specify the full employment level largely because of the difficulty in quantifying the tolerable level of unemployment rate. In many EMEs, data on unemployment are very weak, if not non-existent. It is much more so in populous EMEs like India. Central banks therefore prefer to estimate the desired level of output or the likely rate of increase in output. This, however, may not be sufficient for purposes of targeting, since the estimated value of growth of output has to be related to the capacity of the economy to produce the estimated outcome. Once this premise is accepted, the central banks would need to reduce the variability of output relative to the potential output, which for purposes of convenience will have to be treated as full employment output. In developing and emerging economies, however, it is difficult to specify the potential output, notwithstanding the attempts to estimate potential output growth in some EMEs (see for example, Roldos, Jorge (1997); Donde, Kshitija & Mridul Saggar (1999); and Dhal, Sarat Chandra (1999)). Besides reducing the variability of output (also referred to as output gap), countries prefer low and stable inflation.

Some practical ways of looking at the potential output estimation are, however, possible. As real income grows, the trend level of income would go up and would over time represent what may be regarded as moving towards the economy's maximum sustainable level of output. Such a sustainable output, in the absence of any other scientific method of estimation, could be treated as potential output for purposes of argument. The exercise of reducing the output gap would be rendered possible if the markets are integrated and are led by considerations of the liquidity level and/or the rate of interest.

Is such an exercise possible ? Indeed, it is in practice followed by central banks without being specific and with some nuanced variations. However, to be logically sound and to influence market expectations, the exercise will have to be in the form of a specific rule. The rule, to be effective, must be expressed in terms of a variable over which the central bank has control. One such variable is the money supply with the public.

If money supply growth is manipulated to be equal to the rate of growth of output, then the price level will be stable and inflation rate will be zero. Such a rule is attributed to Milton Friedman (1960). Friedman's guess was that the appropriate money supply growth was about 4 per cent a year, accommodating a 3 per cent growth of real output per year and a 1 per cent annual decline in velocity. But this suggestion was questioned on the ground that central banks cannot directly control money supply but can only indirectly manipulate it. Again, the technology factor embedded in the new payments systems could lead to uncertainty about the effect of money supply growth on prices. It is for this reason some economists like Bennett McCallum (1989) favored a rule in terms of a monetary base or a reserve measure, with suitable adjustments in reserve money velocity (GDP/RM) to reflect the payment technology growth and minimization of nominal GNP growth to take care of cyclical fluctuations in real output.

Neither of these suggestions worked in reality. The quantity variables failed as the financial sector grew with a large number of innovations weakening the influence of money supply on the economy and the link between bank reserves/reserve money and the overall liquidity of the economy. In the United States, the rule therefore is expressed in terms of a short term nominal rate of interest (the federal funds rate) over which the Fed has control.

It is against this background, one needs to study the rule that has gained considerable attention in recent years. The rule has come to be known as the Taylor rule, named after the seminal article by John Taylor (1993). What does the rule say ?

The Taylor Rule

The Taylor rule could be written simply as :

$$R = r^* + p + a\,((y\text{-}y^*)\text{-}1) + b\,(p\text{-}p^*)$$

In the above equation, R is the target nominal interest rate that is policy-centric, r^* is the equilibrium real level of the policy interest rate, y is output, y^* is the potential output level, p is inflation, p^* is the target for inflation, and a and b are the parameters that describe the response of the policy rate to deviations of output and inflation respectively from their potential level and target rate.

The Taylor rule makes the point that it is possible to operate with stabilization of output as a goal, and at the same time provide for average inflation to be consistent with the medium term inflation target. The rule helps to minimize the variability in output and inflation around the potential and target levels respectively. Central banks in IEs work out potential output and fix, at least for internal policy purposes, a target for inflation. In some EMEs, for instance in Chile, the output gap is estimated and an inflation target implicitly laid down. But this by itself does not imply that the Taylor rule can be applied blindly. In reality, despite the enormous amount of discussion on the Taylor rule, it has not been adopted *formally* by any central bank. However, most central banks are aware of it and recognize its usefulness. Nonetheless, there are some limitations. It is said, for example, that the Taylor rule is not valid in open economies where exchange rates could have significant effects on the economy. Also it is argued that the application of the Taylor rule is too narrow and some additional variables such as lagged interest rates, and a variable representing central bank independence may have to be incorporated. Besides, it is observed that the rule may not be applicable to many EMEs in view of the statistical difficulties in estimating the equilibrium real interest rate, besides the potential output, and the politically unfeasible determination of the target inflation. The last of the criticisms, however, is an overstretched one. To be fair to Taylor, he did state that he is not one for interest rate setting under all circumstances. In his view, in EMEs where money demand functions are stable and interest rates are not a fair guide, monetary aggregates could be used.

The Case for Rules as against Discretion

Is it necessary to have rules at all ? Cannot central banks take actions according to the circumstances instead of being constrained by rigid rules ? This question needs to be seen in the light of the argument that central banks under the mistaken impression that output could be maximized in the short run may follow accommodating monetary policies which end up in generating inflation pressures. Such an action would be inconsistent with the objective of maximizing growth with minimal inflation over a period of time and has therefore come to be known as 'time inconsistent' or 'dynamic inconsistency'. Central bankers would need to avoid such a problem (Please refer to Chapter 7 for more details on the time inconsistency problem). This is one of the reasons for favoring rules rather than discretion. Reliance on some policy rules is said to help improve economic performance. A powerful exposition in this regard was made by Kydland and Prescott (1977) who observed that central bankers should not be given discretion not because they are 'stupid or evil' but because they could select a decision which is best only in the current situation but may not be optimal or promoting economic stability. Barro and Gordon (1983) felt that the tendency to cheat to secure benefits from inflation shocks when monetary policy rules are in place, would threaten the viability of the equilibrium that is based on rules. As the interactions between the policy maker and the private agents get repeated, the reputation or credibility would often spur the policymaker to follow the policy rule. In other words, the benefits that could accrue in the short run from inflation shocks would be more than nullified by the gains that low average inflation would afford over the long term. Rogoff (1985) dealing with the point of 'dynamic inconsistency' or 'time inconsistency' argument that central banks seek often to boost output or employment by generating inflation, argues that for monetary policy to stabilize inflation and employment around their mean market-determined levels, societies often would like the central bank to place a large weight on stabilization of the inflation to employment stabilization because that would be welfare-maximizing.

The Case for Discretion

Notwithstanding the dominance of the academic literature on optimal policy rules, central bankers prefer to have discretion in the use of the instruments of policy. The argument often advanced is that there will be continuous inflow of new information about the processes of change in the economic structure and the formation of expectations that have to be added on to the base level information about the current state of the economy. This will imply that application of rigid rules based on historical or past information or abstract hypotheses may not be effective in addressing the current problems as they evolve. More fundamentally, the preference for discretion is because of several other reasons as well. First, there is no certainty about the impact of policy measures. Secondly, the lag structures are not well known. Thirdly, the economic uncertainties due to openness of economies, the quick and significant capital mobility and the changes arising out of the use of new technologies have impacted both on the lag structures as well as on the transmission channels of policy. Finally, the capital mobility and issues of domestic financial sector fragility have compelled central banks in EMEs to view financial stability as an objective equal in importance to the objectives of price stability and output expansion.

Discretion is sought by central banks in EMEs because of the uncertain effects of opening up of the economy. Traditionally, the impact of capital inflows as well as outflows is sterilized by central banks by measures that bring about offsetting changes in bank credit, especially for the private sector. The measures could be in the form of increase in interest rates, reduction of refinance or rise in cash reserve ratios. But sterilization efforts have often been found to be not very effective. Inflows lead to increase in domestic liquidity and often to rise in prices. This in turn generates cost increases and results in lack of competitiveness in foreign trade and in appreciation of the domestic currency vis-à-vis the foreign currencies. More importantly, inflows also mean widening of external current account deficits (i.e., the excess of imports of goods and services over exports of goods and services) often fuelled by fiscal deficits. The growing current account deficits often lead to loss of confidence in the economy, eventually resulting in capital outflows. Such outflows, as the experience of the financial sector crises in some countries of Asia and Latin America in the 1990s has shown, often meant inability to service external debt obligations and sharp cutbacks in both public and private investment expenditures. If, in such circumstances, the banks too are financially fragile and are not able to recover the loans disbursed by them due to failures of their customers to pay back, there could arise financial or systemic crises. Central banks have found it difficult to address such situations of financial instability through pure monetary policy measures. The experience of the 1990s emphasized the need to pursue financial stability as an objective in a more comprehensive manner through an array of measures that go beyond the jurisdiction of central banks. But central banks will have to give central role to financial stability, being the arbiters of the financial development processes and of the stability of the banking systems.

With financial stability occupying a critical place in the array of objectives of central banks, monetary policy making has become complex. For, the larger the number of objectives and thus targets, the greater the difficulty in finding an equal number of effective policy instruments. This is, as stated earlier, in consonance with the Tinbergen-Brainard tradition, wherein it has been well proved that it is important to have n instruments of policy to match n targets : otherwise, the solution would be either over- or under- specified as the case may be. This is perhaps one reason why some central banks have opted for pursuing a single objective such as inflation targeting. But the reality is that there were many financial crises in the world, both in the present day IEs and the EMEs. Central banks need to therefore have discretion in policy making at least to address economic uncertainties in the short run. This will imply that central banks will have to evolve sound monitoring mechanisms to track the evolving economic and financial situations.

Indicators of Policy

Monetary policy makers could be expected to take actions depending on the economic indicators that they monitor to assess the conditions existing in the economy. The indicators triggering action should ideally be neither targets nor instruments but this may not always be possible. All central banks tend to monitor good many macro- and micro-indicators on a regular basis: they are, to briefly mention a few: output, especially of the critically important segments of the economy, nominal and real wages where such information sets are available, monetary aggregates such as narrow and broad money and reserve money, growth in bank credit to private sector, and to a few vital economic activities, industrial sales, imports, private consumption, fiscal position, foreign borrowings, changes in consumer prices and exchange rates. As and when new information flows in, they are added on to the above set of indicators. These however are all macroeconomic indicators. In addition, central banks monitor a number of micro indicators. For example, the financial strength of banks that supervision mechanisms reveal is reckoned in monetary policy making because the level of non-performing assets would often suggest to the central bank the advisability or otherwise of undertaking measures that would have a bearing on the profitability of banks and soundness of the financial system. Again, data on payments — especially the cross border payments — are taken into account because any failure to pay could lead to panics and financial instability.

The question to be asked is whether the set of indicators would help predict future movements in macroeconomic and microeconomic variables. It is not, for example, so important to know whether the change in the price level today follows the trends in the movements of the price level of the past years or months. But it is important to know the incremental predictive content in the vast amount of information that is often collected by central banks about the indications of inflation. In other words, if the current data of price level is not readily available, the central banks should be in a position to make an intuitive judgment about what is likely to be the current price level on the basis of the predictive power of the data located in the bank's data warehouse.

Lags in Policy

The above procedure of making forecasts is often adopted in many central banks, at any rate in industrialized economies essentially to reduce the lags in the *recognition* of the potential problems. The recognition lag would be minimized if the statistical system is efficient in the sense that the data are not only collected on a continuous and frequent basis, stored, monitored but are analyzed for policy purposes. Central banks seek discretion not so much because of the existence of recognition lags as because of lags in execution or implementation of policy. Such lags arise mainly because of (a) institutional constraints and legal shortcomings, and (b) the problem of deciding on the 'size' of the action that may have to be taken. The institutional and legal constraints, however, could be addressed as part of financial reforms, but the determination of 'how much' of action is essential to address the problem is not easy despite the numerical values that one could obtain from the econometric tests of relationships among the variables such as, for example, those included in the Taylor's rule. This is because such tests could be period specific and could well vary when the policy regimes shift or are reoriented. Besides, the fact that economic structures are changing and economic environment is constantly on the churn owing to shifts in the expectations of market participants should caution the central bankers to be conservative while undertaking policy measures. One way that is often followed to resolve this issue is to respond to the recognized problem by undertaking the proposed policy measure in gradual doses, even if the econometric evidence of the past data suggests the need for a sharper change in the policy measure. For example, an increase in output by say z may be possible by a one percentage point decrease in interest rate, according to the econometric tests. If output increase to the extent of z is desired, the policy interest rate will then have to be reduced by 100 basis points. However, very rarely central bankers take such a position. They will, in this case, reduce interest rates by a smaller order and wait for the outcome. Such a gradualist approach would essentially reflect what has come to be known as interest rate smoothing. However, for such an approach to be credible, the central bank would have to signal its intention of having a medium term path of the policy variable that would closely mimic the market expectations. For this reason, it might become necessary for central banks to adopt transparent practices of their monetary policies.

It is generally recognized that the lag between the execution of the measure and the actual outcome — the impact lag — could be long and variable. The impact lags depend on the efficacy of the transmission mechanism of policy assuming the market expectations to be neutral in the meantime. For industrialized economies, these lags are placed anywhere between 12 months and 18 months, notwithstanding the sharp increases in the efficiency of the new payment and settlement technologies set in place in recent years. Estimations of lags for EMEs are rarely in evidence. A study conducted for India showed that the lags are fairly long and large in India, a result that is close to what was pointed out by Milton Friedman (See Nachane, D M and R Lakshmi (1999)).

Instruments of Policy

The instruments of policy that central banks often wield are several. They are generally classified as direct and indirect instruments but the classification by itself is not as important as the ability of the central bank to undertake policies in time and monitor their impact in order to take further corrective actions. In practice the policy instruments in most EMEs boil down essentially to four: the Bank or Discount rate, the open market operations, the changes in the reserve requirements (both primary and secondary), and selective credit controls (Chandavarkar, Anand (1996)). Credit allocative devices are generally not used in EMEs even though there could be guidelines for lending to specific activities or industries or regions, and for promoting the overall social welfare objectives. This is sometimes referred to as 'directed lending' because the guidelines specify the amount of credit so dispensed in relation to either total liabilities or total loans of the banks. Credit allocations are regarded as distortionary from the point of view of resource allocation. In India, lending for priority sectors is required to be 40 per cent of the total net advances of a bank. Such credit directions, if not constrained by interest rate stipulations, may not be as unwelcome as they appear in the first instance during periods when the demand for bank credit from the rest of the economy is relatively weak. The Indian version is a softer version of directed lending compared with the harder version of requiring commercial banks to seek authorization of each and every loan from the central bank beyond an arbitrarily set size-limit. Credit authorization in fact was in existence in India in the 1970s and 1980s. As such authorizations have the potential of being misused, and could in some cases, be unhelpful to growth, no central bank in the EMEs at the present time uses this instrument.

Bank Rate

The Bank or discount rate is the rate at which commercial banks could borrow from or rediscount bills with the central bank of the country. The higher the Bank rate — higher than the short term money market rate such as the interbank overnight rate — the costlier the access to central bank money. In general central banks do not lend on a 'clean' basis: they insist on collateral whose market values do not change significantly from the nominal value of the loan. In most cases there will be margins for lending — margins that take care of the probable loss of the market value during the tenor of the loan. Many central banks also do not allow access to their funds on an automatic basis : they fix criteria for access and often times make the access entirely discretionary. However, in some countries such as India, central banks in order to subserve certain aims such as the development of financial markets or promotion of exports, have allowed refinancing of the loans extended by commercial banks for the specified sectors at rates that are pre-determined at levels that are profitable for commercial banks. General refinancing may not be in place, and may, where permitted, not be automatic. Besides, such refinancing may not be to the full extent of the loans extended for the specified purposes.

Open Market Operations

While the Bank rate is an important policy instrument, by itself it may not be effective unless conditions are created to ensure that banks approach central banks for funds. It is a direct instrument having a bearing on financial intermediation. The traditional thinking is that, to be more effective, the Bank rate should be used along with open market operations (OMO) under which the central banks help to change the liquidity conditions in the economy by operating in the market either as buyers or sellers of government securities. The operations that take place in the secondary markets are more important than the ones in the primary market in government securities. This distinction is important because central banks can enter the primary market only as absorbers or buyers and not as sellers. Besides, primary market transactions need not be open

for all participants: it could be in the form of private placement of securities for funding the government, leading to a
direct and often immediate increase in money supply. This has
happened in many EMEs including India. If increase in money
supply is not perceived as temporary and is taken as a part of
the medium term path of money supply growth, there could
then be significant effects on market expectations. First, the
expected future nominal short-term rates of interest could drift
lower owing to increase in liquidity and lower the expected
long-term nominal interest rates as well. Secondly, the likelihood of higher inflation rate arising out of expansion in money
supply could also lower the expected long-term real interest
rates which, to be credible, would have to imply that the long-
term nominal interest rates would need to be consistent with
a medium term path of short-term nominal interest rates (This
idea is borrowed from Laurence H Meyer's remarks, "Does
Money Matter?", on the occasion of the 2001 Homer Jones
Memorial Lecture, Washington University, St Louis, Missouri;
see Meyer, Laurence H (2001)). In view of the advantage that
is created in the lowering of the expected real interest rates,
and in order to be effective debt managers, central banks in
EMEs tend to buy government securities in the primary market.

The central bank actions in the secondary market, however,
could be liquidity injecting or liquidity absorbing. These are
more in the nature of what is known as the 'structural' form
of OMO. The securities in question could be of Central (or
Federal) or State governments and they could be of different
maturities — ranging from one-year bond to a long term bond
of 20/30 years. Treasury bills of shorter maturities — 7 days,
14 days, 28 days, 91 days, 182 days, 365 days — could also
be a part of the structured OMO, but they are most ideal for
selling and buying in the secondary market as part of what may
be called the 'fine tuning' of OMO for influencing the liquidity conditions and the movements in the short term interest
rate.

Central banks can also resort to what have come to be known as repo operations as part of OMO. The word, repo, is the shortened form of repurchase agreement. The agreement could be sold and repurchased by the central banks. Repos when sold by the central banks would mean that the central banks have borrowed funds from the market. Usually, the sales would be of short-term government securities in the money market on condition that the instruments will be repurchased at a given date (say after a day, or after 3 days, or after 14 days). Such repos are also called gilt repos to distinguish them from repos used widely in the industrialized economies as a borrowing method by large corporations, banks and non-banking institutions. Repos when purchased by the central banks from the money market would lead to increase in liquidity. To put it differently, the banks operating in the money market would be exchanging their government securities against payment of cash on condition that they would repurchase their securities on a given date. Such purchase operations by central banks are called the reverse repo operations in India, though such an expression is not found in the general literature on central banking. Repo transactions (including the reverse repos in the case of India) represent the central bank's act of fine tuning of OMO.

Repos can also be used as part of liquidity adjustment facility (LAF) wherever central banks install such a facility. The Hong Kong Monetary Authority made the use of LAF a viable fine tuning OMO. In India too, LAF was introduced though in a variant form. It was introduced in June 2000 to adjust liquidity and transmit interest rate signals to the markets. Repos under LAF could be used to absorb liquidity and reverse repos could be permitted to inject liquidity. The manner in which LAF works in India is provided in **Box 7** at the end of this chapter.

Repos could be regarded, in a loose sense though, as derived from the prime instrument. But they are not to be treated as hedging instruments in the sense of financial derivatives. Central banks often resort to derivatives such as swap or switch operations wherein the securities of different maturities are changed into a different set or sets of maturities without altering the total size of the public debt. Swaps could occur also across currencies. Let us illustrate how the interest rate swaps work. Suppose a bank borrows long term at a fixed interest rate of say 10 per cent. It then wishes to convert this fixed rate liability into a floating rate liability. To convert, it has to sell a swap, since it would be a floating-rate payment party. It contracts to send floating payments to the insurer equal to say LIBOR (London Inter-bank Overnight Rate) plus 1 per cent. Let us assume that this rate (Libor +1 per cent) would be equal to the insurer's cost of debt when borrowing short term. In return, the bank receives from the insurer fixed payments equal to 11 per cent a year. These fixed payments will then be equal to the bank's 10 per cent cost of debt plus an additional 1 per cent mark up payment. As a result, the bank's net cost of funds (or net payments) after the swap would be equal to Libor. Instead, had the bank engaged in direct hedging by borrowing in the short term floating market where, let us assume, the rate is Libor + ½ of 1 per cent, it would have paid more. Thus, the bank by the swap could save ½ of 1 per cent in financing costs. Similarly, a cross currency swap can also be undertaken entailing the exchange of a fixed rate obligation in one currency for a floating rate obligation in another. On the other hand, typical foreign exchange swaps would occur when there is a simultaneous buying and selling of a currency in approximately equal amounts for different maturity dates. In such an event, the swap prices would be the difference in price between the two maturity dates of the swap.

OMO could be fine tuned to sell / buy any derivative instrument — not necessarily the securities issued by the Government and could well be the securities that central banks in some countries issue on their own. But the central banks should possess such prime securities in sufficient quantities. OMO could also be in terms of foreign exchange swaps but for this the EMEs should have a clear idea of what the sustainable exchange rate is as well as the strength of the link between the money market and the foreign exchange market. OMO however are used often to stabilize the money market rather than the foreign exchange market since the foreign exchange markets cannot be stabilized in cases where the countries that issue foreign currencies do not cooperate. Concerted coordination of policies is therefore advocated for reducing exchange rate volatility in IEs. The same principle holds good in EMEs that are completely open.

The success of OMO would depend as much on the size and depth of the market as on the amount and type of securities that the central bank holds. What is important from the point of view of EMEs is that the OMO should enable the central bank to foster and develop an active government securities market. In most EMEs the primary market would have as participants, the central banks themselves, commercial banks, other financial institutions including primary and secondary security dealers and brokers. The secondary market participants would not differ very much from that of the primary market except that some individuals, and trusts and funds might be interested in transacting in government securities. In order to develop both the primary and secondary markets, it is vital that the auctioning system and the timing of the auctions are properly structured. Where there is no dealership in government securities, it would be useful to set them up mainly because it will be more transparent than what would be the case when there are no security dealers. In so far as the rules and procedures about auctioning, there are no universal rules that need to be adopted. It depends on the legal and institutional structure of the economy concerned. Central banks, however, would have to, in the initial stages of developing an active market, provide technical assistance in the form of training of persons who desire to participate in the auctions and setting up of dealing rooms in the participating entities. Central banks would have to also decide on the kind of institutional structure that needs to be evolved. The structure could be based on the banks participating in the primary segment along with the central bank, or on an elaborate system of primary dealers and secondary (or satellite) dealers specially carved into the financial system, or a hybrid system of having dealers as well as banks participating in the primary segment along with the central bank. In India, there are primary dealers but individual banks could also enter the primary market. The satellite dealers also exist but have not made a mark partly because the secondary market is not yet developed adequately. The government securities market is still dominated by banks and other financial institutions.

Open market operations are most used by central banks in both IEs and EMEs as a major instrument of policy. In several cases, the use of OMO is in conjunction with the use of an official interest rate, be it the Bank Rate or the discount rate or the repo rate, or the rate at which banks could borrow on overnight basis (Fed funds rate). In IEs, where OMO are conducted regularly, the interest rate movements become significant indicators for policy makers to either intervene in the market or stay away from it. In EMEs, on the other hand, the OMO would be a kind of an event in the sense the announcements will often be made not as a part of a time table but at different discrete intervals of time. OMO are often used singly without affecting the official interest rate.

Reserve Requirements

The reserve requirements that central banks of many developing countries stipulate for commercial banks operating in their countries could be of two kinds. One is the primary reserve requirement in terms of cash to be held with the central bank and the other, the secondary reserve requirement in the form of the banks holding government and other specified securities. Both the requirements are expressed in terms of ratio of certain specified liabilities. The former, the variable cash reserve ratio (CRR) is often related to total liabilities, but in some countries (e.g., the US), it is specified in relation to demand or sight deposits. An increase in CRR would reduce the ability of commercial banks to lend or generate assets. The instrument is generally used by central banks to ensure that banks do not create credit indiscriminately or excessively to generate inflationary conditions especially during periods of economic buoyancy or upturn. It also works as a signal to the business community that since banks' lending abilities are constrained, it would have to access the markets or bid higher loan rates for bank financing that has been limited by the additional CRR.

The use of CRR is considered penal since the cash reserves impounded by the central banks are generally not remunerated sufficiently. If the remuneration, however, were made equivalent to the market rate of interest, then banks would have little incentive to compete strongly for increasing their share in the credit market, especially in cases where the CRR is high. It is, on the other hand, argued that cash reserves must be placed with central banks to ensure that there are no payment failures. But this argument is weak in that the banks could be persuaded to keep settlement balances instead of having a statutory CRR in place. It is also doubtful if the minimal balances under CRR would help address bank panics or crisis situations in individual banks for, in most cases of panic or crisis, the cash infusion will in most cases be much larger than the minimal CRR balances that banks maintain with central banks.

The secondary reserve requirement essentially ensures that the share of loan and investment portfolios in the total asset portfolio of banks is rebalanced. Since the investments in government and other specified securities would be statutory and since the securities are supposed to be liquid, a rise in this ratio could imply a corresponding fall in the amounts that banks could lend. Some banks may maintain such liquid securities in amounts that are larger than statutorily specified mainly to permit them to use the excess over the statutory minimum to raise funds for lending purposes.

On the other hand, the statutory liquidity ratio (SLR) could be misused to the advantage of the Government especially where central bank leadership is weak. Governments could persuade, if not compel central banks to raise the SLR, thereby ensuring that commercial banks absorb additional government securities and meet the budget requirements as much as possible. The coupon rate on such securities may also be kept low in order to restrict the interest servicing costs. Governments take such steps whenever they are faced with the problem of financing the fiscal deficits. From the point of view of central banks, persistent upward movement in SLR would imply that development of an active secondary market in government securities would not be possible and banks would find it hard to budget their resources for lending for their own economic viability. However, if the fiscal position is found to be viable, and the banking system is perceived, on the other hand, to be vulnerable and fragile, the use of SLR could be a sound way of overcoming the financial sector stresses. In general, EMEs keep the SLR requirement at a fairly low level and provide for auctioning of Government securities with a view to improving the possibilities of monetary policy conduct through the use of OMO. In some countries (e.g., India) the minimum SLR is by law placed often at fairly high levels mainly as a prudential measure. In India, it is presently at 25 per cent of total liabilities. However, the prices at which the Governments borrow from the market are determined by market forces or in the auctions. Although the SLR requirement is not a theoretically sound arrangement from the point of view of the need to provide freedom to banks in the selection of their asset portfolios, it could reduce the possible emergence of 'adverse selection'. On the other hand, if the values of the securities held by banks decline for some reason or the other, banks may have to find alternative ways of enhancing the quality of their assets portfolio. A sharp fall in asset prices could lead to panic situations and banks will therefore have to continuously watch out the market risks associated with the assets they hold and adopt appropriate hedging mechanisms against any probable erosion of asset values.

Selective Credit Controls

Selective credit controls in EMEs could take several forms. They could be in the form of stipulations about the size of exposures of banks to individual borrowers or groups of borrowers, about the sectors or activities that would have to be supported by bank lending or about the minimum levels of lending to particular sectors or activities (directed lending, as it is some times referred to). Selective credit controls could also be specifically directed towards the margins in lending against inventories of certain commodities or raw materials. Margins would be raised when the central banks find that the inventories are used for speculative purposes or when there are expectations of shortfall in the availabilities of commodities/raw materials in question. Central banks could cover under selective credit controls not only the commodities or raw materials that originate in the domestic economy but also those that are imported. Margins in lending affect profitability and thus dissuade borrowers from borrowing from banks for purposes that are often regarded as unethical or as inimical to social welfare. In general central banks use selective credit controls very sparingly because they not only restrict the degrees of freedom for banks to manage their portfolios but also encourage some of the borrowers to seek credit from the unorganized or curb markets. Where financing of activities is undertaken largely from non-bank sources, sometimes referred to loosely as market sources, selective credit controls would not be effective. In many EMEs, the selective credit controls are used as prudential and regulatory instrument. But those that have direct effects on the size or the direction of borrowing are generally not favored. In India, however, priority sector lending (which is at times loosely referred to as directed lending) is used by the Reserve Bank of India in addition to other instruments of policy such as reserve requirements, open market operations and the Bank rate.

Transmission Mechanism of Policy

The use of any one or a combination of instruments of policy would depend on the channels through which the impact would be transmitted through the economy. Whether the effect would be on prices or output/employment or both and whether the lags are long and variable would have to be determined empirically country by country. There is thus no single transmission channel that is applicable as an effective one for all countries, or even for a group of countries such as the industrial countries or the EMEs and for all times to come. But it is important for the central banks to know the transmission mechanism of monetary policy because it is only then the monetary authorities could be confident of the effectiveness of their actions.

The literature refers to a number of channels — the money aggregates, the interest rate, the asset prices (or the wealth effect), the exchange rate, the credit or the balance sheet channels. The literature has grown sharply since the early 1960s with the emergence of monetarism as counter to the then-prevalent Keynesian preference for supremacy of fiscalism in economic policy-making. The literature has the usual theoretical and empirical parts. The theory part of it is essentially derived from the empirical experiences of the industrialized economies. The Bank for International Settlements (BIS) however made an attempt to bring together the relevance of the transmission channels to some of the emerging market economies but this publication did not provide any new theoretical insights.

There is a general recognition that there are wide differences in the institutional and policy regime structures between the industrialized and emerging market economies. While the differences may not by themselves contribute to new analytical frames, they would help to caution the policy makers in the emerging economies of the limitations to the functioning of the transmission channels and of the need to work out approaches that improve the effectiveness in the conduct of monetary policy.

The main channels of transmission are placed here in a pictorial way for convenience, and for the sake of brevity (See also Frederic S Mishkin, 1995). The monetary aggregates channel is rarely mentioned in the current day literature emanating from the industrialized economies essentially because money supply or other quantitative variables such as the bank reserves or reserve money or excess reserves or free reserves are no longer targeted and also because both the quantity variables and the rate of interest are often fused into the portfolio balance approach. Yet it is useful to distinguish the monetary aggregates channel from the rest, given the importance of money supply and liquidity for determining aggregate spending in most emerging economies at least in the medium term.

A. Monetary Aggregates Channel

(1)   (a) $\Delta\,\text{MS} \rightarrow \Delta\,\text{Yr}$

$\downarrow$

$\rightarrow\ \Delta\,\text{P}$

(b) $\Delta\,\text{RM}$ or $\Delta\,\text{BR} \rightarrow \Delta\,\text{Yr}$

$\rightarrow \rightarrow \rightarrow \Delta\,\text{P}$

Note : In place of BR, ER or FR could be used for explaining the transmission channel.

In the above equations, Yr represents the real GDP, MS represents money supply, P, the price level, RM, the reserve money, BR, the bank reserves, ER the excess reserves, and FR the free reserves, and Δ the change in the specified variable.

The monetary aggregate channel is more a representation of the classical economic thinking, where money supply is exogenously given. The original classical view was that a change in the quantity of money would have an effect on prices, given the full employment of labor and capital. This is represented in a slightly modified way in equation 1 (a) above, by allowing for under full employment conditions to exist. This is typically the essence of the logic of Keynes in his *The General Theory*. Most monetary targeting exercises follow the Keynesian logic since the assumption of full employment is considered to be not realistic.

Equation 1 (b) essentially represents what has come to be known as the money multiplier approach. It shows that it is the reserve money (or its variant expressions, the central bank money or the monetary base or the base money) over which the central banks have control would impact over money supply through the money multiplier and affect eventually both output and the price level. Instead of the reserve money, central banks sometimes target the bank reserves or some variant of reserves (excess reserves or free reserves or reserves that are derived after accounting for borrowing from the central bank) and impact on banks' behavior with respect to asset creation. In other words, banks would be forced to cut down loans or other investments or both if the central bank increases the required reserves. When the required reserves are brought down, it would follow from the above argument, banks would be able to increase their loans. Since loans are a part of bank credit and as changes in bank credit would bring about similar changes in money supply assuming that net foreign exchange asset position of the banking system is constant, the changes in reserves by bringing about changes in money supply via banks' portfolio actions, would affect output and the price level.

B. The Interest Rate Channel

$$(2) \quad r \rightarrow I \rightarrow \Delta Yr \rightarrow \rightarrow \Delta P$$

The above equation is a typical representation of the Keynesian argument that changes in the interest rate represented here by 'r' would influence the cost of capital, causing variations in investment spending represented here by 'I'. The shifts in investment spending in turn lead to changes in aggregate demand and in output. The change in output will impact on the inflation rate (ΔP) with a lag (represented here by two arrows). The lag, however, need not exist in all country-cases. The important thing to note is that during the periods of downturn in economic activity or recession, it is the interest rate softening that is said to trigger investment spending that leads to growth. There could be lags between the time the investment is made and the eventual growth outcome. As already indicated, the lags are supposed to be fairly long and variable in most IEs and are estimated to be about 12-18 months.

C. The Exchange Rate Channel

$$(3) \quad r \rightarrow ex. \rightarrow net\ exports \rightarrow \Delta Yr$$

Equation (3) is valid only where there is international capital mobility or trade and some flexibility in exchange rate regimes. These conditions were widely seen in recent years in IEs and EMEs. Usually, the exchange rate (ex.) would incorporate the interest rate effects. When domestic interest rates rise, domestic currency deposits become attractive relative to deposits denominated in foreign currencies. When domestic interest rates fall, the foreign currency deposits gain at the expense of domestic currency deposits. In the former case, the domestic currency would appreciate and in the latter case, it would depreciate. The higher value of the domestic currency makes domestic goods more expensive than foreign goods thereby causing a fall in net exports. In this case, imports become attractive and exporters would have lost the hitherto available income-incentive to export. The lower value of domestic currency, on the other hand, would help domestic exports by making domestic goods cheaper than foreign goods. The shifts in the value of the domestic currency vis-à-vis the foreign currency would in turn affect aggregate output.

The exchange rate channel has however proved to be somewhat elusive in view of the free capital mobility that has been facilitated in part by the new technology applications whereby at the click of a button of the computers, currencies could be shifted across national borders. A rise in the rate of interest in country T relative to the rate of interest in country Q would attract foreign capital inflows into country T assuming that the macro-economic position in country T is perceived by foreign investors to be good and stable. Such inflows would lead to appreciation of the currency of country T and unless the policy makers in country T take actions to ensure that international competitiveness of the country is protected, there could be widening of trade deficit. Central bank of country T on its part would have to sterilize the capital inflows by actions that bring down the credit demand or by purchasing the foreign currencies in order to build up foreign exchange reserves. In either case, appreciation of the domestic currency relative to the foreign currency would be present affecting the international competitiveness of country T. However, the disadvantage of currency appreciation would have to be weighed against the advantage that may accrue on account of reserve build-up while taking any policy action to neutralize the effects of currency appreciation.

D. The Wealth Effect Channel

(4) $\Delta MS \rightarrow Pe \rightarrow W \rightarrow \Delta C \rightarrow \Delta Yr$

In the above equation, Pe represents the price of equity shares, W represents wealth and C the consumption. The monetarists gave maximum attention to the effects of monetary policy on an array of rates and wealth. When money supply falls (rises), the public would find itself having less (more) money than it wants. It therefore decreases (increases) its spending. One area where the public would spend will be on the stock markets. The demand for equities will, as a result, shift affecting the price of equities. In turn this would affect the value of the financial wealth, and the lifetime resources of consumers. This effect on consumption will influence the real output. Equation (4) can be applied also where other asset prices are involved. For example, assets like real estate would be subject to large spending of households when the households are left with additional money. Real estate price changes could affect the wealth of households dramatically and affect the consumption profiles. The sharp fall in real estate prices in Japan in the early 1990s — the asset bubble as it was referred to — had caused considerable dip in the wealth of the Japanese consumers and proved to be a drag on the aggregate domestic demand.

The wealth effect could also be seen through the Keynesian prism. For instance, the money supply changes affect the Tobin's 'q' through the shifts that occur in the equity prices. The Tobin's 'q' in turn affects investment spending and finally aggregate output.

$$(5) \quad \Delta \, MS \rightarrow Pe \rightarrow q \rightarrow I \rightarrow Yr$$

The Tobin's 'q' is nothing but the market value of firms divided by the replacement cost of capital. If 'q' is high, the market price of firms will also be high relative to the cost of replacement of capital. In other words, new plant and equipment will be cheaper and the companies will therefore issue new equities and get a high price relative to the cost of capital replacement. In case 'q' is low, firms will resist purchasing of new equipments because the market value of firms will be lower than the replacement cost of capital. If at all a firm X wants to acquire capital when 'q' is low, it will buy another firm cheaply and thus acquire 'old' capital. Investment spending does not take place in this situation. Tobin's 'q' can be extended to real estate values as well.

E. The Credit Channel or the Balance Sheet Channel

(6) $\quad$ MP $\rightarrow$ AD $\rightarrow$ BC $\rightarrow$ I $\rightarrow$ Δ Yr

(6a) $\quad$ MP $\rightarrow$ Pe $\rightarrow$ Adv Sel and mor haz $\rightarrow$

$\qquad$ $\rightarrow$ Bank Lending $\rightarrow$ I $\rightarrow$ Δ Yr

(6b) MP $\rightarrow$ r $\rightarrow$ cash flow $\rightarrow$ Adv Sel and mor haz $\rightarrow$

$\qquad$ $\rightarrow$ Bank Lending $\rightarrow$ I $\rightarrow$ Δ Yr

In equations (6), (6a), and (6b), MP would represent monetary policy change, AD and BC represent respectively aggregate deposits and bank credit. They show that monetary authorities could vary the availability of credit, with or without altering the cost of funds at the same time in order to influence eventually aggregate demand. If the funds availability is affected by changes in reserve requirements or by credit controls on lending to select activities or by direct controls on the quantum of credit, then the financial condition of the economy would be akin to what could be described as credit rationing. This would be the case also when OMO affects only the funds availability and not the rate of interest. This would imply that the credit markets are characterized by asymmetric information and could affect the small firms' access to banks. The larger firms in contrast can access not only banks for financing their activities but also stock and bond markets. When monetary policy is such that it decreases (or increases) bank reserves as well as bank deposits, there will be an impact on large firms' borrowing and investment spending, as equation 6 shows. But this is too simple a representation. For, in countries where market financing is dominant and financial innovations abound, such a channel may not be effective. But monetary policy effects can operate through the balance sheet or net worth of firms (Bernanke and Gertler, 1995). The balance sheet channel works the way the equation 6 (a) represents. Equation 6 (a) in fact can be described as the modern theory of banking. When a contractionary monetary policy is undertaken causing equity prices to decline as under the wealth effect channel, the net worth of firms would fall. The fall in net worth means low equity stakes for firms and the firms believe that they could undertake risky investment projects. Such risky projects will lead to increases in adverse selection and moral hazard and hence lenders will cut their lending. This would lead to lower investment outlays and to fall in output.

The adverse selection and moral hazard gets into picture because of information asymmetries. Also it could be due to costly enforcement of loan contracts. It could also take place when interest rates move up as a result of contractionary monetary policy and reduced cash flow as may be seen from equation 6 (b). The balance sheet channel could apply equally well in the case of consumer spending. If monetary policy changes leave liquidity effects on consumer expenditures on durable goods and housing, then the consumers expecting a higher likelihood of financial distress, would rather be holding fewer illiquid assets like housing and consumer durables and more of liquid financial assets. This is because sale of housing and consumer durables during periods of illiquidity may not fetch good prices whereas assets such as bank deposits or bonds may fetch full market value. The expenditures on consumer durables and housing would therefore tend to decline. As a result, aggregate demand would fall, leading to fall in real output. The balance sheet channel thus would arise when lenders are willing (unwilling) to lend as much as the consumers would be willing (unwilling) to spend. In either case, the output effects could be significant.

An Evaluation of the Channels in the context of EMEs

It would be useful to recapitulate the fact that it cannot be a priori determined as to which of the channels would work most effectively in any one country. Besides, a channel that worked well in a country at a point in time may not work well subsequently. What is most important is that identification of channel that is likely to be effective is not so easy. This is particularly so in EMEs for several reasons. For instance, the monetary and fiscal policies may not be easily distinguishable and clarity about the objectives of monetary policy may be conspicuously absent in these countries. Besides, financial markets may not be fully developed and at any rate not adequately integrated, reflecting largely the relatively low sensitivity of households and businesses to interest rate changes. Moreover, there may be a tendency to depend mainly on internal resources rather than on leveraging and outsourcing of resources by firms. Furthermore, the requisite institutional mechanisms may not be present to provide robust and reliable information about the individual borrowers and markets, with the result the bank credit market imperfections would tend to be high, posing potential stress to the banking system. Finally, the policy regimes may not be completely bereft of distortions arising from rate rigidities and allocative devices.

There are not many empirical studies on the transmission mechanism of monetary policy for emerging market economies, barring the one brought out by the Bank for International Settlements in 1999. For India, there was a study made by Vasudevan and Menon in 1978 with data relating to the period 1956-76 and it showed that there was no one channel on which the Reserve Bank of India could place its faith in. The period was characterized by far too many regulations both in the real and monetary and financial sector. The conclusions of the study were vitiated as a result. In the absence of no other study for the recent period, it would appear as if monetary policy is conducted on certain informed judgments. This situation could well be seen also in many other EMEs.

Does it then mean that monetary policy in EMEs would have

to be conducted under the assumption that the transmission channel would exist in what has been termed a 'black box'? This question in fact is posed universally. But central banks have not shown any tendency to unduly worry that their actions would be misinterpreted in the absence of robust empirical work on transmission mechanism. In at least so far as developing countries are concerned, the channel that is viewed by central banks in these countries as most relevant is the quantity channel, namely the monetary base (reserve money) or the money supply channel. If the financial sector in EMEs is not well developed as in other developing countries, and has not witnessed many financial innovations, monetary policy may have to be conducted in a way that the supply of money would passively respond to the demand for money. Fortunately, there is considerable amount of literature on the money supply processes and the relevance of the money multiplier to rely on. The Federal Bank of St. Louis pioneered research in this area throughout the 1960s and excellently reviewed by Rasche (Rasche R H (1972)). The research during this period has shown that there are close links between   reserve money or bank reserves, especially the non-borrowed reserves, and money supply (For definitions of reserves, reserve money and money supply and for derivation of money multiplier, see at the end of this chapter **Box 8**). This approach is commonly used in most developing countries and in some of the EMEs as well.

The supply of money that emanates should equal the demand for money if the monetary sector should be in equilibrium. For this purpose, exercises on the demand for money are crucial. In other words, money demand should be estimated for purposes of monetary targeting (targeting a certain value of money supply as an intermediate target to help realize ultimate target or targets). Money supply could be either a narrow one, favored by Philip Cagan (1982) or broad money, favored by Milton Friedman (See Friedman, Milton and Anna Schwartz (1963)). Whichever definition one adopts, money supply targets based on the demand for money exercises have to be given for the prospective year either in terms of a point estimate or a range as was done in many industrialized economies till the 1980s. (The US abandoned the targeting of money supply in 1982 when the M1 velocity was found to be erratic). Monetary targets were used most effectively by Germany (West Germany before German unification) to signal its anti-inflationary stance till almost the end of the twentieth century. It was also widely agreed that many countries in the continent of Europe used the German mark (since about the early 1980s) as the anchor currency because of the fact that the inflation rate in Germany was low and relatively stable essentially because of the successful control over money supply growth. Money supply targets are also easily understood and could help to influence market expectations.

The literature on the demand for money is perhaps the most voluminous in monetary economics. Estimates of money demand are somewhat easy to generate for any economy, whether or not the interest rate regime is flexible or administered. The main explanatory variables most commonly used in the traditional studies on money demand are income and the opportunity cost of holding money. The latter is expected to capture the potential for substitution between money and financial assets and money and relevant assets. The relevant opportunity cost variables would then be a measure of the rate of interest on financial assets, and a measure of the rate of inflation. One could, however, view the money demand from the point of view of the motives for holding money — for purposes of transactions or for speculative gains. If one were to examine the role of money in the transactions process, as the inventory models have shown, the demand for transactions money would depend on the interest rate, real brokerage charges and the level of real transactions. The asset demand for money, on the other hand, arises from a portfolio allocation decision made under conditions of uncertainty. If it could be combined with transaction costs, the resultant comprehensive demand for money could be better explained.

The empirical exercises relating to the demand for money in India have been very large. Two survey articles by Vasudevan (1977) and by Jadhav (1990) as well as an article by Joshi and Saggar (1995) show that the money demand function in India exhibited stability and was largely scale (income) determined. The results are not surprising considering the fact that the financial sector is not sufficiently deep and is characterized by rigidities in the interest rate structure.

It is not so much the factors behind the money demand that count as the stability of the demand for money function. Poole (1970) gave a framework that clearly suggested that instability in money demand would lead policy makers to move away from monetary targeting. There is almost a unanimous opinion that while money demand functions were generally stable in the US till 1973, they became unstable subsequently mainly because of the financial innovations. Goldfeld (1973) showed that interest elasticities of currency and time deposits to reserves ratio in the money multiplier framework were fairly small in the US economy till the early 1970s. Judd and Scadding (1982) argued that while this was true, the more fundamental source of instability in income velocity was excessive money growth. They observed that since monetary policy did not restrain inflation, short term rate of interest went up. Higher interest rate along with impediments to payment of market yields on demand deposits led to financial innovations. Implicitly, this meant that to the extent that high money supply growth led to money demand instability, and the policy response in such circumstances would have to be to cut down money supply growth to bring about price stability. Hafer and Wheelock (2001) observed that apart from financial innovations, deregulation, other institutional changes and uncertainty about the Fed's commitment to disinflation could explain much of the unstable behavior of the income velocity in the 1980s, leading ultimately to the fall of the famous Friedman policy rule of a constant money stock growth rate.

It was not clear whether monetary targeting as practiced in industrialized economies aimed at only price stability or at nominal GDP. Had it been directed towards nominal GDP targeting, it could have been considered an activist rule that could have provided some answer to the problem of velocity shocks. Monetary targeting for price stability obviously proved to be a passive rule. However, it is difficult to lay down conditions under which one rule policy could be universally favored over the other. For such an outcome to be realized, knowledge about the source of shocks, and their persistence would be required (see Asako, Kazumi and Helmut Wagner (1992).

A more important point of interest in relation to money supply channel is to know whether money at all affects output. Friedman and Schwartz in their monumental work on the history of the US monetary analysis showed that faster money growth tends to be followed by the increase in real output above trend, and deceleration in money supply would be followed by decrease in real output. In their view, the lags however would be long and variable. Benjamin Friedman and Kuttner (1992) however felt that this was not so apparent. King and Plosser (1984) argued that much of the correlations between money supply and output might arise from endogenous response of the banking sector to economic disturbances that may not result from monetary policy actions. There is, however, a general viewpoint that money supply increases would in the short run spur up new economic activities. Barro (1997, and 1998) showed that anticipated money supply changes would not have any impact on output: it is only the unanticipated changes in money supply that would have effects on output. Mishkin (1982) on the other hand found a role for anticipated money as well. Leeper, Sims and Zha (1996), reviewing the vector autoregression models, concluded that shocks from monetary policy side are not that important. Shaghil Ahmed, however, demonstrated that changes in money precede changes in output, and vice versa at different times and therefore there is no clear evidence that output would change in response to variations in money supply (See Ahmed, Shaghil (1993)).

In so far as EMEs are concerned, it is of vital importance to know whether money supply targeting would be valid when expectedly, these economies would be undertaking, as a matter of deliberate policy, measures that would develop and diversify the financial sector and integrate the financial markets. Ronald McKinnon (1973) and Edward Shaw (1973) have shown that financial repression understood to mean rigidity in interest rates would hinder growth. A number of models of financial intermediation in the 1990s showed that such intermediation has a positive impact on growth (Bencivenga, Valerie and Bruce Smith (1991); Greenwood, Jeremy and Bruce Smith (1997); King, Robert and Ross Levine (1993 a); King, Robert and Ross Levine (1993 b); and Roubini, Nouriel, and Xavier, Sala-i-Martin (1992). On the other hand, giving an overview of financial development and growth, Khan and Senhadji (2000 b) argued that even now it is not clear how to develop financial markets and how precisely the development of markets will benefit growth. The latter point of Khan and Senhadji is a valid one and has not been empirically well tested. However, on the basis of the data series of expansion of money supply or other monetary aggregates in relation to growth, most studies show as the recent World Bank report has observed that finance contributes to long term prosperity and diversity and is good for stability and development (World Bank (2001).

Once it is agreed that financial development is necessary for growth and stability and financial innovations would abound, it would be difficult to defend monetary targeting for purposes of policy. In other words, the monetary aggregates channel would have to be given a goodbye. Such a situation would open up possibilities of considering the usefulness of applying other channels of transmission. Let us first take the asset prices or the wealth effect channel. In reality, most central banks do not follow this channel, although they are aware of the problems that asset price changes would often create. The asset prices channel would work where wealth effect operates, and stock markets are well developed and real estate regulations are in place. These conditions are not fully in place in many EMEs. Let us then consider the exchange rate channel. This channel would work best if the economy is opened up fairly well and the role of foreign transactions in the GDP of the economy is substantially high. But as we have already noted, this channel is unpredictable in its effectiveness partly because the exchange rate changes occur not only due to a country's policies but also due to the policies of trading partner countries. Besides, in many cases, the channel is intimately connected with the interest rate channel. The effectiveness of the interest rate channel depends on the stage of financial development and the degree of financial integration. In general, this channel has become somewhat weak in recent years even in industrialized economies with capital mobility, and with the growth of stock markets. However, this channel has the potential to work well in EMEs as households and firms show sensitivity to interest rate channels. But it is the credit channel that seems to be attracting most attention since it would function most effectively irrespective of the share of bank financing in the total financial needs of the economy so long as both bank financing and market financing structures are responsive as much to the current economic conditions as to the expectations of the future working of the economy. The balance sheet or net worth of firms, as well as information asymmetries, and the costs in the enforcement of loan contracts play a part in the working of this channel. Besides, to the extent cash flows are influenced by payment systems and their effectiveness, this channel would have profound influence on monetary policy than any other channel. Where the quick turnover of money and the certainty of the finality of settlement of transactions are assured by efficient payment system, changes that central banks would like to bring about in interest rates would have effects on the behavior of both borrowers and lenders. There will be shifts in the asset portfolios of households, business firms and banks depending on the rate of interest movements and the risk profiles of different tradable assets. These shifts would be facilitated by the efficiency of payments system and central banks will have to therefore consider the implications of payment system for the conduct of monetary policy (See **Box 9** for the relationship between payment system and monetary policy).

All the transmission channels would have effects both on consumption and investment. Thus when the rate of interest goes down, consumption and investment could go up and vice versa. Exchange rate depreciation would imply a rise in incomes in domestic currency terms, pushing up both consumption and investment. Asset price increases will facilitate consumption as well as investment. However, the questions that one needs to ask in this context are several. As the effects on consumption and investment from the operation of each of the channels differ, is it not necessary to know which effect is most dominant and significant ? Again, it is necessary to know whether the effects are generally persistent and stable in values. Further, what are the lags in effects ? Besides, do the lags in effect differ widely as between the channels, and as between the periods? Finally, are the lags in general long and variable and have strong systemic effects ?

Uncertainties Due to Lags

The estimation of lags is crucial since it affects market expectations. It has to be therefore undertaken as a critical empirical exercise by central banks especially those in EMEs. The variations in the lag structure occur on account of institutional, legal and macro-economic policy reasons. For instance, policy shifts to the extent they are not anticipated could bring about uncertainties about the lag structure. These uncertainties could be compounded during periods when financial institutions are evolving. But policy makers need to have an understanding of the lag structure essentially for injecting the dynamic properties to the economic system at work. It helps one to know the ultimate effects as of the terminal period, and if the terminal period happens to be a part of the medium term path, one would have to plan the actions well in advance to be credible and effective.

Central banks in industrialized economies estimate lag structures. But this is not done in many developing countries. Attempts are being done to estimate lags in some EMEs but how robust the estimations are is a matter of debate. Irrespective of the fact that not all central banks have an idea of lag structures, there is very little evidence to show that central banks follow a specific transmission channel. This is not only because there are uncertainties relating to the depth and width of the domestic financial markets, asymmetries of information, inadequate legal and payments infrastructure, and the absence of robust financial institutions and market expectations, but also because of the international face of the transmission of interest rates, exchange rates, inflation, and investor confidence. The cross border effects depend on the degree of openness and as some of the EMEs move towards allowing complete capital mobility, the effects on such EMEs could be substantial and varying in impact at different periods of time. This is an area where future research needs to be focused.

Transparency of Policies and Practices

In most EMEs, transparency is understood mainly in terms of publishing a vast amount of statistical data, speeches of Governors/Deputy Governors/Executive Directors of the central banks, their annual reports and other official publications, and placing all or most of the available data and their publications on the websites. In many cases, the information provided is detailed. Besides, most central banks promptly bring out their monthly bulletins of statistics relating not only to the financial sector but also to the real sector. But central banks in most

EMEs do not normally publish minutes of the meetings of their governing boards or their policy groups. They do not also provide information about the agenda placed in such meetings for discussion. The relationship between the central banks and governments is also not spelt out in sufficient detail: it is often provided in general terms in terms of the laws governing the setting up of the central banks. Very rarely the operational aspects of the relationship are codified in the agreements/understandings and provided through their official documents. As a result, accountability or responsibility for monetary policy actions would be jeopardized. The opaqueness in the relationship arises because of not specifying clearly the objectives of monetary policy and because of unwillingness to lay down definite mechanisms for co-ordination among different tiers of decision making at the levels of the government, the central bank, and other regulatory bodies. For these reasons, imperfections in gathering and processing of information could occur with the result whatever information is published, it would not have any value-addition (See Eijffinger, Sylvester C W, and Marco M Hoeberichts, "Central Bank Accountability and Transparency: Theory and Some Evidence", Paper presented for the Deutsche Bundesbank/CFS Conference on "Transparency in Monetary Policy" on October 16/17, 2000 at Frankfurt, available on website of Bundesbank; and Winkler, Bernhard, "Which Kind of Transparency ? On the Need for Clarity in Monetary Policy-making", Working Paper No. 26, European Central Bank, Frankfurt, August 2000).

Transparency will not be assured merely by dissemination of information. Transparency will be assured only if the central bank explains clearly its objective or objective-set and the rationale of its policy actions for the medium term. Besides, the central bank should institute organizational mechanisms to deliberate on the policy actions to be taken. Such mechanisms could be in the form of monetary policy committees. Their deliberations will also need to be made known to the public. The importance of such transparency practices is recognized in all EMEs. We shall discuss this aspect in greater detail in the next two chapters.

References

Ahmed, Shaghil (1993), "Does Money Affect Output?", *Federal Reserve Bank of Philadelphia Business Review*, July-August, pp.13-28.

Asako, Kazumi and Helmut Wagner (1992), "Nominal Income Targeting versus Money Supply Targeting", *Scottish Journal of Political Economy*, Vol. 39, No 2, May.

Bencivenga, Valerie, and Bruce Smith (1991), "Financial Intermediation and Endogenous Growth", *Review of Economic Studies*, Vol. 58, No. 2, pp.195-209.

Dhal, Sarat Chandra (1999), "Potential Growth in India: Viable Alternatives to Time Series Approaches", *RBI Occasional Papers*, Vol 20, Winter, No. 3.

Donde, K and Mridul Saggar (1999), "Potential Output and Output gap: A Review", *RBI Occasional Papers*, Vol 20, Winter, No. 3.

Friedman, Benjamin and Kenneth N. Kultner (1992), "Money, Income, Prices and Interest Rates", *American Economic Review*, Vol 82, No. 3, pp.472-92.

Greenwood, Jeremy and Bruce Smith (1997), "Financial Markets in Development and the Development of Financial Markets", *Jour of Econ Dynamics*, Vol 21, No. 1, pp.145-81.

Goldfeld, Stephen M (1973), "The Demand for Money Revisited", Brookings Papers on Economic Activity, 3, pp.577-638.

Hafer, R W and David C Wheelock, "The Rise and Fall of a Policy Rule: Monetarism at the St Louis Fe, 1968-1986", *Fed Res Bank of St Louis Rev*, Jan/Feb 2001, pp.1-24.

Jadhav, N D (1990), "Monetary Modelling of the Indian Economy: A Survey", *Reserve Bank of India Occasional Papers*, Vol.11, No.2, June, pp. 83-152.

Joshi, Himanshu and Saggar, Mridul (1995), "The Demand for Money in India: Stability Revisited", *Reserve Bank of India Occasional Papers*, Vol. 16, No.2, June, pp. 79-100.

Judd, John P and John L Scadding (1982), "The Search for a Stable Money Demand Function: A Survey of the Post-1973 Literature", *Jour of Econ Lit*, Vol XX, Sept, pp.993-1023.

Khan, Mohsin and Abdelhak S Senhadji (2000 a), "Threshold Effects in the Relationship Between Inflation and Growth", IMF Working Paper, June, WP/oo/110.

———. (2000b), "Financial Development and Economic Growth: An Overview", IMF Working Paper, WP/oo/209.

Meyer, Laurence H (2001), "Does Money Matter?", *BIS Review*, No. 25.

Nachane, D M and R Lakshmi (1999), "Variability of Monetary Policy Lags in India: An Approach Based on Time-varying Spectra", *Journal of Quantitative Economics*, Vol 15, No. 2, July, pp.111-136.

Rasche, R H (1972), "A Review of Empirical Studies of the Money Supply Mechanism", *Fed. Bank of St Louis Rev*, 54, July, pp.11-19.

Roldos, Jorge (1997), "Potential Output Growth in Emerging Market Countries: The Case of Chile", IMF Working Paper, September, WP/97/104.

Roubini, Nouriel, and Xavier, Sala-I-Martin (1992), "Financial Repression and Economic Growth", *Jour Devpt Economics*, Vol 39, No 1, pp. 5-30.

Shaw, Edward S (1973), *Financial Deepening in Economic Development*, New York, Oxford University Press.

Vasudevan, A, B K Bhoi and S C Dhal (1999), "Inflation Rate and Optimal Growth—Is there a Gateway to 'Nirvana'?" in Vasudevan A et al (eds) (1999), *Fifty Years of Development Economics*, Himalaya Publishing House, Mumbai.

Vasudevan, A (1977), "Demand for Money in India: A Survey of Literature", *Reserve Bank Staff Occasional Papers*, Vol.2, No.1, June, pp.58-83.

Vasudevan, A and Menon, K.A (1978), "On Testing Some Hypotheses Concerning the Transmission Mechanism of Monetary Policy: The Indian Experience, 1956-76" in Reserve Bank of India, *Recent Developments in Monetary Theory and Policy*, Bombay, pp.138-51.

Winkler, Bernhard (2000), "Which Kind of Transparency? On the Need for Clarity in Monetary Policy-making", Working Paper 26, European Central Bank, August.

World Bank (2001), *Finance for Growth*, World Bank, Washington D C, Contributors to this report: Caprio, Gerard, and Patrick Honohan.

Box 7

Liquidity Adjustment Facility in India

Liquidity adjustment facility (LAF) was introduced in India in two stages. The first stage of the LAF was introduced effective June 05, 2000. Under it, the repo rate was made flexible and the fixed repo rate was dismantled. The reverse repo rate was placed at a notch higher than the repo rate essentially to push up short term interest rates with a view to ensuring orderly conditions in the foreign exchange market. During this stage, non-bank financial institutions that were historically participants in the call market as suppliers of funds, were permitted to lend on an average up to 85 per cent of their average daily call money lendings. However, export credit finance facility was left undisturbed. Ideally, the LAF would work effectively when there are no distortions like regular, almost automatic refinancing facilities and the participation of non-bank institutions in the call money market. To progress towards the ideal LAF, the Reserve Bank has had to resort to stage-by-stage approach.

In the second stage, introduced effective May 08, 2001, a few refinements were made. Under it, banks were allowed to have 'normal' liquidity facility at the Bank Rate, and a 'backstop' facility at variable daily rate at 1 percentage point above the reverse repo cut-off rate in LAF auctions or 200 to 300 basis points above the repo cut-off rate. The normal facility would be about two-thirds and the backstop facility about one-thirds of the total limits of standing liquidity support available to banks (and primary dealers in government securities who are for purposes of market development regarded as banks with accounts maintained with the Reserve Bank). But even under this stage, export credit refinance was allowed upto certain specified limits.

The Reserve Bank also reserved the discretion to switchover to fixed rate repos on overnight basis and to introduce longer-term repos upto a 14-day period as and when required. Again, instead of uniform price auctions, multiple price auctions were conducted. Besides, the Reserve Bank released regularly to the wider public information on the scheduled commercial banks' aggregate cash balances maintained with the Bank and the weighted average cut-off yield in case of the multiple price auction. The non-bank institutions' share in the supply of lendings in the call money market has also been reduced.

Source : Annual Reports of the Reserve Bank of India.

Box 8

Bank Reserves, Reserve Money, Money Supply and Money Multiplier

In the literature on monetary economics, one finds good many definitions of different kinds of reserves. Bank reserves are defined as cash held in the vaults of the banks and cash held by banks with the central bank of the country and these are monitored as at the end of the working days. Together with the currency with the non-bank public, they make up reserve money (RM). But when banks borrow from central banks as is the case in many countries, they gain in 'borrowed reserves'. Total bank reserves net of borrowed reserves would be 'unborrowed' or 'non-borrowed' reserves. Excess reserves would be reserves held in excess of the required cash reserves, and if borrowed reserves are deducted from excess reserves, one would arrive at 'free' reserves.

Money supply itself can be viewed the way the analyst wants it to be. For, money supply by definition, would be a part of total liabilities (TL), and would therefore represent monetary liabilities (ML). Thus, one would get 'other' (or what in the Indian context is called 'non-monetary') liabilities by a simple operation: TL – ML = OL (or NML). But there are two most popular definitions of money supply, namely, the transactions definition or the narrow definition and the broad definition. The 'narrow' money would consist of currency with the public and demand or sight deposits, while 'broad' money would be represented by currency with the public and aggregate bank deposits. Since in most countries, time or term deposits are a large component of aggregate deposits, many analysts prefer to work with broad money.

The money multiplier (MM) is essentially a ratio of money

supply and reserve money. In other words, MM = MS/RM. As RM is essentially the cash base of the economy, an increase in RM would lead to an increase in MS by the value of the MM. Thus one could express the money supply determination thus: MS = m RM where m is the value of the money multiplier. It represents the interaction of two major ratios, namely the currency to deposits and reserves to deposits ratios. This may be worked out thus:

(1) MS (M3) = D + C where D = aggregate deposits; and C = currency with the public.

(2) RM = BR + C
where RM = reserve money; and BR = bank reserves.

(3) BR = r(D)

(4) C = k(D)

Substitute (3) and (4) into (2)

(5) RM = r(D) + k(D)

We can express deposits in terms of RM thus :

(6) D = 1/(r+k) * RM

Since we want D plus C, we use (4) and (6) to redefine C in terms of RM

(7) C = k/(k+r) * RM

Substituting (6) and (7) into (1) we get

(8) MS = (k/(k+r) * RM) + (1/(k+r) *RM)

Simplifying (8) we get

(9) MS = 1+k/r+k * RM

This is money supply defined in terms of RM. We can denote the quotient (call it 'm') as

(10) m = 1+k/r+k = MS/RM   where m is the money multiplier. It follows therefore :

(11) MS = m * RM.

Box 9

Payment System and Monetary Policy

Central banks' involvement in payment systems is due to (a) rapid technological changes, (b) dramatic growth of financial activity, (c) enormous expansion of payment transactions both in volume and value terms, and (d) integration of domestic markets as well as globalization of financial markets. As a result, liquidity and credit risks for all the payment system participants (including central banks) have increased. The central banks therefore have to develop rules of operation for the systems designed to reduce systemic risk. Central banks tend to develop and run payment systems especially in respect of large value transfer of funds.

The effectiveness of the indirect instruments of monetary policy that central banks apply as part of financial liberalization depends on the stage of development of financial markets that are used to transmit monetary policy signals. On the other hand, the type of payment instruments used in payment systems, the payment facilities available for market participants, as well as the rules and procedures for payments influence the speed, the risk and the cost of transactions in financial markets. For example, OMO necessitates well developed markets, while also requiring payment and settlement systems that can transfer securities through book entries and settle transactions accurately, speedily and with finality.

Adopting any payment and settlement system has implications for monetary policy implementation. One important issue here involves the cost of liquidity. Also, granting intraday overdrafts in the case of RTGS systems, and pricing and guaranteeing payment facilities would mean that in the trade-off between risk reduction and the effectiveness of monetary policy, the former would have to be given a good measure of importance.

Changes in payment systems can cause changes in the velocity of money and banks' demand for reserves. This will impinge on the conduct of monetary policy, since monetary policy has to ensure that there is adequate liquidity in the financial system.

An important issue about the efficiency of payment system is the payment float. Floats emerge because of delays in the execution of payment transactions. To some extent, availability of funds depends on the instrument used in the transactions. For cash, this availability is immediate; for electronic transfers, it is often less than one day; and for other instruments, it could be more than one day — generally $t+1$ or $t+2$ or $t+3$ days. Credit floats (i.e., when a bank debits a client's account before actually transferring funds to the beneficiary's bank or when the receiving bank delays crediting the beneficiary account) help banks since they are like interest-free loans from banks. Debit floats arise from processing cheques or other debit instruments when a bank credits the payee before receiving money from the payer's bank or when the payer's account is debited with delay after funds are paid to the payee bank. In such a case, the bank customers receive benefits of float at the expense of banks. Floats can exist in the central bank-commercial bank relationship. From the viewpoint of a central bank, floats affect the level and volatility of banks' reserves and complicate monetary policy. A system that reduces floats reduces transaction costs and makes liquidity assessment more definitive. Same day settlement would reduce arbitrage and equalizes interest rates across regions and across activities.

By reducing floats, a robust and efficient payment and settlement system would compel the central bank to manage liquidity, a task that can be best done by regular liquidity forecasts and taking monetary policy actions based on the information provided by such forecasts. However, if flexible exchange rate arrangement is in place, central banks do not conduct foreign exchange operation. This will imply that none of the settlement systems (RTGS or DNS or foreign exchange settlements) would be relevant and monetary policy would be focused on managing liquidity.

Section IV

The New Concerns

6. Financial Stability *155*

- Financial Stability in the context of
  Financial Development

- The Early Warning Signals and Hedging Mechanisms

- Liquidity Forecasts

- Prudential Regulation and Supervision of Banks

- The International Initiatives in Evolving Standards
  and Codes

- Prudent Supervision by Central Banks and
  Other Agencies or by a Superbody?

- International Dimensions of Financial Stability Issues

Box 10 : Early Warning Signals of Crisis

Box 11 : Risk Management in Banks

Box 12 : The Basle Principles for Effective Banking Supervision

Box 13 : Key International Standards and Codes

*Box 14 : The Indian Initiatives in Respect of International
Standards and Codes*

6

Financial Stability

Financial Stability in the Context of Financial Development

Financial stability is the most commonly accepted objective of central banks during the second half of the 1990s and is considered as critical for realizing sustained growth. Essentially because of the currency and financial crises in Latin America, South East Asia, and Russia, central banks and policy makers at the major international financial institutions (such as the International Monetary Fund, the World Bank and the Bank for International Settlements) have taken upon themselves the unenviable task of working out strategies both at the national and international levels to preserve and foster financial stability. At the international level, the Financial Stability Forum (FSF) set up by the major industrialized economies in 1998 has been working to ensure that countries avoid cross border effects of their actions. At the national level, central banks have taken lead. For example, the Bank of England has made changes within its organization to address the problem at the national level and to cooperate with international institutions and other central banks for fostering international financial stability. The Bank of England also has been issuing on a quarterly basis a journal called the Financial Stability Review that deals with issues of financial stability both at the national and international levels. To improve understanding of the issues involved, the international community, in particular the major central banks and international bodies sponsored and held a number of conferences and seminars in different countries emphasizing the international dimensions of financial stability.

Financial stability as a term is understood in relation to financial institutions and financial markets. It is rarely defined. It is described as devoid of instability of financial institutions and markets. This is not a helpful definition but the point to note is that a positive outcome will emerge from being cautious and prudent in the pursuit of policies that affect financial institutions, and markets especially so in EMEs. Pursing financial stability therefore would require an appreciation of the fact that it should be viewed in the context of financial sector development and diversification. Financial stability problem would hardly exist where financial sector is characterized by stagnation and repression. Financial stability would be vulnerable to crisis-like situations when policy regime shifts take place with no trace of transparency. The uncertainties that are associated with such regime shifts could lead market participants (for example, banks) to make their own judgments about the probable actions that their competitors would take in order to optimize their profits. When uncertainties lead to deviations in the market behavior of certain participants, especially the big ones from the normal patterns, the rest of the market participants would tend to imitate and be a part of the 'herd'. Such 'herd behavior', if unchecked, could lead to system-wide crisis. Even if one were to consider such extreme behavior to be uncommon, financial stability could be under stress under two conditions: (a) when financial sector expands at different rates with a variety of instruments having a wide array of risk-return profiles that are outside regulation and supervision and (b) when market practices and trading are unclear and not fully understood by the participants. Payment failures in such situations could trigger panics and runs on banks and eventually force central banks to act as lenders of last resort. If the amounts involved under such crisis situations could not be taken care of by the central banks themselves, the confidence in the economy would be seriously impaired.

Financial stability would be particularly fragile when transparency of operations of banks and other financial institutions is not in evidence and when credit markets are characterized by incomplete information, resulting in adverse selection and moral hazard. When interest rate goes up, low quality borrowers often would be willing to borrow. When banks provide support to such borrowers on the false assumption that the interest payments on such loans would give them higher incomes and larger profits, they make an adverse selection because of the low quality of the borrowings. The return flow of funds to banks would decline, leading eventually to moral hazard and to decline in the supply of credit. To prevent the emergence of liquidity shortage, central banks must have such institutional mechanisms as supervision in place. Besides, the central banks would have to provide a clear idea of what their monetary policy stands for and their role as 'lenders of last resort'. A predictable monetary policy would help banks in avoiding pitfalls of adverse selection.

It is also possible that financial stability would be jeopardized when incentives for compliance and commitment on the part of the borrowers do not exist, leading to absence of renegotiation of loan in the event of default or when bankruptcy laws are not in existence or when procedures for recovery of loans are weak. Recovery laws may be so weak that borrowers may find it convenient and economically sensible to default on the loans taken. Financial stability may be vulnerable to stress also when competition in banking is very severe. In the United States, such competition, especially with several relatively small banks has led to weak financial stability (Davis, E P (1995); and Allen, Franklin and Douglas Gale (2000)).

Financial stability would be under attack if trading in financial derivatives or instruments that resemble financial derivatives is widespread and is without any regulation and surveillance of any statutory authority. The laws that address the concerns of the parties that participate in derivatives trading will need to be sufficiently strong and effective in terms of their implementation and equitable in the treatment of the participants associated with the transactions/trading in derivatives. Central banks will have to be watchful of the procedures followed in the transactions and ensure that the disincentives for not complying with the laid-down procedures and laws are substantial and penal in character.

Financial stability could also be under jeopardy when asset prices collapse. Borrowers' collateral values would decline and the banks' ability to recover the amounts lent in the event of default would be sharply reduced. In most EMEs, the most common collaterals used in the financial transactions are real estate/buildings, and machinery, shares of companies, and foreign exchange deposits. When the market values of these assets decline, the net worth of borrowers would be reduced, giving rise initially to illiquidity situation for borrowers. When such illiquidity is not tackled, it could lead to insolvency of borrowing firms. A payment failure could lead to panics and runs on banks, leading to aggravation of the problem of liquidity shortage. It would therefore be incumbent on the part of central banks in EMEs to ensure that the financial infrastructure embodied in the payment system is run efficiently, and continuously without any gridlocks.

The above discussion, conducted as if only the domestic economic context is relevant, can be extended to capture the international dimensions of financial stability. When exchange rates are volatile, or when foreign inflows do not follow a steady pattern or when foreign debt incurred by governments or by firms in EMEs is perceived to be unsustainable, financial stability would be under severe stress. Most currency and financial crises in EMEs could be traced to improper sequencing of economic reforms. The reasons for crises could be several. For instance, total liberalization of capital account of the balance of payments (i.e., capital mobility both into and outside the country) cannot be sustained unless it is supported by sound macro-economic framework and structural and institutional policies. Pursuing a rigid or pegged exchange rate regime could, when there is a speculative attack on the currency, cause runs on banks. High external current account deficit (deficit on account of trade in merchandise and other services) could lead to currency attacks, particularly if the deficit is perceived to be unsustainable. This had happened in Thailand towards the early part of 1997 when Thailand had in place fixed exchange rate system. Large and unsustainable fiscal deficits, high external debt position, the large proportion of short term external debt in total external debt raising doubts about external asset-liability matching, insufficient bank supervision, limited and inadequate prudential regulations on banks, and absence of appropriate regulations on stock markets have all been found to be some of the factors that caused financial crises in the 1990s. (An attachment is provided at the end of this book to give a bird's-eye view on the Asian Economic Crises).

When capital inflows take place in the initial stages of financial liberalization, countries get benefited because they help to bridge the foreign exchange gaps. If the inflows are not in the nature of direct investments, and are more in the form of portfolio investments, then the inflows should be treated as temporary and as likely to flow out if the portfolio investors perceive investments in the stock market in the concerned emerging economy to be not financially profitable. Foreign direct investment flows are likely to be more stable. In either case, the inflows would last as long as the policy framework is sound. Once the foreign investors perceive the economic prospects of the emerging economy to dip, they will cause capital outflows. Large capital outflows, as the past experiences show, have destabilized investment plans of emerging economies and sharply reversed growth prospects. The most affected social groups in such situations would be the poorer ones. The large capital outflows will cause considerable illiquidity initially and could lead to insolvency. If a country is regarded as vulnerable to financial illiquidity or insolvency, then all countries that are closely linked with it through trade in merchandise or services or through financial markets could also be affected adversely. Such 'spill over' effects were seen in the episodes of the experiences of some of the East Asian countries in the 1990s. A payment failure by the crisis-hit country would affect the financial balance sheets of the countries linked with the said country. This could lead the international rating agencies to reevaluate the credit worthiness of all the countries related with the crisis-hit country. Such a reevaluation itself could engender a 'contagion' of crisis in all the related countries. Most EMEs, being exposed to international commodity and financial markets, would have to be wary of the interactive and interlinked domestic and international processes that have a bearing on the financial stability of their national economies.

The Early Warning Signals and Hedging Mechanisms

The systemic crises that occurred in the 1990s (in Mexico, Thailand, Korea, Indonesia, Argentina, Brazil, Russia) were the extreme in the sense they were severe cases. From the point of view of policy-making at the levels of both the Treasury and Central banks, it is important to nip the crisis in the bud when symptoms of crisis arise. Such symptoms, often referred to as 'early warning signals' (EWS), are closely monitored and used for policy actions (see **Box 10** for early warning signals, sometimes also referred to as leading indicators of crises). It must however be recognized that instituting an EWS mechanism would not by itself assure financial stability. For, EWS often takes the form of data scanning and analysis and may not fully capture the sentiments and expectations of markets.

It would be obviously illogical to consider every unfavorable signal or a cluster of signals as foretelling a financial or systemic crisis. Nevertheless, central banks will have to know the sources of the imminent problems. For example, *it is essential for them to first distinguish the liquidity issue from the solvency issue and treat illiquidity as the first priority for policy action.* When a policy action to resolve illiquidity fails and leads to insolvency, the liquidity crisis would turn into a systemic crisis in the financial sector. This would suggest that financial stability in the domestic economy would be under severe stress when liquidity management principles are not adequately adhered to. From the central banks' point of view, it is important that introduction of financial sector reforms does not lead banks and other financial institutions to adopt practices that are relatively risky and are characterized by mismatches between liabilities and assets. Where markets are not deep, banks would find it difficult to trade their assets, especially during times of high demand for credit and growing financial disintermediation. If expectations of liquidity of assets are not present, trading in assets cannot take place. That is why in countries where efforts are continuously made to develop and diversify financial markets, central banks will have to ensure that there is enough market liquidity. However, till the economies reach a stage of reasonably high degree of financial integration, assets will face different degrees of tradeability. In other words, markets would exist for some assets and not for all assets. To put it differently, there need not be single equilibrium in the financial sector as a whole but multiple equilibria. In such circumstances, effecting changes in the methods of valuation of assets as part of financial sector reforms (that is, as part of banking regulation) or volatility of asset prices could lead to considerable fluctuations in the liquidity structure of banks. Banks will have to adopt appropriate strategies to ensure that they are sufficiently liquid by managing portfolios in a manner that tradeability is assured in respect of most of the assets they hold. In the process of portfolio management, banks have to pay attention to minimize the variety of risks that are associated with interest and principal repayment defaults, market valuation changes, as well as operational problems (See **Box 11** on Risk Management).

There is a general impression that financial stability would be secure if central banks not only understand the cyclical as well as structural problems faced by banks on a continuous basis but also take steps to enable banks to overcome such problems. This is where considerable amount of research would have to be conducted in central banks on the risks that the financial sector would face at the system level as well as at the level of some of the critical components of the sector. Since banks are directly under the control and regulation of central banks, the financial and economic analysis of banks would have to be strong and thorough in the central banks. But this alone may not be enough. It might become necessary for central banks to conduct research on the developments and the expectations of stock markets and of the corporate entities that depend crucially on market financing for expansion and diversification.

On their part central banks will need to be transparent about the mechanisms they adopt to guide banks to adopt risk and liquidity management techniques. Central banks may also have to play a proactive role in providing technical assistance and training in risk management techniques. They also may have to be clear about the mechanisms that would be set in place to enforce prudential regulations. Transparency about the surveillance and supervisory systems would be particularly helpful in influencing market expectations.

The relationship between regulations and supervision and liquidity in the economy is critical and is not fully understood. It is well known that liquidity in the economy is influenced by both supply of and demand for credit. More often than not, central banks focus on supply of credit and assume that the demand for credit adjusts itself to it at the *given* market rate of interest. In other words, an increase in the market rate of interest would imply excess of demand for credit over credit supply and vice versa. The demand for credit, however, could be elusive. It is determined by the behavior of lenders and borrowers. The behavior is influenced by bank regulations and supervision — the true indirect instruments of monetary policy. But regulations and supervision also impact on bank reserves just as the conventional instruments of policy such as the open market operations, the bank rate, and reserve requirements do. This is one fact that is not adequately appreciated in most discussions. The size of bank reserves ultimately determines the supply of credit and through it the liquidity position. Thus the regulations and supervision have a bearing on both the demand for and supply of credit whereas the conventional policy instruments influence only the supply of credit. Keeping this point in view, central banks will have to ensure that there is sufficient liquidity. For this purpose, central banks will need to make estimations of liquidity requirements of the economy on a daily basis, and if need be twice in a day, and inject or absorb liquidity as dictated by the needs.

Liquidity Forecasts

In reality, central banks in both industrialized and emerging market economies make liquidity forecasts every day. For this purpose they would need to make estimations of cash flows (both in and out of the financial system). To illustrate:- Cash outflows out of the banking system (inclusive of the central banks) would have to be gauged from the likely amounts on account of (a) the expected absorption of dated and short term government securities and treasury bills, (b) absorption of repos, (c) the likely withdrawals of deposits for payment of taxes, (d) payments due on the amounts borrowed from abroad by banks/government/corporate entities either by way of principal repayments or by way of interest payments or both, (e) the trend growth of bank credit, (f) special needs of bank financing due to seasonal operations (due for instance to food procurement operations by government agencies as in India) and (g) trend growth of import payments. The factors enumerated here are essentially indicative and not exhaustive.

Cash flows into the banking system could consist of items such as (i) the available repos for sales, (ii) the likely amounts that will be redeemed on maturity of government securities and treasury bills in auctions as well as repos, (iii) the trend improvements in bank deposits, and (iv) the trend expansion of export receipts. Again the factors mentioned here are not exhaustive.

Once the liquidity forecast exercise is made, central banks will have to estimate the amounts that they could make available to banks under their discretionary powers, namely, through refinancing facilities or special funding facilities generally against collateral of eligible securities (usually government securities). The decisions about what to do with the amounts due from banks on account of the loans provided in the past period, and about the likely amounts that would be available to central banks on account of statutory and cash reserve requirements of banks arising from expansion of deposits and other liabilities will be critical ones since they could shift liquidity positions of banks, sometimes dramatically during periods of upturn of economic activities. Estimations of these amounts when juxtaposed with net liquidity requirements will provide a basis for central banks to decide as to whether liquidity should be injected into or withdrawn from the system.

On paper the above suggested liquidity forecast exercise would look formidable, but most central banks undertake it as a matter of daily routine, sometimes twice a day, once at around the beginning of the day when transactions in money and other financial markets begin to pick up, and again sometime during the peak time of the daily transaction. Oftentimes, the way the interest and exchange rates behave would indicate the discrepancies between the cash inflows and cash outflows.

Central banks ensure that the liquidity needs are fully met so that the markets do not fail owing to any possible defaults and interest rates do not increase sharply. If businesses face illiquidity, banks would be the first to face its effects because any delay in meeting the demand for regular borrowers or in discharging the withdrawal of deposits across the counter would immediately give rise to perceptions that the financial strength of banks is not sufficiently strong. Banks would, when faced with liquidity crunch if not illiquidity, have to either reduce their commitments on additional or new credit or sell off some of their assets to accommodate the new demands for credit, or raise interest rates to ration funds available for credit or seek credit from the central bank. But the latter solution is not easy to implement. A sharp hike in interest rate on loans by any one bank would be viewed by markets as a sign of financial weakness of the bank and place the rest of the banks in a position of comparative strength at least temporarily. On the other hand, if some banks are closely linked with the bank that raised its loan rate, then they would be concerned about the return flow of the funds that they lent to the bank in liquidity bind. In other words, the central bank would have to closely monitor the banks' responses to the market conditions but as this cannot be done on a day to day basis except when the final settlement of interbank accounts occurs at the level of the central bank, it may have to resort to some amount of gathering of market intelligence in addition to tracking the movement in interest rates. Many central banks in EMEs consider the inter-bank call money rates to be the best guides about the liquidity situation in the economy.

Prudential Regulation and Supervision of Banks

From the point of view of central banks, it is necessary that banks comply with all the necessary prudential requirements. Most EMEs have followed the Basle Principles of Bank Supervision (See **Box 12**) while specifying the prudential supervisory requirements. The areas on which emphasis is laid are the capital adequacy norms, asset classification procedures and methods, income recognition principles, market valuation of assets, and recovery mechanisms to reduce the non-performing assets of banks. A medium term path would have to be laid down to see that banks improve their financial position. Since central banks cannot conduct at short notice and in high frequency, on the spot supervision (the onsite supervision as it is often referred to) of all the banks, particularly when the banks are far too many with a large number of branches, they would have to undertake off-site supervision mechanisms by devising appropriate data formats to collect information about a large number of variables such as the banks' latest cash flow position, new loans and investments, the liabilities incurred, the off-balance sheet items, capital adequacy, profitability, bad loans and bad investments, recoveries of old loans, share-holding patterns, risk and liquidity analyses conducted, and the principles adopted by banks to reduce the asset-liability mismatches. Central banks in EMEs often tend to rely both on on-site and off-site supervision. From the individual bank-wise prudential indicators, central banks work out what has come to be known as aggregate micro-prudential indicators (AMPI) for the banking system as a whole.

It is important to know what these indicators are. Essentially, they represent those that help one to know the inherent strength of each bank and when the quantities under each indicator for all the banks are added on (i.e., aggregated), one would get the AMPI. The indicators could be divided into a number of categories, of which the first six are the capital adequacy (C), asset quality (A), management soundness (M), earnings (E), liquidity (L) and systems and controls (S). The letters in the parentheses here amount to the well known CAMELS. In addition, indicators that provide sensitivity to market risk and other market-based indicators are considered.

The details of the indicators under each of the categories are generally carefully seen by most central banks in EMEs. They are :

Capital Adequacy :

Capital ratio, namely the capital to assets ratio
The frequency distribution of capital ratios for the aggregated banking system

Asset Quality :

Lending Institution
Sectoral credit concentration
Foreign currency denominated lending
Non-performing loans and provisions
Loans to loss-making public sector entities
Risk profile of assets
Connected lending
Leverage ratios

Borrowing Entity
Debt-equity ratios
Corporate profitability
Other indicators of corporate conditions
Household indebtedness

Management Soundness :

Expense ratios
Earning per employee
Growth in the number of financial institutions

Earnings and Profitability :

Return on assets
Return on equity
Income and expense ratios
Structural profitability indicators

Liquidity :

Central bank credit to financial institutions
Deposits in relation to monetary aggregates
Segmentation of inter-bank rates
Loans to deposits ratios
Maturity structure of assets and liabilities
Measures of secondary market liquidity

Systems and Controls :

Procedures and systems for risk management
Audit, compliance and internal inspections systems within the banks
Management Information Systems and vigilance mechanisms

Sensitivity to Market Risk:

Foreign exchange risk
Interest rate risk
Equity price risk
Commodity price risk

Market-based Indicators :

Market prices of financial instruments including equity
Indicators of excess yields
Credit ratings
Sovereign yield spreads

Since the AMPIs capture the essence of the balance sheet of the entire banking system, it also reflects at a point of time, the impact of any changes in monetary measures or magnitudes, such as the exchange rate, or the interest rate. In recent years, most central banks in industrialized economies have attempted to quantify such linkages through sensitivity tests — the stress tests as they have come to be known because they test the stress on the system caused by changes in certain macroeconomic variables. Some EMEs have shown inclination to move toward conducting such exercises within their central banks.

It must however, be noted that while stress testing is useful, it would not be feasible to conduct them regularly and monitored at high frequencies. The indicators that are regularly monitored are really the macro-economic ones such as those related to the real economy, fiscal, monetary and credit sectors, external sector developments and asset and commodity prices. There can of course no one standard list of variables that central banks follow. In general, central banks follow the traditional approach of going into details of each and every major sector of activity and supplement the details with some additional factors such as the macroeconometric analyses of trade and financial market spillovers. Economists at the central banks study the course of macroeconomic indicators and draw broad conclusions about the state of the economy at different points of time. While these analyses point to general policy requirements, they would not be helpful in respect of specific policies that might be needed to preserve or enhance, if need be, the stability of the banking system. Nor do macroeconomic indicators (MEIs) necessarily provide sufficient information about the fragility of the banking system or of any one bank that is critical to the banking system. In fact one could also contend that MEIs may not also throw adequate light on the impending liquidity and systemic problems, as the experience of the recent currency and financial crises of the 1990s in Mexico, and some South East Asian countries has shown.

If MEI-based models were regarded as not reliable, it would become necessary to find ways of strengthening the central banks' analyses of financial stability issues. One of the ways of doing so is to link AMPIs and MEIs in a logical way to arrive at what may be called the macroprudential indicators (MPIs). But there are not many worthwhile studies so far on such a linkage, although the Bank of England has been known to be taking into account both AMPIs and MPIs rather than any fixed model to study the financial stability issues. The European Central Bank (ECB) has set up a working group on macroprudential analysis and has identified the existing data gaps constraining the compilation of information on MPIs. This is the type of analysis that central banks in EMEs may have to also do on a regular basis in the near future.

The International Initiatives in Evolving Standards and Codes

It is not enough to have prudential regulations and supervision on commercial banks alone. For, as the experience of the financial crisis in Thailand during the middle of 1997 showed, the failure of non-bank financial companies that borrowed in substantial amounts from banks, especially the financially weak banks, led to some bank failures as well. The financial companies' failure was in turn attributed to collapse of real estate prices. The Thai experience suggests that regulations and supervision over all financial entities, and not merely commercial banks, would be necessary to foster financial stability. Adverse selection process can occur in the case of non-bank financial entities as well due to inadequate and asymmetric information and could lead to inappropriate market expectations. Market expectations often play a key role in the initial stages of financial liberalization when the regulatory mechanisms may not be sufficiently strong. When the Mexican crisis broke out in 1994 almost all of a sudden, it was felt by a number of keen observers of international economic and financial scene that markets could have anticipated the problems had there been sufficient and timely information on all the macroeconomic variables and taken corrective actions. Foreign investors would in particular be hard hit by currency crisis situation because of information inadequacies and asymmetries. The International Monetary Fund therefore initiated early in 1995 among its members a drive towards creating, improving and disseminating all macro-economic and other information about their economies that market participants both at home and abroad would seek. The IMF wanted the members to agree to some standard in data provision by countries on some agreed areas of interest. In the typical language of the IMF, the members were requested to "subscribe" to the standards and for this purpose created a set of data formats. Within the standards, there are two varieties — the Special Data Dissemination Standards (SDDS) devised specifically for those members of the Fund that seek private market financing, and the General Data Dissemination Standards (GDDS) that become applicable to those Fund members who do not have access to private markets. Essentially, the standards, be they SDDS or GDDS, related to the data on major macroeconomic indicators. It took sometime for the membership of the Fund to understand the full implications of the data dissemination standards that were evolved. The data provided to the IMF would be available to other countries from the publications as well as from what was called the IMF's 'bulletin board' to which countries would have access through electronic means. To the extent possible, standardization of the terms used, the coverage of data, and the items included under each activity-area would be done under the standards-approach. For example, bank credit to the government would be defined to cover all banks' direct loans to governments as well as their investments in government securities. The inclusion of the central banks under the term 'banks' is for example an important standardization practice. Where practices and institutional contexts differ, the precise meaning of the terms employed by the country concerned would be conveyed to all those who seek such information through appropriate footnotes and other notes.

Even before the data standards got stabilized, there occurred series of currency and financial crises in some countries of South East Asia in 1997 and 1998 and in Brazil in 1998. There were clearly differences in the nature of the crises. Moreover, none of the crisis-situations in the 1990s were anticipated well in advance by the international financial community. Each of the crisis-situations had imposed high costs on the economies concerned. The costs were in terms of loss of growth, and employment, sharp decline in investment and capital outflows. The crisis in each country had domestic system-wide effects. Many of them also had, to the extent dictated by openness of the economies, spill-over effects on countries that were linked with the crisis-hit country by trade and through the financial market transactions. Given the high costs in overcoming the crises and given the systemic impact of the crises, the industrialized economies had, in association with multilateral and professional bodies such as the IMF, the World Bank, and the Bank for International Settlements, set out to lay down detailed mechanisms to foster financial stability in domestic economies and across countries. A Financial Stability Forum (FSF) was created, with emphasis being placed on elimination of information asymmetries and on adoption of stricter and efficient prudential regulations over financial institutions and markets. This was in a sense a reiteration and a reaffirmation of what the industrialized economies had been seeking to establish on a wide scale since the middle of the 1970s after the Herstatt Bank crisis in the then West Germany. Transparency rules and practices in macroeconomic policies and standardized international standards and codes based on the best known and widely adopted market practices in the major markets were considered as critical and as required for adoption in order to foster and strengthen financial stability by all the industrialized and emerging market economies.

The questions that arise in this context are several. What, after all, are the standards? What are the areas where standards need to be implemented? Are they already in existence in some countries or are they themselves evolving ? If they are not already given, how does one implement them when markets are being developed and as some markets are growing with diverse market participants ? The truth is that many of the standards are generated by international technocrats working in multilateral institutions such as the IMF and World Bank and in professional associations on the basis of their observance of the market practices in markets that are fairly deep. But there is no certainty that the observed market practices would resolve all conceivable problems that arise in the course of a wide array of financial transactions. Nor is it certain that all market participants even in the industrial country markets fully understand each element of the standards. Again, if there are too many standards, they cannot be implemented. It is therefore necessary to identify the critical ones among them. The discussions in the international forums including the multilateral financial institutions, and some major private sector creditors showed that the standards in fact could be far too many, well exceeding fifty, and clearly beyond the capacity of the countries to comply with each of them.

It was inconceivable that only IMF or the World Bank or the Bank for International Settlements could have worked out all the critical standards and ensured that member countries would comply with all of them. The whole exercise required some concerted and cooperative action on the part of those whose influence in international financial markets is immense. It is against this context, a number of major IEs with the help of the IMF, World Bank, and Bank for International Settlements (BIS) created the Financial Stability Forum which in turn brought into the fold the major international professional bodies having national affiliations such as those which dealt with accounting, auditing and securities trading. At the same time, an official group of 20 industrialized and emerging market economies, called the Group of Twenty or simply the G-20, was formed in 1999 under the initiative of the US Government, to focus on issues of financial stability and other economic and financial issues that have a bearing on the international financial system. The G-20 consisted of the following countries: the United States, the United Kingdom, Japan, France, Germany, Italy, Canada, Russia, Argentina, Australia, Brazil, China, India, Indonesia, Korea, Mexico, Saudi Arabia, South Africa, Thailand and Turkey. The criteria for choosing countries and classifying them as 'systemically important' have not been made clear but both the openness and the population size must have been reckoned in the matter. The G-20 is an informal and a close-knit group without any regular secretariat of its own. It has a two-tier structure — one at the Ministerial level and the other at the Deputies' level. At the Ministerial level, the discussions are conducted among the Ministers of Finance and Central Bank Governors of the Group. At the Deputies' level, senior representatives of the Ministries of Finance and central banks conduct discussions and report to their respective Ministers. The G-20 asked the FSF to clearly identify those international standards and codes of transparency practices that could be regarded as *key* to fostering financial stability and report to it. A Working Group was formed to identify the key standards and recommend for implementation. Mr Andrew Sheng, who was the Head of the Securities commission in Hong Kong, was made the Chairman of the Group. The Sheng Group's identified standards and codes are given in **Box 13**. The G-20 endorsed the recommendations. The IMF and the World Bank accepted them and adopted them as an important element in their work on promoting financial stability among their member nations.

It is worth noting that of the ones that have been widely treated as the key ones, the most widely known one relates to the core principles of bank supervision that have been laid down by a committee at the Bank for International Settlements. This has come to be known as the Basle Committee. The core principles are essentially twenty-five. These may be recalled from Box 12. These are to be complied with by all the commercial banks within the national boundaries and the national bank supervisors are expected to ensure that the compliance is full.

Each standard/code/core principle (to be henceforth referred in this book as standards or as standards and codes, for purposes of simplification) is explicitly stated and defined. The standards are widely notified and placed on the websites of the agencies entrusted with the work of evolving standards in the areas identified as key areas. The standards are in effect a set of principles that markets are expected to follow so that financial stability could be fostered. But it does not automatically mean, as the Sheng group pointed out, that implementation of international standards and codes would lead necessarily to financial stability but could help to foster it. In fact there are no theoretical or empirical exercises to show that there is a definite link between the two (See Vasudevan, A (2001)). This point about the lack of theory or empiricism was explicitly acknowledged subsequently by the group on incentives to foster implementation of standards and codes headed by Axel Nawrath, appointed by FSF as a sequel to the Sheng Group. Apart from the lack of link between implementation and realization of financial stability, a number of issues cropped up in respect of implementation of standards. First, it is not clear, at least not as yet, that financial stability would be best fostered *only if* countries implement *all* the 12 identified standards and whether implementation of a few of them would be adequate for the purpose. Secondly, within each standard, there are a large number of principles or items, making it very difficult for implementation in full by every country at a given point in time. For example, of the twenty-five Core Principles of Bank Supervision, some countries comply with most of them and not all of them and yet do not face any noticeable problems of financial instability. India was identified as such a case as early as 1999. Thirdly, some of the standards cannot be implemented by some of the emerging market economies because of institutional and legal constraints. Fourthly, it is possible to envisage differences in the perception of compliance of standards by different market participants, in which case the certification of compliance by the national authorities may not be sufficient to give confidence about setting in financial stability. Finally, implementation of standards would have to be supplemented by appropriate financial sector reforms that encompass macroeconomic, institutional and legislative areas in the countries that are characterized by close financial integration.

There is not enough evidence that all the 12 identified key standards have been implemented in full in most countries, including the industrialized countries. The IMF and World Bank have been asked by the international community to report about the implementation of the standards and codes by the industrialized and emerging market economies. The IMF and World Bank have been reporting to their respective Executive Boards their assessments of financial stability in industrialized countries and in EMEs by observing the implementation of standards in each key area recommended by the Sheng group. Such Reports On compliance to Standards and Codes are referred to in the IMF language and in the literature on the international financial architecture as ROSCs. The reports are, with the permission of the national authorities, are disseminated by the Bretton Woods twins, the IMF and the World Bank, so that the markets would be fairly clear that any financial stability problems that may emerge in these countries are not on account of non-compliance with best international market practices but on account of other reasons. This exercise is said to be useful but not all countries agree to such wide dissemination of ROSCs, partly because markets could be myopic and could act irrationally when reports contain any observation that is open to different perceptions and produce uncertain outcomes. ROSCs however do not comment on the imminence of financial instability if a standard or a part of any one standard is not complied with. In certain cases, ROSCs may not be able to cover all the key areas for which standards have been recommended. For example, some countries may not have developed markets in certain financial segments (for example, insurance in the case of India where regulations and supervisory mechanisms are being evolved) and therefore the standards would not apply to them. There are also countries where financial markets are in different stages of evolution and development. It would therefore be difficult to generalize and state that non-compliance with any one of the 12 identified key codes would necessarily imply that financial stability is jeopardized.

Ideally, emerging market economies should make their own assessments of compliance with international standards and provide clear and unambiguous information about the legal and institutional constraints that might be at work. The Reserve Bank of India did such a self assessment in respect of the Basle Core Principles of Effective Bank Supervision and placed the results on its website. While such initiatives are commendable, they may not be enough. To gain international credibility to the exercise of working towards financial stability, EMEs should, besides disseminating their own assessments, agree to the financial stability assessments of IMF and World Bank. In many cases of financial stability assessments, IMF and World Bank undertake what is called stress testing or vulnerability testing by picking up a number of variables and subject them to sensitivity analysis. For example, how the profitability of banks would be affected by a unit increase in interest rates would be one part of such sensitivity analyses. These tests are useful but may not necessarily be sufficient to provide possible approaches to avoiding financial instability.

One of the significant developments of the 1990s is that industrialized countries as well as many emerging economies have agreed to implement the standards. A number of EMEs, however, expressed their difficulties in implementation of the agreed key standards due to differences in institutional and legal structures, and due to the fact that the international standards themselves are evolving. For example, India expressed reservation about the ability of the standards to ensure financial stability but had committed herself to the idea of fostering the implementation of international standards to the extent possible at this stage. The rationale of the Indian response to the question of implementation of international standards could be considered as an interesting example of an emerging economy that is attempting to reconcile the national market practices and the shifts in the institutional and legal positions engendered by financial sector reforms with the specified international standards. The fact is that in the process of development of the financial sector it would be difficult to ensure that all the international standards are fully complied with within a short-to-medium term horizon (See **Box 14** for the Indian initiatives in the matter). But a somewhat extended medium term path would have to be laid down to see that the international standards are implemented ultimately in all the key areas.

Prudential Supervision by Central Banks and Other Agencies or by a Superbody?

Central banks have traditionally supervised commercial banks and other financial entities that fall within their jurisdictions as provided for in the legislations of the land. But questions have been raised that as central banks are also regulators and are consequently in a position to influence the behavior of market participants, the supervision (which entails monitoring the norms of behavior) that central banks would undertake could pose a moral hazard. It is therefore suggested that supervision should be given to an agency outside of the central bank even though this would imply higher costs. In the context of EMEs wherein financial sector development and diversification would be evolving, it is suggested that supervisory arrangements would need to be clearly specified before hand for purposes of fostering financial stability. This is because the new financial services are catered to either by a number of new institutions or at one place by a few of them and it would be essential that the distinction, if any, between a regulator and a supervisor in relation to any one type of activity (like banking, securities, or insurance) is made widely known to the concerned institutions as well as to the public.

What are the possible options relating to the supervisory arrangements ? There are at least three alternatives. It is possible to envisage multiple supervision agencies including the central bank, or have supervision functions of all financial sector activities vested with the central bank, or have all supervisory tasks performed by a separate agency created for the purpose. The supervision would essentially cover prudential and systemic aspects but it could also span over the very conduct of business. In prudential type of supervision, the health of individual financial institutions would be under scrutiny. For instance, the balance sheets of institutions would be looked into with reference to their compliance of some broad parameters (such as the capital adequacy, asset classification, income recognition, provisioning norms, and credit concentration norms) that would have been laid by the regulators. The idea is to contain the possibility of spill over effects of a weak or fragile institution over the rest of the economy and to give a sense of comfort and protection to consumers. In the case of systemic supervision, a broader view of the economy has to be taken into account in that the health and ability of financial systems to withstand shocks would be carefully examined. In supervising over the conduct of business, focus would be placed on customer relationships including consumer protection, information disclosure, and fair business practices (See Narain, Aditya and Saibal Ghosh (2001)).

The arguments for having the supervisory tasks performed only by central banks are familiar but worth noting in brief. First is the general observation that central banks collect enormous amount of data on the financial sector and track all the major variables relating to the real sector and are therefore in a better position to form relatively objective views on the market expectations and take necessary actions. Secondly, most central banks provide payment and settlement services and are in a position to quickly monitor the payment failures and stresses at different markets and institutions. Payment supervision or surveillance would help give unique insights on the liquidity position in the economy prior to the final liquidity outcome. Thirdly, being considered as the lender of the last resort (LOLR), a central bank will get prior intimation about the borrowing requirements of any one bank, an advantage that helps the central bank to take necessary actions in quick time to obviate the liquidity or systemic crisis situation. Finally, cooperation among the central banks is well known and established, and the spill over or contagion effects could be avoided if central banks take concerted action on the basis of the 'superior' information that they have about the working of institutions and markets.

On the other hand, the main arguments for not locating the

supervisory functions with the central bank would be essentially two : (a) the moral hazard argument arising partly from the expectation that both depositors and creditors of institutions supervised by the central bank would expect that they would be treated equally in the event of failure of an institution and partly because of the central bank's own failure in not laying down the rules regarding the treatment of institutions in the event of failure; and (b) the dilemma that central banks face while taking monetary policy action based on the supervisory information, viz., that the action may affect institutions in different ways and in different degrees and could encourage the affected institutions to set right the anomalies, thereby leaving doubts about the credibility of the action originally taken.

Would a unified supervisor help overcome the disadvantage of having supervision undertaken by the central bank ? A few countries have experimented with this method, the most notable being the United Kingdom where the Financial Supervisory Authority (FSA) was created in 1998. Given the limited experience of the working of the unified supervisory bodies, it is difficult to be definitive about the efficacy of a separate and often supposed to be an autonomous body. In EMEs, however, it is not easily possible, at least prima facie, to have such a separate entity for several reasons. The costs of having a separate body for supervision could be high. There may not also be enough trained staff to undertake supervision tasks in a competent manner. Moreover, the financial markets are yet to be fully integrated and may not be sufficiently sophisticated. Most institutions in EMEs are relatively less complex. Besides, a separate supervisory body if created by the governments would tend to carry political color and may be less objective than the central banks that often enjoy fairly high public confidence.

What if there were to be multiple agencies for supervision as is the case in many EMEs. This is so in the United States and the US financial sector is none the worse for it. The existence of multiple supervisory agencies would imply a clear need for coordination of their activities and sharing of information. Such a coordinating mechanism would not succeed without active central bank role in economies where bank financing is important, if not the dominant. This is because central banks are known to have considerable 'superior' information on all the sectors of the economy and on the international financial markets. But to be effective as well as credible, the coordinating mechanism that is entrusted with the central bank should be backed by sound legal framework. Besides, the supervision authorities would have to deal with each sector by the benchmarks set by international standards and codes referred to earlier and the regulations of the regulatory authorities relating to the medium term path of achieving the benchmarks.

In the case of India, several agencies conduct supervision and regulation of the financial activities. The *main* ones are the Reserve Bank of India, the Securities and Exchange Board of India, and the recently formed Insurance Regulatory and Development Authority. There are also specialized institutions such as the National Bank of Agricultural and Rural Development, the Industrial Development Bank, the Small Industries Development Bank of India, and the National Housing Bank that often team up with the Reserve Bank of India to supervise and regulate the institutions that fall under their areas of operation. The Reserve Bank of India on its part works as an operational mechanism of the supervision guidelines and rules provided by the Board for Financial Supervision, created in 1994 as an autonomous body under the aegis of the Reserve Bank. The Governor of the Reserve Bank of India acts as the Chairman of the High Level Committee on Capital Markets. In an important sense, the Committee represents the main coordinating mechanism that focuses on the functioning of the money, government securities, private debt and equity markets. It is too early to pronounce judgments about the efficacy of the existing mechanisms. As the financial sector grows and diversifies further, it is to be seen whether the existing mechanisms are adequate to meet serious vulnerabilities in the financial sector without further toning up the legal framework presently surrounding the supervisory and regulatory arrangements.

International Dimensions of Financial Stability Issues

The spill-over effects of financial crisis in a country could be substantial where countries in a region are linked by trade and other financial market activities. The experience of the crises in Mexico, Thailand, Korea, and Indonesia in the 1990s has demonstrated that apart from the spill-over effects there were also 'contagion' effects. Contagion builds over the spill-overs and would aggravate when reevaluation of ratings of a country is attempted by international investors when that country falls in a region that is affected by crisis situation or crisis-like situation. Large capital outflows that occur as a result from the region would affect adversely the economic prospects of the region as a whole. But within the region, the adverse effects would differ from country to country. The experience of the 1990s showed that while crisis resolution is important, crisis prevention is necessary.

The costs of the system-wide crisis are high. Countries would not be able to resolve the crisis situations by themselves. They would need external help. The international financial institutions such as the IMF and World Bank, concerned about the wide implications of the systemic problems that crisis-cases leave, have tried to provide some support out of their own resources, catalyzed resources from other member countries, and promoted the idea of having transparency practices and international standards and codes in place. The international opinion on financial crises has turned round to the view that unless countries follow sound macro-economic policies, and undertake structural reforms, they would not be able to attract private capital flows. This would imply that exchange rate regimes would have to be flexible, and capital account liberalization has to be well paced and structured keeping in view the sustainable external debt and liquidity positions. Orderly debt 'workouts' (i.e, rescheduling of debt, and structured repayment schedules with initial capital infusion for example) and payment 'standstills' (i.e., temporary suspension of payments on the due dates of redemption of debt) may have to be attempted to avoid systemic risks. It has also been widely recognized that as no one international institution can undertake the task of restructuring the economies affected by financial crisis all by itself, that task has to be undertaken with both public and private sector participation and involvement in debt workouts.

Crisis management has to be a part of the overall strategy of addressing the overall crisis issues. It is clear that the policy framework that countries adopt as part of such a strategy has to be credible and implemented in full so that capital would flow in. But it is not enough to place the burden of preventing crisis situations only on the member-countries. Crisis prevention also requires that responsibility is placed on the international financial institutions to govern well and respond expeditiously to the evolving situations. It is in this context, a number of proposals were made for reform of IMF and World Bank. A number of other proposals also came up for creating what has come to be known as the new international financial architecture (NIFA).

The proposals in respect of NIFA came from both official bodies, academic and reputed financiers. Eichengreen (1999) provided a fairly comprehensive review of the proposals in this regard. What is most interesting is that in all the proposals, there is recognition, either implicit or explicit, that crises generally occur subsequent to financial liberalization, in particular relating to interest rate liberalization, unregulated lending, and capital account convertibility. The East Asian financial crises in particular have demonstrated that it is necessary to have robust banking regulation and to revisit the usefulness of complete capital account convertibility in the context of financial sector development. Controls on capital inflows were advocated as a corrective mechanism. Controls could be in the form of taxes, as practiced by Chile in the 1980s, or in line with James Tobin's famous idea of throwing 'sand in the wheel' advocacy of taxes on outflows : they were strongly suggested as better options than increasing interest rates or depreciating the home currency for preserving monetary and financial stability. But it must be recognized that the proposed measures cannot be carried out beyond a point. For example, currency traders could disregard the taxes on capital inflows. Similarly, if quantitative restrictions on capital outflows are placed, foreign investors may get scared. Therefore, it had become a practical proposition for countries to be committed to financial liberalization as a medium term policy but have in place in the short run some degree of capital controls till they are confident of addressing speculative attacks.

Besides the advocacy of some degree of capital controls, there were a number of proposals for bringing about new international financial architecture. One of them was for setting up of a global central bank; yet another for establishment of an International Supervisory, regulatory and rating agency. There were some proposals for setting up an International bankruptcy court. This proposal along with the one for an international debt insurance authority were too specific and were not pursued because it would be difficult to get international agreements for creating additional organizations in addition to the existing international financial institutions. Besides, the proposals do not give assurance that they would help prevent recurrence of currency and financial crises. Then there was the proposal to have exchange rate movements within certain limits, referred to as a target zone. The target zone concept has a long history but it was not acceptable because of the difficulties in defining what the target zone is. Besides, defending the currencies with limited reserves or with reserves accumulated with debt-creating capital account transactions (such as foreign currency loans) would aggravate volatility in exchange rates.

There were also specific proposals for reform of the IMF and World Bank but none of them got support from the major IEs because of the rigidities that the proposals tend to introduce. Replacement of IMF and World Bank cannot be an alternative by itself because the institution or institutions that replace the existing international monetary and financial system may not function any better. Most of the proposals that emanated particularly after the crisis in Thailand in 1997 have been more or less shelved by the middle of 2000 on grounds of pragmatism. The latest indications are that international efforts to resolve crisis situations can come about only if countries in the first place take actions necessary to prevent crisis situations from developing and turning into systemic ones.

References

Abrams, R K and M W Taylor (2000), "Issues in the Unification of Financial Sector Supervision", IMF Working Paper no. 213, Washington DC

Allen, Franklin and Douglas Gale (2000), *Comparative Financial Systems*, Mass, MIT Press.

Crockett, Andrew (1997), "Why is Financial stability a Goal of Public Policy?", in *Maintaining Financial Stability in a Global Economy*, a symposium by the FRB, Kansas city, Wyoming.

Davis, E P (1995), *Debt, Financial Fragility, and Systemic Risk*, London, Oxford University Press.

Goodhart, C (2000), "Whither Central Banking ?", 11th CD Deshmukh Memorial Lecture, RBI, Mumbai.

Narain, Aditya and Saibal Ghosh (2001), "Bank Supervisory Arrangements — International Evidence and Indian Perspective", *Econ.& Pol Weekly*, Vol XXXVI, No. 37, Sept 15-21, pp. 3543-53.

Peek, J, E Rosengren and G M B Tootell (1999), "Is Bank Supervision Central to Central Banking?", QJE, pp. 629-653.

Reddy, Y V (2001), "Issues in Choosing Between Single and Multiple Regulators of Financial System", *RBI Bulletin*, June, pp.707-26.

Sinclair, Peter JN (2000), "Central Banks and Financial Stability", BoE *Quarterly Bulletin*, November, pp.377-91.

Vasudevan, A (2001), "International Standards and Codes", Econ & Pol Weekly, May 19-25.

Box 10

Early Warning Signals of Crisis

Solutions to crisis situations would differ depending on the causes of the crisis. It is often argued that more important than the crisis resolution is the need to prevent crises from happening. The crisis prevention approach has two elements : (a) to have a system by which the policy makers would monitor continuously the macroeconomic and other variables so as to detect the possible emergence of crisis situations, and (b) to undertake measures that are expected on the basis of the received theory to address the problems that could emerge in different areas from the monitoring exercises. The monitoring exercises are in effect the early warning signals (EWS), sometimes also serving as the leading indicators of crises. Reliance on EWS does not mean that there is a mechanism to predict crisis situations. EWS should be considered merely as indicators of vulnerability or financial stress.

Kaminsky, Lizondo and Reinhart (1997) (referred to as KLR) proposed that several indicators need to be monitored. These indicators would normally exhibit an unusual behavior in the periods preceding the crisis. When an indicator exceeds a certain threshold value, it would be considered a warning signal that a crisis is likely to occur in the following period (usually two years). The literature on the subject shows that the main indicators to be monitored could be large. KLR gave a large list of indicators under ten broad heads, including the one on political variables which cannot be easily specified and measured. The indicators other than the political variables are :

Capital account : international reserves, capital flows, short term capital flows, foreign direct investment, and the differential between domestic and foreign interest rates.

Debt profile : public foreign debt, total foreign debt, short term debt, share of debt classified by type of creditor and by interest rate structure, debt service and foreign aid.

Current account : the real exchange rate, the current account balance, the trade balance, exports, imports, the terms of trade, the price of exports, savings and investment.

International variables : foreign real GDP growth, interest rates, and price level.

Financial liberalization : credit growth, the change in the money multiplier, real interest rates, and the spread between bank lending and deposit rates.

Other financial variables : central bank credit to banks, the gap between money demand and supply, money growth, bond yields, domestic inflation, the 'shadow' exchange rate, the parallel market exchange rte premium, the central exchange rate parity, the position of the exchange rate within the official band, and the ratio of broad money to international reserves.

Real sector : real GDP growth, the output gap, employment/ unemployment, wages, and changes in stock prices.

Fiscal variables : the fiscal deficit, government consumption, and credit to the public sector.

Institutional / structural factors : openness, trade concentration, and dummies for multiple exchange rates, exchange controls, duration of the fixed exchange rate periods, financial liberalization, banking crises, past foreign exchange market crises, and past foreign exchange market events.

The coverage under each category could be substantial, and more exhaustive than what was suggested by KLR. But most policy makers would select a manageable number of indicators for monitoring purposes. The literature also shows that in any currency crisis episode, there were never more than 12 indicators having significant 'signalling' effects. This outcome would be inevitable, irrespective of the scope of the expressions, 'signal' and 'threshold' that one agrees to.

Source: Kaminsky, Graciela, Saul Lizondo, and Carmen Reinhart (1997), *Leading Indicators of Currency Crises,* Working Paper 79, July. International Monetary Fund, Washington DC.

Box 11

Risk Management in Banks

Deregulation of financial markets and the increasing internationalization have increased the range of activities that banks could undertake. At the same time, these factors have exposed the banks to a number of risks. New trading and derivative activities have added newer risks to the traditional ones. Banks are hard pressed to do proper risk identification and risk classification, and to develop necessary technical and managerial skills to assume risks. The regulators on their part are faced with problems in measuring and controlling the risks associated with the provision of financial services.

Banks face mainly four types of risks : market risk, credit risk, legal risk, and operational risk. In addition, there is systemic risk arising due to a serious disruption in the working of a major bank which in very quick time could spread to other banks or to the entire financial system.

The credit risk arises mainly from lending operations. They are centered in on balance sheet assets, both domestic and overseas, and in off balance sheet transactions. What is needed to overcome the credit risk is a sound domestic and overseas credit administration. The interest rate risk arises from (a) mismatched positions, (b) dealings in public bonds, and (c) management of securities in the investment account. This risk as well as the foreign exchange risk and liquidity risk will need to be addressed by appropriate market trading, securities investment accounting, fund management and asset-liability management. Operation risk and EDP risk will have to be addressed by strong business operations and EDP risk monitoring and management systems. Management risk essentially requires to be taken care of by management policies, internal controls, profit/loss management, accounting policies, and contingency plans. Systemic risk, on the other hand, has to be addressed in a comprehensive manner through management and internal controls, sound market and business operations, ALM, and EDP risk systems.

Banks and regulators have traditionally concentrated on credit and market risks. Computer aided credit management techniques and scoring systems were developed in this regard. J P Morgan's CreditMetrics is one of the first readily available portfolio models for evaluating credit risk. The CreditMetrics approach enables a bank to consolidate credit risk across its organization and provides a statement of value-at-risk (VAR) due to credit caused by upgrades, downgrades, and defaults. Besides the CreditMetrics, neural network techniques are often utilized as powerful analytical tools to identify and quantity risks.

In more recent times, banks are exposed to operations risks, i.e., the set of risks that banks share with other financial intermediaries or commercial entities: product liability risk, business interruption risk, technology risk, image impairment risk, directors' liability etc. Most of the operations risks are not insurable and banks have therefore been coping with these risks through the creation of internal controls and contingency plans.

Regulation of financial markets, in particular the risk-taking activity of banks, is necessary to preserve and nurture public confidence in the banking system. These measures can be classified as preventive and protective regulation. Preventive regulation includes rules governing capital / liquidity adequacy and permissible business activities. The Basle Committee on banking supervision have developed risk-based standards as part of preventive protection. The protective regulatory measures on the other hand include deposit insurance and emergency measures taken by regulators in the wake of bank failures. There are essentially three regulatory approaches to deal with the market risk. They are : (a) the building block approach (BBA) ; (b) the internal models approach (IMA); and (c) the Pre-commitment Approach (PCA). BBA is a set of wills that assigns risk charges to specific assets or portfolios. The 1988 Basle Accord Credit Risk Capital Standards represent an example of BBA. The IMA implies that capital charges are based on market risk estimates models (like the VAR). The market risk exposure is then multiplied by a certain scaling factor (determined by the regulator) to decide the regulatory capital chart for market risk. The PCA implies that each bank precommits to a maximum loss exposure over a designated horizon, which can be one quarter or even a shorter period. The maximum loss commitment becomes the bank's market risk capital charge. If the bank incurs trading loss in excess of its capital commitment, it is subject to penalties by regulators. The nature of regulatory punishment could take different forms including (i) a fine penalty, (ii) additional capital penalty, and (iii) supervisory actions such as review of banks' risk management system, increasing back testing, close monitoring and restrictions on trading activity.

Sources : Bank of Japan (1997), "Checklist for Risk Management", *Quarterly Bulletin,* May, pp.58-91; Kupiec, P and J. O'brien (1995), "Model Alternative", *Risk,* June, 8; and Reserve Bank of India (1997), *Report on Trend and Progress of Banking in India, 1996-97,* pp.22-23.

Box 12

The Basle Principles for Effective Banking Supervision

Effective and strong banking regulations and supervision are considered a public good that is needed to complement the market forces that are at work to ensure prudent banking in any country. A weak banking system would threaten financial stability, both domestically and internationally. In order to strengthen financial systems especially the banking systems, the Basle (at times Basel) Committee on Banking Supervision that was established by the central bank Governors of the group of Ten Countries in 1975 after the Herstatt Bank crisis, had formulated a set of 25 basic principles. These have come to be known as the Core Principles and have been widely accepted as providing a benchmark for assessing whether the supervisory system is effective or not. These principles could be classified into 7 categories : (a) preconditions for effective banking supervision; (b) licensing and structure; (c) prudential regulations and requirements; (d) methods of ongoing banking supervision; (e) information requirements; (f) formal powers of supervisors; and (g) cross border banking

(a) Preconditions for effective banking supervision

1. A system of banking supervision, to be effective, should have clear responsibilities and objectives for each agency involved in banking supervision. Each such agency should possess operational independence and adequate resources. Besides, a suitable legal framework for banking supervision is necessary, including provisions relating to authorization of banks and their ongoing supervision, powers to address compliance with laws as well as safety and soundness concerns; and legal protection for supervisors. Also arrangements for sharing information among supervisors and protecting its confidentiality should be in place.

(b) Licensing and Structure

2. The permissible activities of licensed banks subject to supervision should be clearly defined, and the use of the word 'bank' in names must be controlled as far as possible.

3. The licensing authority must have the right to set criteria and reject applications for establishments that do not meet the set standards. The licensing process should consist, at the minimum, of an assessment of the bank's ownership structure, directors, and senior management; its operating plan and internal controls; and its projected financial condition, including its capital base. Where the proposed owner or parent organization is a foreign bank, the prior consent of its home country supervisor should be obtained.

4. Banking supervisors must have the authority to review and reject any proposals to transfer significant ownership or controlling interests in existing banks to other parties.

5. Banking supervisors must have the authority to establish criteria for reviewing major acquisitions or investments by a bank and to ensure that corporate affiliations or structures do not expose the bank to undue risks or hinder effective supervision.

(c) Prudential Regulations and Requirements

6. Banking supervisors must set prudent and appropriate minimum capital adequacy requirements for all banks. Such requirements should reflect the risks that the banks undertake and must define the components of capital, bearing in mind their ability to absorb losses. At least for internationally active banks, these requirements should not be less than those established in the Basle Capital Accord and its amendments.

7. An essential part of any supervisory system is the evaluation of a bank's policies, practices and procedures related to the granting of loans and making of investments and the ongoing management of the loan and investment portfolios.

8. Banking supervisors must be satisfied that banks establish and adhere to adequate policies, practices, and procedures for evaluating the quality of assets and the adequacy of loan-loss provisions and loan-loss reserves.

9. Banking supervisors must be satisfied that banks have management information systems that enable management to identify concentrations within the portfolio, and supervisors must set prudential limits to restrict bank exposures to single borrowers or groups of related borrowers.

10. To prevent abuses arising from connected lending, banking supervisors must have in place requirements that banks lend to related companies and individuals on an arm's-length basis, that such extensions of credit are effectively monitored, and that other appropriate steps are taken to control or mitigate the risks.

11. Banking supervisors must be satisfied that banks have adequate policies and procedures for identifying, monitoring, and controlling country risk and transfer risk in their international lending and investment activities, and for maintaining appropriate reserves against such risks.

12. Banking supervisors must be satisfied that banks have in place systems that accurately measure, monitor, and adequately control market risks; supervisors should have powers to impose specific limits or a specific capital charge (or both) on market risk exposures, if warranted.

13. Banking supervisors must be satisfied that banks have in place a comprehensive risk management process (including appropriate board and senior management oversight) to identify, measure, monitor, and control all other material risks and, where appropriate, to hold capital against these risks.

14. Banking supervisors must determine that banks have in place internal controls that are adequate for the nature and scale of their business. These should include clear arrangements for delegating authority and responsibility; separation of the functions that involve committing the bank, paying away its funds, and accounting for its assets and liabilities; reconciliation of these processes; safeguarding its assets; and appropriate independent internal or external audit and compliance functions to test adherence to thee controls as well as applicable laws and regulations.

15. Banking supervisors must determine that banks have adequate policies, practices, and procedures in place, including strict 'know-your-customer' rules, that promote high ethical and professional standards in the financial sector and prevent the bank being used, intentionally or unintentionally, by criminal elements.

(d) Methods of Ongoing Banking Supervision

16. An effective banking supervisory system should consist of some form of both on-site and off-site supervision.

17. Banking supervisors must have regular contact with bank management and thorough understanding of the institution's operations.

18. Banking supervisors must have a means of collecting, reviewing, and analyzing prudential reports and statistical returns from banks on a solo and consolidated basis.

19. Banking supervisors must have a means of independent validation of supervisory information either through on-site examinations or use of external auditors.

20. An essential element of banking supervision is the ability of the supervisors to supervise the banking group on a consolidated basis.

(e) Information Requirements :

21. Banking supervisors must be satisfied that each bank maintains adequate records drawn up in accordance with consistent accounting policies and practices that enable the supervisor to obtain a true and fair view of the financial condition of the bank and the profitability of its business, and that the bank publishes on a regular basis financial statements that fairly reflect its condition.

(f) Formal Powers of Supervisors

22. Banking supervisors must have at their disposal adequate supervisory measures to bring about timely corrective action when banks fail to meet prudential requirements (such as minimum capital adequacy ratios), when there are regulatory violations, or where depositors are threatened in any other way. In extreme circumstances, this should include the ability to revoke the banking license or recommend its revocation.

(g) Cross-Border Banking

23. Banking supervisors must practice global consolidated supervision over their internationally active banking organizations, adequately monitoring and applying appropriate prudential norms to all aspects of the business conducted by these banking organization world-wide, primarily at their foreign branches, joint ventures, and subsidiaries.

24. A key component of consolidated supervision is establishing contact and information exchange with the various other supervisors involved, primarily host-country supervisory authorities.

25. Banking supervisors must require the local operations of foreign banks to be conducted to the same high standards as are required of domestic institutions and must have powers to share information needed by the home country supervisors of those banks for the purposes of carrying our consolidated supervision.

Sources : Basle Committee on Banking Supervision (1996), *Core Principles for Effective Banking Supervision,* Bank for International Settlements, Basle, Switzerland; International Monetary Fund (1998), *World Economic Outlook, May 1998,* Washington DC

In order to have convergence of supervisory norms and practices and in the light of the debate over the limited usefulness of universally standardized capital adequacy norms, the Basel Committee on Banking Supervision had released its New Capital Accord in January 2001. The Accord reflected the feedback received from a few banks indicating the need for substantial upgradation of the existing management information systems, risk management practices and procedures, and technical skills of the staff. There would be a final round of consultations with members of the Committee and this is expected to end in 2002. The final Accord will probably take effect by 2005.

The revision as provided for in the New Capital Accord has several features. While the current definition of capital and the minimum requirement of 8 per cent of capital to risk-weighted assets has been retained, the Accord will be extended on a consolidated basis to holding companies of banking groups and will refine the measurement of risks. The measurement of market risk has been also retained. However, the Accord emphasizes the measurement of operational risk and credit risk (either by the standardized or the internal rating-based [IRB] approaches). In case of the standardized approach, although the risk measurement would be the same, there would be four categories for claims on corporate entities — 20 per cent, 50 per cent, 100 per cent, and 150 per cent — of risk weight as against the present uniform risk weight of 100 per cent. The IRB approach, on the other hand, will be allowed to use its internal estimates of the borrower's creditworthiness to assess credit risk in the portfolio subject to strict methodological and disclosure standards. The Accord also sets out disclosure requirements in several areas, including the way the banks calculate their capital adequacy and their risk assessment methods. The New Accord is expected to foster a healthy market based banking system.

Source: Basel Committee on Banking Supervision (2001), The New Basel Capital Accord, Bank for International Settlements.

Box 13
Key International Standards and Codes

The advocacy for implementation of international standards and codes and transparency practices has become sharp in the context of the need for crisis prvention and for containment of financial stresses and vulnerabilities. Inappropriate macroeconomic policies, weaknesses in financial structure and institutions, institutional rigidities and distortions have been as the main contributors to crises. The growing internationalization of financial markets and the application of computer networking systems have unleashed the dimension and intensity of crises. Implementing international standards would, it is said, help EMEs to develop prudent policies, enhance transparency, and improve infrastructure that is related to institutions as well as market development. In the process, the domestic financial systems are expected to become resilient. In turn, they would, because of financial integration, help improve international financial stability.

The idea of application of standards was first triggered in the wake of the criticism that the Mexican crisis of 1994 was essentially a reflection of asymmetric information about the economy's policies and reactions to economic events. The idea was extended in response to the financial crises of 1997-98. The expression, 'standards ad codes' is used to include transparency practices in macro policy-making, and core principles relating to regulatory and supervisory systems and market infrastructure. The initial enthusiasm for developing standards was so large that every aspect of financial sector activity was to be considered. The number of such identified standards amounted to 43. Of these, the Task Force on Implementation of Standards with Mr Andrew Sheng as the Chairman, which was constituted by the Financial Stability Forum (FSF), favored twelve as the key standards. The Reserve Bank of India was represented on the Task Force. The key standards would have to be implemented, as held by the Sheng's Task Force, with a measure of flexibility both by the industrialized economies and emerging market economies. What this essentially implied is that implementation has to be in the light of the country circumstances — the stage of economic reforms, the availability of the required specialized human skills, the enforceability of laws, the level of technology, and the degree of 'openness'. The Task Force's report was first placed before the G-20 (consisting of governments of industrialized and emerging economies). The report was also considered by the International Monetary and Financial Committee (IMFC, which was earlier known as the Interim Committee) in April 2000. The IMFC adopted it. The Task Force's identified twelve key standards are as follows :

Subject Area	Key Standard	Issuing Body
Monetary and Financial Policy Transparency	Code of Good Practices on Transparency in Monetary and Financial Policies	IMF
Fiscal Policy Transparency	Code of Good Practices on Fiscal Transparency	IMF
Data Dissemination	Special Data Dissemination Standard / General Data Dissemination Standard	IMF
Insolvency	Principles and Guidelines on Effective Insolvency and Creditor Rights System	World Bank
Corporate Governance	Principles of Corporate Governance	OECD
Accounting	International Accounting Standards	IASB
Auditing	International Standards on Auditing	IFAC
Payment BIS & Settlement	Core Principles For Systemically Important	CPSS-
Market Integrity	Forty Recommendations of the Financial Action Task Force on Money Laundering	FATF-OECD
Banking BIS Supervision	Core Principles for Effective Banking Supervision	BCBS-
Securities Regulation	Objectives and Principles of Securities Regulation	IOSCO
Insurance Supervision	Insurance Core Principles	IAIS

IMF = International Monetary Fund; OECD = Organization for Economic Coordination and Development; IASB = The International Accounting Standards Board; IFAC = International Federation of Accountants; CPSS = Committee on Payment and Settlement Systems in the Bank for International Settlements; FATF = Financial Action Task Force; BCBS = Basle Committee on Banking Supervision; IOSCO = International Organization of Securities Commission; IAIS = International Association of Insurance Supervisors.

Box 14

The Indian Initiatives in Respect of International Standards and Codes

India is one of the few countries which had taken initiative in studying the relevance of the international standards and codes in the light of the existing and the planned legal, infrastructural and institutional setting in the country and in exploring ways of fostering the implementation of the international standards in a flexible manner. The initiative was taken both by the Government of India and the Reserve Bank of India. The initiative was taken in the form of setting up a Standing Committee on International Standards. This Committee in turn appointed working groups for each key standard. Each working group was chaired by an expert who is currently not associated with either the Ministry of Finance or the Reserve Bank of India.

The working groups have submitted their reports and these reports have been placed on the Reserve Bank's website for generating public awareness and debate and discussion.

Simultaneously, India has been placing on the website its own assessment of its compliance with the international standards as for example in the area of banking supervision. India has also agreed to have external assessment of compliance with the international standards and codes.

The main recommendations of the different Advisory Groups are summarized below to give an idea of not only the extent of compliance as at the time of the writing of the reports of the Advisory Groups but also the kind of initiatives that still need to be taken for full compliance.

1. *The Advisory Group on Transparency in Monetary and Financial Policies (Chairman : M. Narasimham)*

The Group recommended that the Government should set out objectives to the central bank, with parliamentary endorsement and accord it the necessary autonomy to fulfill its responsibilities if necessary by amending the Reserve Bank of India Act. The Group also adopted the view that the Government should consider setting a medium term objective of monetary policy namely, the inflation rate to the central bank. In the view of the Group, there has to be some fiscal responsibility in that it would provide the central bank with reasonable headroom for operating monetary policy. The Group recommended the setting up of a monetary policy committee (MPC) consisting of Governor, Deputy Governors, and three other members drawn from the Central Board who are knowledgeable in the areas of macroeconomics, monetary analysis, central banking policy, and operations in banking and finance.

2. *The Advisory Group on Fiscal Transparency*
   (Chairman: Montek Singh Ahluwalia)

The Group held the view that current fiscal practices at the level of the Union Government satisfy the minimum requirements of the Code in several respects. The remaining deficiencies will be substantially addressed once the Fiscal Responsibility and Budget Management (FRBM) Bill is enacted. The Group recommended amplifying the scope of the FRBM Bill to include the essential elements of budget law, list macro-economic assumptions regarding GDP growth, inflation, export and import growth, the current account deficit, saving and investment rates, and project major categories of revenue and expenditure for two years ahead. The Group also required that the Reserve Bank end the practice of providing direct support to government securities at the primary issue stage, within the next three years. The other important recommendations relate to improved reporting on contingent liabilities, major tax expenditures and quasi-fiscal activities, quantification of fiscal risks, fuller discussion of the consolidated position of central and state governments, availability of information on the overall public sector balance, government equity and outstanding loans to public sector enterprises, Oil Pool Account deficit, and simplification of the tax structure with greater use of information technology. Fiscal practices at the level of the States (provinces) were, in the view of the Group, generally felt short of the standards achieved at the level of the Union Government. The Group recommended that the Finance Secretaries Forum could review the report and determine a set of minimum standards on transparency, which all State Governments should achieve within a three-year period.

3. *The Advisory Group on Data Dissemination*
(Chairman: A. Vaidyanathan,
vice the late Pravin M Visaria)

The Group held that there were a large number of data categories under which India had been disseminating information more frequently and with a shorter time lag than those prescribed by the SDDS. The Group concurred with the position taken by the official agencies that India should opt for 'flexibility' option pertaining to the data on labor market as it would be difficult to generate quarterly data on employment, unemployment, and wages/earnings using the International Labor Organization's concepts, and classifications because of the prevalence of the large agricultural sector and sizeable unorganized segments in the non-farm sector. The Group encouraged that the standard on the international investment position (IIP) be complied with by end-September 2002. So far as the template on international reserves and foreign currency liquidity is concerned, the Group observed that the data put up by India compare favorably with those of many other countries and a view has to be taken for disclosing such information based on the disclosure of information as practiced by many other developing countries. The Group proposed compilation of forward-looking indicators, viz,. the surveys of business expectations and greater co-ordination between various agencies with a view to refining data dissemination in respect of general government operations for total public sector operations including the data for these two sub-sectors.

4. *The Advisory Group on Banking Supervision*
   (Chairman: M S Verma)

Assessing the Indian regulatory and supervisory practices with those brought out by the Basel Committee's Principles on Bank Supervision (see **Box 10** above), the Group concluded that the level of compliance is of a high order, and where there are significant gaps, they could be remedied within a reasonable time-frame with the help of necessary amendments to laws. The Group stressed the need for making directors on bank boards conversant with issues such as risk management and for setting accountability standards for boards and greater transparency and disclosures in respect of their constitution and functioning. A recurring theme in the Group's report is the need to put in place reliable risk management systems in banks. The Group also emphasized the need for action in areas such as performance-related compensation, quality of management information systems and in increasing the awareness about risks involved in and controls required in working in a computerized environment. For improved supervision of financial conglomerates, the Group recommended that the Reserve Bank consider introducing formalized co-ordination between different regulators, with one of the regulators designated as a primary regulator with clear responsibilities. The Group also called for greater coordination and sharing of information among supervisors across borders. The Group held the view that in future, the methods of supervision should be increasingly risk-based with reliance on directions of the boards of the banks and on external auditors. As already noted, the Group's report came out after the Reserve Bank had published its self-assessment report on the compliance with the Basel Principles on bank supervision. And the Reserve Bank had been also actively involved with the discussions on the revisions in the Basel Principles.

5. *The Advisory Group on International Accounting and Auditing* *(Chairman: Y H Malegam)*

The Group reviewed the availability of various accounting and auditing standards in India and compared them with the corresponding international standards. In India, while the International Accounting Standards (IAS) served as a benchmark from the point of view of statutory recognition, the US Generally Accepted Accounting Principles (US GAAP) served as a yardstick from the practical perceptions of the investors. With regard to the Indian auditing standards, the standards issued by the International Auditing Practices Committee (IAPC) of the International Federation of Accountants served as the reference point. The Group noted that the Accounting Standards Board of the Institute of Chartered Accountants of India (ICAI) had, at the time of the submission of the report, issued 19 standards that were on par with those of international standards subject to differences owing to country-specific applicable laws, customs usages, and trade practices. The Auditing Practices Committee of ICAI had issued 20 statements on Standard Auditing Practices and four additional statements on auditing that were anchored on the international standards. The Group also discussed issues that need to be addressed in future relating to bridging the gap between the Indian accounting standards and IAS, the need for a single standard setting authority, and the need to position an effective implementation procedure for the accounting standards in India.

6. *The Advisory Group on Payments and Settlement System* (Chairman: M G Bhide)

The Group recommended extensive legal reform especially empowering the Reserve Bank to supervise the payment and settlement system, institution of a framework for ensuring at least the Lamfalussy Standards for the deferred net settlement and suitable framework for RTGS systems. The Group was of the view that the Reserve Bank should eventually come out of the role of a payment systems provider except for funds settlement. The Group recommended, inter alia, the introduction of rolling settlement in the liquid segment of the equity market, allowing current account facility with the Reserve Bank to the clearing corporations for ensuring settlement facility on the books of the Reserve Bank as an interim measure pending the eventual grant of a limited purpose banking licence to them with appropriate prudential guidelines thereon, building up of an institutional mechanism for centralized collection of information, their dissemination, and prudential guidelines for implementing cross-margining across markets in order to deal with problems arising from participants undertaking multiple exposures in various markets at any point of time and permitting securities borrowing and lending systems for institutions in both the debt and equity segments in India. The Group also recommended the establishment of a clearing agent abroad by the Clearing Corporation of India (CCI), institution of a separate guarantee fund for foreign exchange clearing, appropriate integration between the participating banks and the CCI and their interface with the RTGS systems. At the time of the writing of the report, however, the Reserve Bank was actively involved with the task of evolving the RTGS system and the changes that need to be put in place for the RTGS to be effective.

7. *The Advisory Group on Insurance Regulation*
(Chairman: R Ramakrishnan)

The Group was of the view that the Indian position of allowing foreign companies to operate through joint venture arrangements with Indian companies with share holding not exceeding 26 per cent in the paid up capital of the insurer, was broadly comparable with the international practices. While the Indian requirements in respect of minimum capital requirements, deposit requirements, business plan and reinsurance were adequate, the Group recommended that minimum capital levels could be fixed for each class of business rather than on aggregate basis. The Group favored the 'file and proceed' requirements in respect of new insurance products adopted in India, but recommended that the actuarial certification, premium rate tables and benefit design should be treated as public information in the interest of transparency. With regard to actuarial and solvency issues, the Group observed that the Indian standard is on par with the international norm in the matter of estimating the liability under life insurance policies, while that in relation to solvency margin requirements is actually more stringent. While there do exist certain gaps in evaluating general insurance technical reserves, the Group was of the view that these could be addressed in due course. The Group recommended that unit-linked life insurance business could be brought under the definition of life insurance business, with closer co-ordination between the regulators. While the Indian standard regarding the taxation of life insurance companies is at par with the international practice, the Group proposed that the transfer to the catastrophe reserve could be allowed in certain cases to be made out of pre-taxed profits.

8. *The Advisory Group on Securities Market Regulation*
(Chairman: Deepak Parekh)

Comparing the Indian situation with the principles laid down by the International Organization of Securities Market Regulation (IOSCO), the Group recommended that the authority of the Securities and Exchange Board of India (SEBI) should be enhanced. SEBI may need to be provided with disgorgement powers to effectively deter market players from regulatory violations. The Group highlighted the need for strengthening the legal framework. For example, inclusion of both regulatory responsibilities and the authority to carry them out in the same legislation, and a shift from institutions-specific framework to market-specific regulation were required. In respect of mutual funds, the Group underlined (a) the need for bringing the Unit Trust of India under the purview of SEBI, (b) introduction and implementation of international accounting principles across the mutual fund industry, and (c) reduction of discretion of the asset management company in adopting valuation of thinly traded/non-traded securities. The Group favored the demutualisation of stock exchanges as a necessary step for promotion of fairness and investor protection as the conflict of interest inherent in the current ownership and governance structures of many stock exchanges could render self-regulation ineffective. The Group emphasized the need to strengthen inter-regulator cooperation preferably by bestowing legal status to the High Level Group on Capital Markets. The Group also observed that regulatory cooperation would be effective only if there is sharing of information about specified markets on a regular and automatic basis among the regulatory functionaries.

9. *The Advisory Group on Corporate Governance*
(Chairman: R H Patil)

The Group observed that since most of the Indian companies belong to the East Asian 'insider' model, where the promoters dominate governance, it is essential to bring reforms quickly so as to make boards of corporates/banks/ financial institutions/public sector enterprises more professional and truly autonomous. As the statutory framework for corporate governance has already been enshrined in the Companies Act, the Group felt that it is desirable to amend the Companies Act suitably for enforcing good governance practices in India. To improve governance mechanisms in public sector units, the Group recommended transferring of the actual governance functions to the boards from the concerned administrative ministries and strengthening the boards by streamlining the appointment process of directors. Further the Group underlined the need for public sector banks to main a high degree of transparency in regard to disclosure of information. The Group also made a number of recommendations in a variety of areas — the business group's areas of responsibilities of the board to stake holders/shareholders, selection procedures for the appointment of directors of the board, size and the composition of the board, committees to oversee the practice of corporate governance, disclosure and transparency standards, role of shareholders, role of auditors etc. spanning the institutional categories of the private corporate sector, banks and the development financial institutions, and Central and State public sector enterprises that were set up under the Companies Act.

10. *The Advisory Group on Bankruptcy Laws*
   (Chairman: N L Mitra)

The Group recommended a comprehensive bankruptcy code incorporating the provisions relating to reorganization, winding up and liquidation of a corporate entity, and settlement of all other related issues including cross-border insolvency. The Group suggested the repeal of Sick Industrial

Companies (Special Provisions) Act and abolition of Board for Industrial and Financial Reconstruction (BIFR). The Group also favored the institution of a dedicated high court bench as bankruptcy court and the replacement of the office of the Official Liquidator with a professional bankruptcy institution known as the 'Trustee'. The Group also recommended the evolution of an effective trigger point for bankruptcy, time-bound bankruptcy proceedings, prioritization of claims and orderly and effective insolvency procedures. The Group further recommended a special procedure for banks and financial institutions and for the institutions in the businesses like insurance, non-bank financing, telecommunications etc. For public sector undertakings and Government companies, the Group recommended the same procedure as applicable to other corporate entities.

The reports of all the Advisory Groups appeared between the third quarter of 2000 and the fourth quarter of 2001. They all recognized the critical importance of amending the prevailing laws

---

Source : Annual Report of the Reserve Bank of India, 2000-01. There is no instance of any other emerging market economy that has done such extensive professional work relating to the country's position relating to the various international standards and codes vis-à-vis the accepted international standards and codes.

7

Autonomy and
Organization Issues

Issues in Autonomy and
Independence of Central Bank

The subject of autonomy and independence of central banks
has assumed critical importance in the 1980s and a large part
of the 1990s in the context of the need for undertaking comprehensive macroeconomic and structural reforms by both the
Governments and central banks for fostering growth with price
and financial stability. In the process of implementing reform
measures, there would arise many occasions when interactions
between the government and the central bank could impinge
on the freedom of central banks to undertake actions to achieve
their own objectives. The constraints to central bank action
could be endogenous or could be exogenously imposed by
governments on central banks on a variety of considerations,
both economic and political. The subject thus lies on the sensitive borderland of domestic political character and economic
considerations. This helped economists to give respectability
to the subject by modeling and empirical exercises.

There is, however, no clearly accepted definition of central
bank independence. And autonomy and independence are
often used interchangeably, although, conceptually speaking,

central banks could have autonomy without being independent of the government. In this chapter too, we shall not make a distinction between the two terms. It is generally recognized that central banks could be considered as independent if governments do not exercise control on matters relating to central banks' (a) personnel and management; (b) financial budgets and their management; and (c) policy pursuit. Even in these three areas, it is doubtful, however, whether even the most 'independent' of central banks could act on their own without consulting, if not being wholly led by the governments in power. Of the three areas, the last mentioned one relates to monetary policy making having a vital bearing on the societal welfare while the first two areas are essentially in the nature of operational and organizational efficiency and viability. Although the three areas are not mutually exclusive, it is on the area of policy pursuit that higher emphasis needs to be given in the discussions on autonomy than on the other two areas.

Besides the typical monetary policy functions, central banks also perform several non-monetary functions. Exchange rate management, lender-of-the-last resort functions, prudential supervision of specified financial institutions as well as markets, management of foreign exchange reserves, public debt management, besides the quasi-fiscal functions like the subsidization of specific sectors and equity participation in financial institutions, deposit insurance and licensing could be cited as examples of non-monetary functions. All these have influence on the degree of central bank independence (Swinburne, Mark and Marta Castello-Branco (1991)). Conflicts could arise in the performance of non-monetary tasks and monetary policy functions in which event the central bank independence would be called into question. In all probability, the issue would be reviewed essentially to ensure that there is no moral hazard. Such reviews could well lead to redefining the allocation of some of the tasks or setting up different agencies to perform certain specific tasks, as for example, a debt management office or a separate bank supervisory authority.

Before discussing the three areas separately, it is important to note at this point that the modern interpretation of the theoretical argument for central bank independence is different from the compulsions that led to the evolution of central banks. For example, in the 18th and the 19th centuries, governments needed support to finance wars and therefore bestowed special privileges to those banks that provided such financial help. The Bank of England, as Bagehot argued, was made the central bank of England essentially because of its accommodation of the financing needs of the government (See Walter Bagehot's *The Lombard Street*). The early central banks had monopoly in note issue, management of metallic reserves, and had maintained reserves of commercial banks. The reserve maintenance gave the central banks powers to run the payment system and also to provide temporary additional liquidity to commercial banks that seek such financial support. In the event, central banks turned into bankers' bank. This evolution tended to lead to concerns among central banks about the health of commercial banks and the overall conditions in the economy. But as conflicts arose as between the concerns about banks' position and the general economic position on the one hand, and the central banks' own commercial operations, central banks tended to move away from competitive activities and to concentrate on what could be termed as genuine central bank functions. No wonder therefore that most central banks in the 20th century were set up as noncompetitive entities by special legislations. This development clearly signaled the fact that central banks' main operations will have to be distinct from ordinary commercial banking and to be away from the political pressures from the governments.

The theoretical basis for central bank independence lies in the fact that it would help sort out what has come to be known as time inconsistency problem referred to in Chapter 5. Drawing on the seminal writings of Kydland and Prescott (1977) and Barro and Gordon (1983), this problem is explained thus : A policy would be time consistent if an action proposed to be taken at time t for time t+1 remains optimal for implementation when t+1 actually arrives. The new information that central banks get between the period t and t+1 would still not make a difference to the optimal policy action that was planned to be taken at time t+1 (Walsh, Carl (1998)). If the public does not believe in the central bank's commitment to control prices or control money, then the central bank will have no incentive to let money supply expand temporarily to increase the level of output/employment.

It is often argued that central banks that believe in discretion in policy making would tend to have inflationary bias. Such a bias, as Barro and Gordon would argue, could however be reduced or eliminated if there are fixed rules in monetary policy. This would imply a firm commitment on the part of a central bank to a lower order of inflation. But if there is economic uncertainty, there has to be a feedback rule for central bank to respond to shocks in an optimal manner.

The question is who would frame the rules and how do the rules get enforced. Besides, how does one ensure that the rule that is framed enables the central banker to make a firm commitment and to enforce the rule. In case the rule is forced upon the central bank by the Government or by lawmakers, then its enforceability could be a problem. The rule therefore has to be endogenously generated by the central banks themselves. Or, as the Rogoff's 1985 model has indicated, the society may appoint a central banker to pursue the objective of price stability by eliminating the inflationary bias and containing inflation variability, as one would normally expect. This is because the gains from lower inflation would exceed the losses that arise on account of high output variability. As the rate of the time preference of a central bank would be such that its objective function (essentially meaning price stability) would be time consistent in a dynamic sense, the conservative central banker would be seen as independent and his action cannot in such circumstances be overridden.

Legislation can always be the easy way by which the central
bank could be made independent. But in practice there can
be nothing like absolute independence. Even in the erstwhile
West Germany which represented a case of highly independent
central bank, when there was a difference of view between the
Head of the Government and the President of the Deutsche
Bundesbank on the question of fixing the par value of the
currencies of West and East Germany in the context of the
German unification, the President of the central bank had to
quit his position on grounds of health. The Government's view
on the exchange rate prevailed in the end. However strong the
legislation is for making central banks independent, there can
be no assurance or adequate incentive to pursue a totally
independent monetary policy. However, one way of providing
incentive is to adopt a contracting approach wherein an optimal contract would have to be set in place between the government (as the principal) and the central bank (as the agent).
The contract would be for attaining a given objective of monetary policy. The contract would be such that the central bank
would be faced with a penalty on ex post basis if say, the
inflation outcome is sharply higher than the originally planned
price   increase, unless there are factors that are beyond the
control of the central bank. (See Walsh, Carl (1995); also
Persson, T and G Tabellini (1993)). The penalty would be spelt
out within the contract. In this context, it was also suggested
that a targeting approach could be adopted whereby the political principals of the central bank would impose explicitly
an inflation target and make the central bank governor accountable for meeting the target. In other words, central banks would
be free to wield whatever instrument of policy they prefer to
achieve the targeted objective. This was in fact attempted in
New Zealand where there was a Policy Targets Agreement (PTA)
between the Reserve Bank of New Zealand (RBNZ) and the Government about the inflation target that of course could be
renegotiated if there is deviation for reasons that are beyond
the control of the Governor of RBNZ. In general, the optimal

contract has a chance of eliminating inflationary bias and provides the central bank with instrument (not goal) independence.

Let us now take up the three areas where central bank independence is involved. If policy independence is to be realized,
then there is a need for central bank leadership to be committed to the objective function of the central bank. This would
imply the presence of personnel independence and the criti-
cality of financial autonomy. Personnel independence would
mean that government's representation in the governing board
of the central bank, and terms and conditions of appointment
of Governor and Deputy Governors, and the dismissal of the
governing board would have to be specified without any
ambiguity (i.e., without any exception clauses). These aspects
are often legislated in most countries but they need to be looked
into afresh from the point of view of making the governing
boards more independent and accountable. Indeed many EMEs
will need to amend the original legislations for this purpose.
Financial autonomy would imply that government's access to
the central bank financial support should not be direct and
unquestionable. Nor should such access be even 'indirect'
through processes that often characterize the management of
public debt. For, the aim of the government should be to ensure
that central banks do not indulge in quasi-fiscal activities (such
as subsidizing certain sectors or credits or subscribing to the
equity capital of public financial institutions) and do not
maximize profits solely to transfer the entire corpus of profits
to the government. But as this may not be feasible in some
EMEs, it would be useful to work out limits on government
borrowings from the central bank either directly or indirectly
for each year in the initial stages of financial liberalization
program and after a medium term of say 3 years or so, provide for central bank discretion in respect of holding of government securities or direct lending to government. This is
where independence of central banks in pursuing their monetary policy would matter most. The approach suggested here
to have limits initially on government borrowing and subse-

quently discretion could be attempted even in countries that had a fairly long history of direct monetization of fiscal deficit. This approach has been set in place in India since April 1997 with one important focus, namely, the discretion to provide credit to government whenever the government deposits with the Reserve Bank fall below a critical minimum has been denied to the Reserve Bank after the medium term period. (Please see Box 5 for details about the experience in India with ad hoc treasury bills).

There have been numerous attempts to show that independent central banks are successful in containing inflation and improving real economic performance (See Alesina, A (1988); also Alesina, A and Lawrence Summers (1993); and Eijffinger, Sylvester C W, ed. (1997)). Alex Cuckierman reported that central bank independence and inflation for a sample of 20 OECD countries through simple regressions : they showed that the estimated effect of central bank independence on inflation is both statistically and economically significant (Cukierman, A (1992)). Japan however proved to be an exception to the outcome reported by Cukierman. The Bank of Japan was never regarded as an autonomous institution and yet could realize very low inflation rates in the 1980s and 1990s. For EMEs, no such empirical exercises are available. There is also very little of explicit evidence to show that central banks in EMEs enjoy autonomy and independence from their Finance Ministries in reality.

Much depends on how the central bank independence is measured. In academic writings on the subject, an index is often constructed for the purpose. The index to be meaningful would have to have appropriate elements and weights attached to each of the elements. There are at least four areas that are given prominence in the construction of comprehensive indices in most of the writings. For instance, the position of the chief executive officer (Governor or Managing Director or Chairman), his appointment, his dismissal, the nature of the tasks that he performs, and the tasks that he could additionally undertake are often considered as major elements in such index-construction exercises. Again, the policy formulation processes (the body or board that formulates monetary policy, the authority in taking the final monetary policy decision and resolve conflicts within the board, and the role of the government in budgetary process) as also the objectives of the central bank are considered as important components of the index. But in the context of EMEs, it is very important that the constraints and limitations that need to be placed on lending to government are reckoned as a component.

It is difficult to swear by the superiority of any one central bank independence index over the other. But there are suggestions that although the Fed is legally independent and is considered by popular perception to be highly independent of all central banks of the world, it may not turn out to be so, and could well be lower than the score that European Central Bank or the Deutsche Bundesbank of the present day would get, going by the outcomes shown in the work of Cukierman.

It must be recognized that given the nature of the issue, measurement of central bank independence can never be a complete exercise. For example, what will be the role of central bank's goal of promoting financial stability and how does it appear in the index construction are not easy to know. But this is an important aspect that has not been given adequate emphasis in most academic writings on the subject. Again, the index may not consider the powers that central banks wield in deciding on the type of assets that they want to choose, their valuation methods and accounting rules and policies, and the participation of the central bank in the decisions concerning the exchange rate regime and policy. But they are important if one were to evaluate the effectiveness of the financial sector reforms that central banks in EMEs commit themselves to.

Should Decision Making Processes be Left out of Central Banks?

The issue of independence of central banks needs to be seen in the context of the very structure of the central banking system in place. There could be centralized central banking systems wherein the central bank is headed by Governor assisted by Deputy Governors and in some cases by Executive Directors as well. All policy decisions are taken by the Boards of Directors of central banks. However, the Governor and Deputy Governors being members of the Board and the Governor being the Chairman of the Board would wield enormous influence in the final decisions that are taken by the Board. In decentralized systems, there will be central banks for each region or province of the country and the Chairman of the heads of the central banks would, by presiding over the policy making committees or boards, spearhead the main decision making. Theoretically speaking, the Chairman could be voted out by the majority in the Board. In fact, such an event took place in the 1980s once when Paul Volcker was the Chairman of the Fed. But such instances are very rare. The decentralized system in vogue in the United States has shown that it has worked satisfactorily within the constraints imposed by the political structure and arrangements in the country. Such a decentralized system is rarely attempted at in EMEs. But it can work effectively if there exist definitive set of rules regarding the issue of currency, its distribution and supervision of the financial system. Such rules are generally not laid down. No wonder therefore, that barring the US experiment, there is no other decentralized central banking system in the world.

The question as to which of the systems would work best came up when the idea of having an European Central Bank (ECB) emerged in the 1990s. There are even today, the national central banks (NCBs) in those parts of Europe that have agreed to abide by the principles of monetary integration. The ECB, however, is a centralized central banking system, functioning as "single brain of the Eurosystem to be obeyed by all the other members (the NCBs)". The ECB Governing Council has 6 Executive Board members and the Governors of the participating NCBs. The Council formulates the monetary policy of the European Community including decisions concerning intermediate monetary policy objectives, key interest rates, and the supply of reserves in the system, and establishes the necessary guidelines for their implementation. These guidelines are meant for the NCBs. The six members of the Executive Board include the President and the Vice President of the ECB.

The Fed's Open Market Committee (FOMC) is the main monetary policy making organ of the Fed. It is akin to ECB Governing Council and it meets once in 6 weeks. The FOMC is composed of 7 Governors and the twelve Presidents of the regional Federal Reserve Banks. Of the 12 Presidents, only five have the right to vote. As a result, the majority lies with the Board of Governors sitting permanently in Washington. In an effective sense, the Fed's decisions are as centralized as the ECB. There are as stated earlier no models of decentralization among EMEs, and almost all central banks in EMEs work in a centralized set up, with constraints on their actions imposed exogenously.

Why did the ECB prefer centralization ? This is because decentralization would have produced several distortions in the monetary integration framework. The first concerns the use of monetary policy instruments and procedures. Reserve requirements, for example, have been imposed mainly with a view to safeguarding the ability of NCBs to play a role in the practical implementation of the single monetary policy. Since reserves are remunerated, no wedge is created between the return on deposits and that of other financial assets. Reserves are thus of no use for the purpose of controlling monetary aggregates. The main use of reserves is to create liquidity buffer that banks could utilize in order to absorb liquidity shocks. This buffer is vital because it obviates frequent fine tuning interventions by the central bank in the money market to stabilize the short term interest rates. Such interventions would not normally be wrong but the procedure for conducting open market operations (OMO) in a decentralized way would take considerable time (estimated to be more than 12 hours) and could therefore create problems in tackling within this period of 12 hours any unforeseen liquidity shocks. Hence ECB undertakes the laborious task of allotting tenders and announcing the tender results while the NCBs do the settlement of the transactions. As reserve requirements exist, banks hold a buffer of liquidity to absorb any unanticipated liquidity shocks, thereby reducing the need for frequent central bank intervention. In an important sense, the reserve requirements ensure that ECB does not become an operating agency of monetary policy.

The Bank of England (BoE) presents an interesting model, bordering on centralized system. In the model, there is a Monetary Policy Committee (MPC) that is housed in and serviced by BoE under the Bank of England Act 1998. The UK Chancellor of the Exchequer (equivalent to the Finance Minister in most EMEs) retains the power to set the inflation target for the MPC in numerical terms. In general, the target is not changed essentially to protect the operational independence of BoE. The Treasury also retains reserve powers permitting it to take back the monetary management role from the MPC at the discretion of the Chancellor. But exercise of such a power is subjected to ex-post Parliament ratification but as this is not easily possible, effectively the power exists only in name. The MPC members are drawn from within the BoE (five in all including the Governor and Deputy Governors) and from outside (numbering four with renewable 3-year terms of office). Each member is individually accountable in that the practice of taking a formal vote on interest rate setting at the meeting of the Committee was adopted. The information about which member voted for which of the propositions on the table (e.g., whether the rate of interest should be raised or lowered) is also published within two weeks of the vote being taken. The members of MPC are judged by their professional competence and independence. They are not to be viewed as representatives of any regional or industrial or sectoral interests.

The MPC of BoE has so far worked as independent of political authorities but this was essentially rendered possible by the enlightened policy environment. But so long as this is not enshrined in law, the independence of MPC could change when the political environment shifts (Buiter, Willem H and Anne C Sibert (2001)).

The ECB experiment, however, is a unique case in that it formally gives greater operational and target independence than what one could see in the case of the Bank of England. It has shown that centralization of monetary policy making is possible, thereby proving that decision outside of the national central banks is not sub-optimal. What is most important is that it shows that central banks could be independent of political interference. Since the governments of the monetary union responsible for the formation of ECB are far too many, they just cannot interfere with the day to day functioning of ECB and are in any case bound by the monetary integration agreement (Maastricht Treaty). ECB lays down the inflation target to achieve. The Treaty has not given reserve powers to the Treasuries either. A change in the Treaty is also not easy since it requires unanimity of views. However, it must be recognized that the ECB works in a rule based and disciplined frame that may not be replicable in other countries, simply because well structured rules may impinge on discretion of central banks that often function in a world of uncertainty. Yet, central bank independence may have to be pursued within the framework of the given central banking systems (perhaps a mix of centralized and decentralized systems) in emerging market economies for reasons of accountability and for influencing market behavior.

Independence, Accountability and Central Bank Governance

Central banks are often regarded as institutions that operated in a veil of secrecy or ambiguity (See Garfinkel, M and S. Oh (1995)). Where unanticipated monetary policy is perceived to be effective in influencing output or employment, disclosing only partial information may be interpreted by market participants as the central bank's proclivity to keep some information private so as to retain the possibility of springing inflationary surprises (See Canzoneri, Matthew (1985)). This line of reasoning has been often used by the Fed to justify that information about the FOMC meetings and their deliberations should not be disclosed as requested by some market participants (Goodfriend, Marvin (1986)). This view was justified when price stability was not the sole objective. It could be justified also where the central bank is not independent. But by disclosing full information, central banks often benefit from the fact that they would be in a better position to interpret current developments.

But why is it central banks tend to be less than transparent ? By providing full and symmetric information, central banks often regard that they deprive themselves of the possibility of following a different policy from the ones announced. But transparency could still exist even when discretion rather than the rule is the main feature of the policy frame. By providing the necessary information to markets, central banks could influence the expectations of the participants and indicate that policy surprises would be exception. Such an approach would increase credibility and enhance the reputation of central banks.

Transparency practices are being increasingly emphasized in recent years especially after the Mexican currency crisis of 1994. But do these practices differ from one central bank to the other ? In its comprehensive form, transparency refers to an environment in which the objectives of policy, its legal, institutional and economic framework, policy decisions and their rationale, data and information relating to monetary and financial policies and developments are provided widely to the general public in an understandable manner and on a timely basis. These practices, by helping to promote efficient market expectations, create an environment for setting in place sound policies. Such outcomes would in turn promote financial stability.

Mere statement of objective(s) is not sufficient to prove that transparency practices are set. Central banks will need to pursue numerical target(s) and provide evidence of the steps being taken to move towards mechanisms for realizing the objectives. For instance, the quarterly inflation reports published by BoE provide the technical work done to improve understanding about the inflation target and to give basis to members of the MPC while taking policy decisions such as the determination of an appropriate nominal official interest rate. Such reports are being published by a number of central banks in other IEs as well. A few EMEs are now attempting to publish inflation reports.

Dissemination of information through publications of the central bank is a commonly seen phenomenon. The Annual Reports of the central banks being public documents and often presented to governments or parliaments contain the working and functioning of central banks in the given economic environment of the year. Besides these reports, monthly and weekly publications and speeches and statements of Governors and Deputy Governors are also placed often in the public domain: all these add to transparency. Websites are being increasingly used by central banks as the best vehicles of communication with the public both domestically and outside the national boundaries. Some central banks also encourage seminars and symposia for discussion on monetary and financial policy matters with academics, policy makers and market participants. They tended to invite professionals from outside their countries as well. For example, the Federal Bank of Kansas City, the Bank of England, and the Riksbank of Sweden are known to sponsor such seminars.

Adoption of transparency practices often leads to ex ante control and accountability, the elements that are most cherished in most democratic societies. While ex ante control implies standards and principles laid down in advance by societies, accountability would imply willingness to listen to criticism and respond to questions about the past and future behavior. If the ex ante control is loosely defined and has escape clauses (that is the circumstances under which the targets or rules could be deviated are not specified and deviations are not treated as exceptions), then accountability will be poor and bad performance could be justified ex post. If accountability has to be of high quality, not only should there be publications and website notifications, but also some hearings in Parliament or its committees as in the United States and the United Kingdom about banking and finance matters where central bank governor's actions and views are sought and are closely scrutinized, may have to be tried. If this is not possible in the state of the evolution of the political institutions, then one could at least provide for participation of a government representative in the decision making body of the central bank and the publication of the minutes of the meetings containing the viewpoints of the participants of the meetings of the decision making body would be helpful in enhancing accountability. Summary minutes of the monetary policy committees along with the votes of the members in favor of or against the finally arrived decisions are published by the United States and the United Kingdom. The US goes as far as to publishing detailed minutes of the FOMC along with the votes of the members of the committee. The publications of the detailed minutes would however take some time. But the immediate transmittal of the main decision of the policy making committees to the wider public would greatly influence market behavior even though it is well known that markets would on the basis of the past records predict the behavior of different members of the monetary policy committee with respect to the main policy option and act accordingly. Such market expectations tend to build some pressure on the members to be consistent in their behavior and not deviate from their past voting pattern even if circumstances warrant actions otherwise. But this may not be as insurmountable a problem as is often made out to be. In any case, the fact that central banks commit themselves to publishing the detailed minutes of the meetings, albeit with lags, could itself help promote policy rationale and thereby the efficacy. Over time, such detailed minutes would help the analysts of financial markets in understanding as to how policy making process works and what kind of information has gone into the process.

Better governance of central banks will flow from control and accountability, provided the central banks are independent and are clear of their objectives and of the context in which they operate. The EMEs operate in the context of financial sector development, diversification and integration and as such will be required to go beyond the traditional view of monetary policy pursuit and be prepared to undertake structural reforms of the financial sector. Since most financial sector reforms to be effective require to be complemented by reforms elsewhere in the fiscal and real sectors as also in the labour and exchange markets, there is a need for central banks to be given sufficient powers to implement what is regarded as necessary for attaining allocative efficiency and non-inflationary growth.

Independence in the Context of the Implementation of International Standards/Codes

Central bank independence is recognized by the international financial institutions like the IMF, World Bank, and BIS, as well as by the international financial markets as important for transparency and effective conduct of monetary and financial policies. As seen in Chapter 6, the IMF has sponsored an international standard in respect of this area of standards (see the chapter on financial stability) but it is not clear whether implementation of this standard would be impeded in case the central bank is not legally and operationally independent. While independence helps improve accountability, there is no guarantee that it will necessarily lead to higher levels of transparency and clearer enunciation of the central bank objectives and policy stance. But once it is decided to implement this international standard, a number of policy decisions will have to be taken and implemented in other areas of macroeconomic policies and in creating appropriate infrastructure in support of it. For instance, it would not be possible to make monetary policy credible without clearly defining the objectives of policy and without specifying the stance of policy before hand. The legal, and payment infrastructure would have to be strong and robust to support central bank independence. The central bank-parliament relationship would also get delineated. The limits on government seeking financial support from the central bank would also get set. There would be also certainty in the tenure of offices of Governors and Deputy Governors. Again aspects relating to the processes of monetary policy formulation would get clarified. For instance, whether public debt management should be undertaken by the central bank or by a separate agency would be the question that would be resolved, although, in the process, this would place pressure on the government to accept a fair amount of fiscal transparency and responsibility. The institutional setting for monetary policy formulation within the central bank would have also got sorted out. Whether there should a monetary policy committee or an open market committee is a matter that would be addressed along with the associated issues of transparency practices relating to the deliberations of the committee meetings. Finally, the acceptance of the international standard would also require the central bank to work out appropriate relationship with other financial institutions including other regulatory bodies in pursuit of its own monetary policy and of the objective of financial stability.

At this point of time, EMEs seem to have very little of choice but to agree to implement the international standard relating to the Code of transparency practices in monetary and financial policies. But EMEs could, in implementing the international standard, exercise some flexibility keeping in view the unique legal and institutional settings of their countries. Such an approach should, however, be widely made known, for it is likely to help the concerned the emerging economy in a number of ways. First, the investors' expectations would be better formed. Secondly, the investors' confidence in the viability as well as capability would get a boost because the chances of the economy facing problems of financial instability would be lower. Finally, to the extent compliance to the standard helps promote price stability as targeted, the possibilities of realizing output and employment expansion would be relatively strong.

References

Alesina, A (1988), "Macroeconomics and Politics", in Stanley Fischer, ed., NBER Macroeconomics Annual, Cambridge, MIT Press, pp.11-55.

Garfinkel, M and S Oh (1995), "When and How Much to Talk: Credibility and Flexibility in Monetary Policy with Private Information", *Jour of Mon Economics*, Vol 35, pp.341-57.

Swinburne, Mark and Marta Castello-Branco (1991), "Central Bank Independence: Issues and Experience", IMF Working Paper, June, No. 58.

8

Conclusions

THIS book is essentially analytical in its orientation. But wherever possible, the Indian experience and realities have been cited to give credence to the analytical insights on the evolving operational principles of central banking. The cited Indian experience may be taken as representing some of the important characteristics of economies that are undertaking large scale macroeconomic and structural and institutional reforms. This generalization obviously cannot be valid for each and every emerging economy but to the extent the insights about the Indian experiences are of value for some EMEs and for those developing economies that closely mimic the EMEs, the conclusions that one could draw from the preceding chapters and the tasks ahead for central bankers in these economies would be of interest for advanced students with interest in policy matters and for analysts in policy-making bodies and financial institutions.

Central banks in both industrialized and emerging economies have had to operate in the last twenty years in economic and financial environment that has been vastly different from the one obtaining before the 1970s. Central banks in IEs have adapted themselves quickly to the changing economic circumstances. They have also been keeping themselves ready to address the new challenges as they emerge either due to technology shocks or economic uncertainties arising out of market expectations and other exogenous factors. Academic writings on central banking have also taken altogether different hue. Most of these writings emerged from the West. Good many central banks in IEs supported research projects on the changing nature and dimensions of central banking in the context of global financial sector integration. Central banks in EMEs have been attempting to see whether they could draw lessons from the experiences of IEs and adapt the operational principles to the institutional and legal structures that are either readily available to them or amenable to transformation to structures that would closely resemble the financial markets of industrialized countries. The analytics of the academic writings on the subject would have a bearing on the actions that central banks in EMEs take and it is therefore essential that central banking for emerging market economies be seen as a close cousin of central banking in IEs at this point in time.

The new concerns and challenges of central banks in IEs and EMEs have been of a rich and wide variety. Most central banks have had to also reorient their traditional functions, reengineer their procedures and processes and infrastructures in order to maximize their objective functions. Currency issuance and distribution is a part of the payment system but its role would diminish as a number of other paper-based and electronically led payment modes become accepted media of settling transactions. Besides, as the process of financial liberalization picks up and internationalization of financial markets grows, cross border transactions will increase and they would normally be conducted through the use of electronic media. Central banks in EMEs have in the circumstances no other option than to encourage the development of efficient payment and settlement systems so that the gains from lubricating the financial sector and improving the transmission channels of policy are advantageously exploited. It should be recognized that a modern payment and settlement system such as the RTGS could be set up by service providers but the capital and maintenance costs of operation will be high in the initial stages and cannot be easily absorbed by economic units in emerging economies. Besides, the design and rules of the settlement systems need to be developed and enforced by regulators of the banking system, namely the central banks for reducing risks. For this reason, the central banks in EMEs may have to take initiatives initially in setting up appropriate settlement systems, DNS or/ and RTGS system. From the point of view of reducing risks and fostering financial stability, it is best to move towards setting up RTGS system. Once the markets understand the discipline of the systems, and the established systems stabi- lize, central banks in these countries could move away from the provision of payment and settlement systems and outsource them as in some of the industrialized countries. But supervi- sion and surveillance of the payment system may still have to be a function of the central bank or an appropriate designated authority in EMEs and perhaps in IEs as well. Since financial stability is a prime concern, and since data on the movement of funds would be the first indicator of the problems involved in the settlement of transactions, it is best that central banks undertake payment oversight. As EMEs will be increasingly contributing to and participating in the internationalization of financial markets, the rules of the payment and settlement systems will have to be consistent with the best international practices. Compliance with the international core principles of payment system will therefore have to be top priority. Cen- tral banks in EMEs will also have to continually monitor the developments in payment systems across countries and take part in the discussions on reviews of the payment system core principles whenever they take place. They need to be aware of the changing technology applications as well as the market procedures and practices. They need to also share information with other central banks on matters that pertain to payment oversight in order to see that irregularities and wrong appli- cation of core principles do not occur and payment failures are eliminated.

It is a fact that the objective functions of central banks in some EMEs could not be stated in clear terms for both statistical and extra-economic reasons, but the experiences in the last 10 years or so have shown that clarity about objectives would have to be in place for market participants to form expectations and act as per their own calculus of risks and rates of return. It does not seem to matter in practice whether one should have only one objective or have multiple objectives of monetary policy: the fact is that most EMEs have multiple objectives for some reason or the other. Most statutes by which central banks have been established in EMEs do not provide for pursuing only a single objective. Again, the jury is not yet out as to whether a superior outcome from the point of view of the general welfare of a society would emerge by pursuing only one objective. Moreover, the economic uncertainties have sharply increased, rendering the pursuit of a single objective largely problematic. For example, inflation targeting which in the early 1990s caught the fancy of a number of central banks and academics has, by 2000/2001, lost much of its glamour, partly because of the unfortunate Japanese experience of almost zero inflation alongside negligible growth in recent years and partly because the inflation performance in most industrialized economies that pursued more than one objective during the 1990s has been low and stable. The economic uncertainties also contributed to lack of consensus as to which of the objectives could be worked out operationally and on a priority basis. In so far as the transmission of the intended effects of monetary policy is concerned, the conventional monetary aggregates channel may not have the expected impact in transitional stages when the financial markets are growing and are increasingly sensitive to rates of return. On the other hand, the interest rate channel employed in many IEs mainly for purposes of inflation control may not work as effectively as one would theoretically assume, because of lack of *adequate* financial integration and the associated information inadequacies and asymmetries. Even in IEs, this channel has tended to become weak mainly because of growing economic uncertainties and shifting market expectations. In fact, central banks in IEs where single objective is pursued have found that optimal control methods cannot be adopted where forward looking transmission lags have to be determined. Such optimal control methods would imply that there has to be a manageable model with clear specifications, a structure of shocks, and loss functions. But model and shock specifications influence the optimal control horizons. That leaves the determination and adoption of loss functions. Even these exercises are beset with far too many difficulties and complexities. The question that is often posed in the context of autonomy and accountability of central banks is that whether there can be a collective loss function for the monetary policy committees or policy boards. Most central banks and governments in IEs therefore preferred to make a general specification of the objective (of price stability) and not bind the committees or boards to any a priori rule.

This brings us to the debate on rules versus discretion. The debate has lost much of its sting notwithstanding the continuing academic interest in it simply because no central banker would like to be devoid of discretion in her actions. The consensus view now emerging among most central bankers is that it is best to view the debate not as confrontational but as assimilating. In other words, rules *and* discretion rather than rules versus discretion would be the practical approach to adopt. In any case, discretion does not mean total freedom: constraints to action would exist because of the compulsions to influence market expectations and discipline. Nor should rules be interpreted as rigid. It is possible for central banks, be they in IEs or EMEs, to state the medium term paths for some of the financial variables (e.g., interest rates) and prices and allow for tolerable range of deviations to occur in them in the short term essentially because of the existence of uncertainties.

Most Central banks have also become increasingly conscious

of the need for having transparency practices and are moving toward setting in place standards that are consistent with the international standards and are, during the process of liberalization, in line with their own institutional and legal structures. But as institutional and legal settings too are subject to changes owing to the on-going reforms, the transparency practices that have to be set in place would ultimately have to converge with the accepted international standards and codes. Markets must follow the discipline that the regulators monitor and the regulators in their turn must keep the markets informed of the initiatives they take in respect of the implementation of standards. This is a critical requirement for market expectations to be formed and to be stable.

Most central banks in EMEs find it hard to grapple with the diverse and complex problems that are associated with financial sector development and diversification. They have no choice but to pursue financial sector reforms that they have undertaken. It is here the central banks will have occasions to interface with government at different tiers (federal or central, provincial or local), banks and other financial intermediaries, and other market participants including domestic corporate entities and foreign institutions. Financial sector reforms will imply not mere creation of new institutions or markets or financial instruments; they also require that flexibility be imparted in the existing markets by liberalizing both 'quantities' and 'prices' in a sequential way and at speeds that do not engender macro-economic imbalances. Creation of new institutions is expensive and time consuming while introduction of new instruments should be allowed with great deal of scrutiny of the possible pitfalls and with appropriate supervisory and regulatory mechanisms in place. Growth of financial markets would depend to a large extent on the confidence of market participants in the stability and direction of policies. Often the central banks by clearly showing evidence of their commitment to financial sector reforms could foster market development, much more effectively than governments. The signals the central banks emit provide the clue to the build up of confidence. The best litmus test of confidence in the economy is to see whether the markets are stable and not volatile. Absence of volatility will encourage central banks to go ahead with reforms. One of the aspects of reforms would be for central banks to be careful in assessing their own regulatory and supervisory capacities and work out strategies for fostering financial stability. This implies that central banks need not be super regulators and/or super supervisors of the entire financial system. Instead, they should be willing to be players, major ones at that, to coordinate their own regulatory and supervisory actions with those of other regulators and supervisors in the system.

An issue that was touched upon at several places in the previous chapters pertains to the critical importance of good, unbiased information system. Informational problems are not only at the heart of adverse selection and moral hazard; they are also present in policy-making processes. Good policy responses from central banks would not be forthcoming unless the central banks collect a wide variety of robust information, sift them and analyze them regularly for policy purposes. In many EMEs, the statistical wings of central banks are fairly well endowed in terms of the number of staff but, as the currency and financial crises experiences of the 1990s have shown, the type of information collected and analyzed had not been sufficient to provide sufficient clues in time about the simmering or incipient problems. This is where the central banks in EMEs will have to make special efforts to strengthen their statistical and research base.

One question that has not been dealt with in this book but has often cropped up in recent discussions relates to the sudden upsurge of new technologies and their impact on consumers of banking and financial services. It is rhetorically asked as to whether there will be a need for a central bank say in the next decade. It is a tantalizing idea to think of a world without central banks. But is it possible to have a world without money? So long as transactions are conducted and there has to be a medium of accounts and exchange, there has to be some institutional set-up to ensure that the transactions are final and settled to the full satisfaction of all the participants concerned. That institution could be given any name but could well be termed the central bank. It is also probably too far fetched an idea to believe that the central bank can be rendered redundant by assuming that problems in transactions that are conducted on a contemporaneous or on a future payment basis can be resolved by some ready made or even customized software applications. However good these applications are, they cannot replace human ingenuity that is required to address day-to-day problems and the evolving financial and economic situations. What is more, a central bank is required to ensure that the financial sector is sufficiently liquid and that severe illiquidity and insolvency issues are resolved to safeguard the financial system. In fact, it is the job of central bankers to prevent panics.

The Asian Economic Crisis of the 1990s

THE Asian Economic Crisis that began, historically speak ing, with Thailand abandoning the defense of its currency, the baht, was one of the severest ones that engulfed a large part of the Asian region without any prior notice. It was most discussed in academic circles, as well as in policy making bodies and forums. Since it was not anticipated, its impact was dramatic especially as the theoretical as well as the empirical literature that existed prior to the crisis did not prima facie seem to be sufficient to provide plausible explanations. New approaches to currency and financial crisis were necessitated by the fact of this failure.

The Asian crisis is not mere currency crisis as the one witnessed in Mexico in 1994. Nor is it the debt crisis that began with the Mexico defaulting in 1982. It was a combination of currency and financial sector crisis with wide ranging effects on the real economy and on the international financial markets. Its effects were across national boundaries but, fortunately, confined within the region (East Asia).

While the discussions on the Asian crisis tended to be some times acrimonious, the policy implications for EMEs have been considerable. They also led to issues concerning the soundness of macroeconomic and structural reforms, the international economic cooperation, governance of international financial institutions, and the new international financial architecture as well as institutional mechanisms to continually monitor and discuss financial stability matters.

The Asian crisis essentially concerns five countries — Indonesia, Korea, Malaysia, the Philippines, and Thailand, although Hong Kong, Singapore, and Taiwan were also affected to some extent by it for a brief period. During the large part of the 1980s, the five crisis-hit countries had grown on the average at rates ranging between 6 per cent and 10 per cent a year. The highest rate was recorded by Korea at 9.6 per cent and the lowest rate of 1.1 per cent was by the Philippines. In the period 1990-96, barring the Philippines, the rest of the crisis-hit countries maintained fairly high growth rates. But even the Philippines on the average improved the rate of growth from 1.1 per cent in the 1980s to 2.8 per cent a year during the period 1990-96. The remaining four crisis-hit countries grew at an average annual rate of 8-9 per cent in the recent period. Such extraordinarily high growth rates were achieved with relatively tolerable inflation rates, fiscal surpluses, and high saving and investment rates.

The average annual inflation rates during the years 1990-96 compared favorably with the 1980s and they were: Indonesia: 8.6 per cent (8.1 per cent in the 1980s); Korea: 6.4 per cent (3.8 per cent in the 1980s); Malaysia: 3.5 per cent (2.0 per cent in the 1980s); the Philippines: 10.5 per cent (15.4 per cent in the 1980s); and Thailand: 5.1 per cent (3.1 per cent in the 1980s). Saving rates during the 1990s (up to 1996) were higher on the average than those in the 1980s in Indonesia, Korea, Malaysia and Thailand. In the case of the Philippines, the saving rate was stable in both the periods. Interestingly enough, the average investment rates in 1990-96 were higher than those in the 1980s in respect of all the five countries in question. The averaged investment-saving gaps in the recent period were quite substantial in all the countries : in Indonesia, it was 3.3 percentage points; in Korea, 2.1 percentage points; in Malaysia, 7.4 percentage points; in the Philippines, 4.9 percentage points; and in Thailand, 6.7 percentage points. The gaps reflected the large average current account deficit in relation to GDP during 1990-96 in the case of three countries: Malaysia (6.0 per cent), the Philippines (4.2 per cent), and Thailand (6.9 per cent). During the same period, the current account deficit in relation to GDP averaged 0.5 per cent in the case of Korea, and 1.7 per cent in respect of Indonesia. In fact, in the case of Korea and Indonesia, the current account to GDP ratio turned out to be a surplus in 1996.

The excess of investment over saving was on account of private sector's plans rather than the government's fiscal position. Barring the Philippines, the remaining four crisis-hit countries had fiscal surpluses in the years 1994-96. The large private sector deficit was financed largely by borrowings from abroad. The external debt incurred was of a short term nature and with the exception of Malaysia, the short term debt as per cent of total reserves exceeded 100 per cent in the case of Indonesia, the Philippines, and Thailand and over 200 per cent in the case of Korea in 1995 and 1996.

The large investment boom and the fairly high growth rates gave respectability to the development strategies adopted by the countries in the region. The region was open to foreign trade and capital movements. In fact these outcomes made East Asia, a region of economic miracles. So enamored were the foreign investors that capital inflows into the five countries of the region averaged over 6 per cent of GDP between 1990-1996. They ignored the fact that exchange rates showed little variation in Malaysia, the Philippines and Thailand, and small but very predictable changes in Indonesia and Korea. This was clearly suggestive of the fact that central banks in these countries were willing to absorb risks of exchange rate movements on behalf of investors. The elimination of exchange risk however did encourage capital inflows. But as capital inflows increased, the prices of non-tradables tended to drift upward, with the result the exchange rates appreciated in real terms. Barring Korea, real exchange rate appreciated in 1996 in the remaining four countries. Export growth, by virtue of the fact that most goods manufactured by the region were highly labor intensive and were in excessive supply partly because of the competition from China, slowed in the US dollar terms in the mid-1990s. In fact, it dropped sharply in 1996. As a result the external current account deficits widened. As these deficits increased, there was a perception that external debt sustainability may not be realized, especially as a large share of foreign borrowing was in the form of short-term debt. This seemed to be at the core of the pressure exerted on the exchange rate. The regime of exchange rate pegs in the region could not cope with the speculative attack on the currencies. In addition, the domestic lending quality was poor and concentrated in areas that did not yield stable and high rates of return. The financial market deregulation apparently gave to banks and near banks highly distorted incentives to borrow abroad and lend domestically for real estate, property and the purchase of equity funds. The collapse of prices of stocks and real estate that occurred in some countries (for example, Thailand) led to sharp vulnerability in the financial system. Unfortunately, the financial deregulation which led to entry of a large number of banks and other financial entities was not complemented by rigorous financial regulation and supervision. The regulatory systems in the central banks in vogue were not suited to the regime of financial liberalization. As Radelet and Sachs (1998) argued: "Regulatory reforms tended to be partial and incomplete". The weaknesses of banks and financial companies came into open when the exposures to assets whose prices fell were high. Payment failures of financial institutions were widespread and assumed systemic proportions.

The first country that suffered the excesses of investment boom unaccompanied by appropriate exchange rate and regulatory regime was Thailand. The first speculative attack on the Thai baht occurred in early 1997, to be precise in February 1997. But the Bank of Thailand intervened heavily, and held on to the parity, with some external help. It was erroneously thought that the situation could be thwarted if there was some indication of fund support from outside to the extent necessary. Such a support would, it was felt, provide a psychological boost and calm the markets. Accordingly, the Bank of Thailand entered into a cooperative agreement of fund support from other central banks in the region. But this measure proved to be effective only temporarily. In May 1997, the baht once again came under pressure. But the Bank of Thailand continued to support the fixed rate regime while the international financial community clearly preferred that Thailand move to flexible rate regime. The acrimony surrounding the policy options led to greater market uncertainties. As Thailand's foreign exchange reserves declined sharply, Thailand had to abandon the exchange rate peg and allow the baht to float in July 1997.

The collapse of the Thai baht sent shock waves to the rest of the region and speculative attacks began to mount on the Philippine peso, the Malaysian ringgit, and the Indonesian rupiah. While this is factually correct, the Thailand experience is not a story of the classical currency crisis. The classical currency crisis could be defined as one that occurs when a speculative attack on the exchange value of a currency results in a sharp depreciation/devaluation or in the authorities defending the currency. The defense of the currency would occur either by placing large amounts of foreign exchange reserves or by raising sharply the interest rates. The defense of the currency did not succeed also partly because of the fact that the US dollar had rapid appreciation after 1995. There was panic among the international creditors to withdraw funds from Thailand and move away to relatively safe havens. The massive capital outflows from Thailand that occurred as a result dwindled the foreign exchange reserves. The sharp contraction in the international market confidence in the economy and the constrained ability of the domestic financial institutions to lend and support the economic activities, coinciding unfortunately with the collapse of asset prices, led to serious liquidity shortages. The illiquidity, in the absence of central banks' intervention in the form of liquidity injection, was faced by firms including those that were solvent and had sufficiently strong net worth.

By end-September 1997, the baht as well as the rupiah had depreciated by over 35 per cent over the levels at the beginning of the year. For the ringgit and peso too the depreciation was effectively close to 30 per cent. In the case of Malaysia, the large public investment projects and strong consumption growth led to the widening of the external current account deficit that in turn, following the float of the baht in July 1997, placed pressures on the Malaysian currency. In regard to Indonesia, incentives given to the firms owned by the ruling family to borrow for undertaking risky and unviable projects created problems akin to those that arise when there is adverse selection. The information about the external debt was not systemically compiled, leaving the impression that financial vulnerability was much more severe than what the official balance sheets of banks and other financial institutions would suggest.

Speculative pressures on the currencies of Taiwan, Singapore and Hong Kong began to build up by October 1997 because of the depreciation of the currencies of Thailand, Malaysia and Indonesia, the countries with which their linkages were strong. Singapore had let its currency to depreciate, albeit moderately. Taiwan had to allow its currency to float. Hong Kong had faced it by monetary tightening and hiking interest rates and operated the principles of currency board to the letter. The last currency to face the attack was the Korean won. Essentially because of depreciation of the currencies in the region, Korea's international competitivenss had suffered a loss. Besides, the large corporate entities, called the chaebols, had faced bankruptcies owing to excessive external borrowing and build-up of overcapacities. Their debt equity ratios were extraordinarily high. The corporate bankruptcies led to significant fall in external financing with the result the foreign exchange reserves plummeted. Monetary policy was tightened briefly but relaxed very soon when the government felt that high interest rates would adversely impact on the highly leveraged corporate entities. By December 1997, the Korean won had depreciated by over 20 per cent against the US dollar and the foreign exchange reserves declined by about $6 billion.

The experiences of these East Asian countries show that the crisis situations were marked not merely by currency attacks but also by the fact that the financial system was rendered highly vulnerable. The ensuing financial crisis took on a systemic character, reflecting disruption of financial markets and large adverse effects on the real economy.

The crisis was not foreseen by economists or by international financial institutions or by the respective governments/central banks. Crisis management or crisis prevention thus became an ex post phenomenon. The theoretical models available till then were scanned through by the writings that appeared mostly after the middle of 1997 and more prominently since early 1998. As the economic fundamentals were found to be sufficiently strong at least till 1996, the 'first generation' models of balance of payments a la Krugman were clearly not good enough to explain the crisis. The 'second generation' models (see Obstfeld, 1994, 1996) suggest that currency crises could occur even when the fundamentals are sound. In these models, crisis would be self-fulfilling in which policy action would justify investor pessimism. To be more explicit, the self-fulfilling crises occur when the sheer pessimism of a significant group of investors provokes a capital outflow that eventually leads to the collapse of the exchange rate system, thereby validating the negative expectations. The actions of economic agents thus determine the movements from one equilibrium position to another. These models thus emphasize that there would be multiple equilibria because of the interactions between government policies (either to defend or to abandon the exchange rate system, for example) and the perceptions of private economic agents about the possible use of expansionary fiscal policies by governments to overcome the economic slowdown. Anticipating such a policy, private agents would react by attacking the domestic currency, thus accelerating the collapse of the exchange rate system.

The 'second generation' models could be two types. There are models of herding behavior stressing the fact that information costs could lead foreign investors to take decisions based on limited, often asymmetric information. Their actions would be led by market rumors rather than by firm information base. There are on the other hand models emphasizing contagion effects based on the fact that groups of countries in a region may have common policy characteristics or objectives and are closely interlinked. Thus when one country faces a crisis situation, investors may perceive high downside risks of investment in the neighboring countries. Or, the international rating agencies may reevaluate their previous ratings of the neighboring countries and provide fresh ratings, with added emphasis on the incipient problems, if any, that investors may face.

The fundamentally unnecessary panicked reversals in flows of capital would point to what may be called the intrinsic nature of instability in international lending and investment. When capital markets cannot provide fresh funds for borrowers to be current in servicing their debt obligations, there occurs liquidity crisis. The borrowers may have sufficient net worth and could well be solvent. But so long as liquidity is not forthcoming, there is no way that the borrowers can service their debts.

The reason why the crisis in East Asia attracted so much attention is that the costs imposed on the concerned countries were very high. The costs were in terms of the fairly long duration of the crisis, the extent of the financial meltdown, as also the loss of output, employment and other real sector variables. It took almost 15 months for Thailand to recover. The crisis in Indonesia was of a fairly longer duration partly because of the information asymmetries. The crisis in Korea was perhaps of the shortest duration, with recovery in sight in about 9 months from the time of the first sign of the crisis in October 1997. In Malaysia and the Philippines, the duration of the crisis was anywhere between 13-14 months. Exchange rate depreciations as already noted were strong, especially so in Indonesia. The behavior of share prices in dollar terms showed a real meltdown of over 90 per cent in Indonesia and between 70-85 per cent in the rest of the crisis-hit countries. The financial system was most stressed. In Thailand, for example, out of the 90 finance companies, 58 were suspended from operation by the end of July 1997 and were closed, barring two suspended companies. Thailand had to also temporarily 'nationalize' a few problem banks in order to avoid further systemic problems. 16 banks were closed in Indonesia while 10 merchant banks in Korea were closed. All the countries in the region had recorded negative GDP growth in 1998. Inflation rates also surged up, especially so in Indonesia. On the whole, the costs of the crisis were very high in Thailand and Indonesia, and least in the Philippines.

Given the high costs of the crisis situations, the concerned countries could not cope with them by themselves. The International Monetary Fund (IMF) together with other creditors took up the task of meeting the problems posed by the crisis situations. The responses of IMF however were most vociferously questioned by a number of writers as too conventional, giving prominence to most elements of the stabilization and structural programs. Radelet and Sachs (1998) especially argue that the market confidence did not get any boost by the IMF responses that favored fiscal contraction, restructuring of financial markets through closing of financial institutions, raising interest rates that did not douse the 'extreme creditor panic', announcements of large bail-out packages that did not guarantee readily available short term fund support, secrecy surrounding the number of IMF arrangements, and undertaking trade liberalization, privatization and such other policies. And what is more, the IMF arrangements carried far too many conditions and left out private creditors.

The acrimonious discussion that followed the rescue packages and the IMF conditionality was perhaps responsible for a positive relook at the very viability of the international financial system. What is also interesting is that the role of the central banks vis-à-vis currency board was discussed seriously for avoiding the currency volatility. As some of these issues were already dealt with in the chapters of this book, it is enough if we state here by way of conclusion that the Asian economic crisis was an important wake-up call for countries to be vigilant about their own policies and for the international financial community to mitigate risks and bring advantages of globalisation across countries.

Select References

Agenor, Pierre-Richard, Marcus Miller, David Vines and Axel Weber (eds) (1999), *The Asian Financial Crisis*, Cambridge University Press, Cambridge (UK) and New York.

Dadush, Uri, Dipak Dasgupta, and Marc Uzan (eds) (2000), *Private Capital Flows in the Age of Globalization*, Edward Elgar, Cheltenham, UK and Northampton, MA, USA.

Krugman, Paul (1979), "A Model of Balance of Payments crises", *Journal of Money, Credit and Banking*, Vol. 11, pp.311-25.

Obstfeld, Maurice (1994), "The Logic of Currency Crises", NBER WP 4640, Cambridge, Mass.

Obstfeld, Maurice (1996), "Models of Currency Crises with Self-fulfilling Features", *European Economic Review*, Vol.40, pp.1037-47.

Radelet, Steven and Sachs, Jeffrey D (1998), "The East Asian Financial Crisis: Diagnosis, Remedies, Prospects", *Brookings Papers on Economic Activity*, 1, pp.1-74.

Rakshit, Mihir 2002), *The East Asian Currency Crisis*, Oxford University Press, New Delhi.

$\mathcal{S}$elect References[†]

Aiyagari, Rao S. and R. Anton Braun (1998), "Some Models to Guide the Fed", *Carnegie-Rochester Conf Series Public Policy*, 48, 1-42.

* Akerlof, G.A (1970), "The Market for Lemons: Qualitative Uncertainty and the Market Mechanism", QJE, 84, 488-500.

Akerlof, G.A, W.T. Dickens, and G.L. Perry (1996), "The Macroeconomics of Low Inflation", *Brookings Papers on Economic Activity*, No.1, 1-76.

Alesina, Alberto and Lawrence H Summers (1993), "Central Bank Independence and Macroeconomic Performance: Some Comparative Evidence", JMCB, 25 (2), 151-62.

Allen, F (1983), "Credit Rationing and Payment Incentives", *Rev Eco St* 50 (4), 639-46.

* Amato, J.D. and Gerlach, S (2001), *Modelling the Transmission Mechanism of Monetary Policy in Emerging Market Countries Using Prior Information*, Bank for International Settlements, Basle.

Andersen, Leonall C and Carlson, Keith M (1970), "A Monetarist Model for Economic Stabilization", *FRB St Louis Rev*, April 52 (4), 7-25.

---

† This part may not include all the references given within the text of the book as some references are also given at the end of most of the chapters.

* These references are recommended readings.

! **Legend** is given at the end (page 261)

Backus, David and John Driffill (1985), "Inflation and Reputation", AER 75, 530-38.

* Bagehot, Walter (1873), *Lombard Street: A Description of the Money Market*, William Clowes and Sons, London. Reproduced in Volume 9 of The Collected Works of Walter Bagehot, edited by Norman St. John-Stevas, The Economist, London, 1978.

Ball, Laurence (1997), "Efficient Rules for Monetary Policy", NBER WP 5952.

Ball, Laurence (1998), "Policy Rules for Open Economies", NBER WP 6760.

Ball, Laurence (2000), Policy Rules and External Shocks, NBER WP, 7910, September.

Baltensperger, E (1978), "Credit Rationing: Issues and Questions", JMCB, 10 (2),170-83.

Barnett, W. and K. Singleton eds., (1987), *New Approaches to Monetary Economics*, Cambridge, Cambridge Univ. Press.

* Bank of England (1999), *Economic Models at the Bank of England*, London

* Bank of England (1999), "The Transmission Mechanism of Monetary Policy, *BoE Qly Bul*, May, Vol 39 (2), 161-70.

* Bank for International Settlements (1998), *The Transmission of Monetary Policy in Emerging Market Economies*, BIS Policy Paper 3, BIS, Basle.

Bank for International Settlements (1999), *Bank Restructuring in Practice*, Policy Paper No. 6, August, Basle.

Bank for International Settlements (2000), *Core Principles of Payment and Settlement Systems*, Committee on Payment and Settlement Systems, Basle.

* Barro, Robert J (1977), "Unanticipated Money Growth and Unemployment in the United States", AER, 67, March, 101-15.

Barro, Robert J (1978), "Unanticipated Money, Output, and the Price Level in the United States", JPE, 86, August, 549-80.

Barro, R.J. and D.B. Gordon (1983), "A Positive Theory of Monetary Policy in a Natural Rate Model", JPE, 91, 589-610.

* Barro, Robert J ((1995), "Inflation and Economic Growth", *BoE Qly Bul* 35 (2),166-76.

Batini, Nicoletta and Andrew Haldane (1999), "Forward-looking Rules for Monetary Policy", in John B Taylor, ed., *Monetary Policy Rules*, Univ of Chicago Press.

Bekaert, Geert, Campbell R Harvey, and Christian Lundblad (2001), Does Financial Liberalization Spur Growth, NBER WP 8245, April

Bernanke, B (1990), "Financial Fragility and Economic Performance", QJE 105 (1), 87-114.

Bernanke, B. and A.S. Blinder (1992), "The Federal Funds Rate and the Channels of Monetary Transmission", AER, 82 (4), 901-21.

* Bernanke, B.and M. Gertler (1995), "Inside the Black Box: The Credit Channel of Monetary Policy Transmission", JEPer, 9 (2), 27-48.

* Bernanke, B and M. Gertler (1999), "Monetary Policy and Asset Price Volatility", in FRB of Kansas City, *New Challenges for Monetary Policy*.

Bernanke, Ben S. and Ilian Mihov (1998), "Measuring Monetary Policy", QJE, 113 (3), 869-902, August.

Bernanke, B. and Frederic Mishkin (1992), "Central Bank Behavior and the Strategy of Monetary Policy: Observations from Six Industrialized Countries", NBER *Macroeconomics Annual*, 7, 183-228.

* Bernanke, B. and Frederic Mishkin (1997), "Inflation Targeting : A New Framework for Monetary Policy", NBER WP, 5893.

Bernanke, B. and Michael Woodford (1997), "Inflation Forecasts and Monetary Policy", JMCB, 29 (4), 653-84.

* Bernanke, B.S., T.Laubach, F.S. Mishkin, and A.S. Posen (1999), *Inflation Targetting : Lessons from the International Experience*, Princeton, Princeton Univ. Press.

Blejer, Mario I., and Marko Skreb, eds. (1999), *Central Banking, Monetary Policies and the Implications for Transition Economies*, London, Kluwer Academic.

Blinder, A.S (1998), *Central Banking in Theory and Practice*, Lionel Robbins Lecture, Cambridge and London, MIT Press.

Bordo, M.D (1990), "The Lender of Last Resort: Alternative Views and Historical Experience", *FRB Richmond Eco Rev*, 76 (1,), 18-29.

* Brainard, William C (1967), "Uncertainty and the Effectiveness of Policy", AER, 57, 411-25.

Bryant, J (1980), "A Model of Reserves, Bank Runs and Deposit Insurance", JBF, 4, 335-44.

Budd, A (1998), "The Role and Operations of the Bank of England Monetary Policy Committee", EJ, Vol. 108 (451), 1783-95.

Buiter, Willem H and Anne C Silbert (2001), "Designing a Monetary Authority", in Santomero, Anthony M, Staffan Viotti and Anders Vredin (eds), *Challenges for Central Banking*, Kluwer Academic Publishers, Boston/Dordrecht/London.

* Cagan, P (1958), *The Demand for Currency Relative to Total Money Supply*, NBER, New York

Cagan, P (1972), *The Channels of Monetary Effects on Interest Rates*, NBER, New York

Campbell, J (1995), "Some Lessons from the Yield Curve", jEPer., 9, (3), 129-52.

Canzoneri, Matthew, B (1985), "Monetary Policy Games and the Role of Private Information", AER, 75, 1056-70.

Capie, F., C.Goodhart and N. Schnadt (1994), "The Development of Central Banking", in F.Capie, C.Goodhart, S.Fischer, and N.Schnadt eds., *The Future of Central Banking*, The Tercentenary Symposium of the Bank of England, Cambridge, Cam Univ Press.

Carlson, Keith M (1986), "A Monetarist Model for Economic Stabilization: Review and Update", *FRB St Louis Rev*, October, 18-28.

Cecchetti, S.G (2000), "Making Monetary Policy: Objectives and Rules", OREP, 16 (4), 1-31.

* Cecchetti, Stephen G (1997), Central Bank Policy Rules: Conceptual Issues and Practical Considerations, Cambridge, NBER WP 6306.

* Chandavarkar, Anand G (1996), *Central Banking in Developing Countries*, Macmillan London

Christiano, L.J. and M. Eichenbaum (1995), "Liquidity Effects, Monetary Policy and the Business Cycle", JMCB, 27, 1113-36.

Christiano, L.J. and C.J. Gust (1999), Taylor Rules in a Limited Participation Model, NBER WP 7017.

Christiano, L.J., M. Eichenbaum, and C.L. Evans (1998), "Monetary Policy Shocks: What have we Learned and to what End?", NBER WP 6400. Also in Taylor, J.B. and M. Woodford, eds., *Handbook of Macro-economics*, Vol.1, Amsterdam, North-Holland, 1999.

* Clarida, R., J.Gali, and M. Gertler (1998), "Monetary Policy Rules in Practice: Some International Evidence", EER, 42, 1033-68.

* Clarida, R., J. Gali, and M. Gertler (2000), "Monetary Policy Rules and Macroeconomic Stability: Evidence and Some Theory", QJE, CXV (1), February, 147-180.

Clarida, R., J. Gali, and M. Gertler (1999), "The Science of Monetary Policy: A New Keynesian Perspective", JEL, XXXVII (4), December, 1661-1707. Also NBER Working Paper No. 7147.

* Cukierman, Alex (1992), *Central Bank Strategy, Credibility and Independence*, MIT Press, Cambridge.

Cukierman, Alex and Allan H Meltzer (1986), A Theory of Ambiguity, Credibility, and Inflation under Discretion and Asymmetric Information", *Econometrica*, 54, 1099-1128.

De Kock, M H (1939), *Central Banking*, Staples Press Ltd. London, 3rd ed 1954.

DeLong, J Bradford (2000), "The Triumph of Monetarism?", JEPer, Winter, 83-94.

Dittmar, R., W T Gavin, and F E Kydland (1999), "The Inflation-output Variability Trade-off and Price Level Targets", *FRB St.Louis Rev.*, January/February.

Dornbusch, Rudiger, Carlo A Favero and Francesco Giavazzi (1998), The Immediate Challenges for the European Central Bank, NBER WP 6369.

* Eichengreen, Barry (1999), *Toward A New International Financial Architecture — A Practical Post-Asia Agenda*, Institute for International Economics, Washington DC.

* Eijffinger, Sylvester, ed. (1997), *Independent Central Banks and*

Economic Performance, Cheltenham and Lyme UK and USA, Edward Elgar

* Eisner, Robert (1999), "Central Banking in Theory and Practice", JEL. 37 (1), 191-93.

* Enoch, Charles, and Anne-Marie Gulde (1998), "Are Currency Boards A Cure for All Monetary Problems?", *Finance and Development*, December, Vol 35, no.4

Estrella, Arturo and Frederic S Mishkin (1997), "Is There a Role for Monetary Aggregates in the Conduct of Monetary Policy?", JME 40, 279-304.

Faust, Jon and Lars E.O. Svensson (1998), "Transparency and Credibility: Monetary Policy with Unobservable Goals", NBER WP 6452.

* Federal Reserve Bank of Kansas City (1996), *Achieving Price Stability*, FRB of Kansas City Symposium Series.

Feldstein, M, ed (1999), *The Costs and Benefits of Price Stability*, University of Chicago Press for NBER

Fischer, Stanley (1990), "Rules versus Discretion in Monetary Policy", in Benjamin M Friedman and Frank H Hahn, eds., *Handbook of Monetary Economics*, Vol. II, North Holland, Amsterdam and New York, 1165-84.

Fischer, Stanley (1996), "Why are Central Banks Pursuing Long-run Price Stability?", in FRB of Kansas City, *Achieving Price Stability*, 7-34.

* Fischer, Stanley (1995), "Modern Approaches to Central Banking", NBER WP 5064.

Fratianni, Michele, Jurgen Von Hagen, and Christopher Waller (1997), "Central Banking as a Political Principal-Agent Problem', EI, 35 (2), April, 378-93.

* Friedman, Benjamin M (1990), "Targets and Instruments of Monetary Policy", in Friedman, B M and Frank Hahn, eds., Handbook of Monetary Economics, Vol II, Amsterdam, North-Holland.

* Friedman, Milton (1956), "The Quantity Theory of Money: A Restatement", in M. Friedman,ed. *Studies in the Quantity Theory of Money*, Chicago, Univ Chicago Pr.

Friedman, M (1959), "The Demand for Money: Some Theoretical and Empirical Results", JPE, 67 June 327-51.

* Friedman, M (1960), *A Program for Monetary Stability*, NY, Fordham Univ Press.

* Friedman, M (1968), "The Role of Monetary Policy", AER 58 (March) 1-17. Reprinted in Snowdon, Brian and Howard R Vane, eds., *A Macroeconomics Reader*, 1997, Routledge, London and New York.

* Friedman, M (1970), "A Theoretical Framework for Monetary Analysis", JPE 78,193-238.

Friedman, M and Anna J Schwartz (1963), *A Monetary History of the United States, 1867-1960*, Princeton, N.J., Princeton Univ Press for the NBER.

* Fry, Maxwell (1999), "Central Banking and Economic Development", in Blejer, Mario I and Marko Skreb (eds), *loc.cit.*

* Fry, Maxwell, Isaack Kilato, Sandra Roger, Krzysztof Senderowicz, David Sheppard, Francisco Solis, and John Trundle (1999), *Payment Systems in Global Perspective*, Routledge in association with the Bank of England's Centre for Central Banking Studies, London and New York.

Fry, Maxwell, D.Julius, L. Mahadeva, S. Roger, and G. Sterne (2000), "Key Issues in the Choice of Monetary Policy Framework", in L.Mahadeva and G. Sterne, eds., *Monetary Frameworks in a Global Context*, London, Routledge.

* Ghosh, Atish R, Anne-Marie Gulde, and Holger C Wolf (1998), "Currency Boards: The Ultimate Fix?", IMF WP 98/8, Washington, International Monetary Fund.

* Goodfriend, Marvin (1986), "Monetary Mystique: Secrecy and Central Banking", JME, 17, 63-92.

Goodfriend, M (1997), "Monetary Policy comes of Age: A 20th Century Odyssey", *FRB Richmond Eco. Qly*, (Winter), 1-22.

Goodfriend, M, and Mervyn King (1988), "Financial Deregulation, Monetary Policy and Central Banking", in W. Harag and R.M. Kushmeider, eds., *Restructuring Banking and Financial Services in America*, AEI Studies, No. 481, Lanham, MD, USA.

* Goodhart, Charles (1988), *The Evolution of Central Banks*, MIT Press, Cambridge , Mass, and London.

Goodhart, Charles A E (1994), "Game Theory for Central Bankers: A Report to the Governor of the Bank of England", JEL, 32, March, 101-14.

Goodhart, Charles (1995), *The Central Bank and the Financial System*, Cambridge, MIT Press.

Goodhart, Charles (1999), "Central Bankers and Uncertainty", *BoE Qly.Bul*, Vol.39 (1), February.

Goodhart, C and D.Schoenmaker (1993), "Institutional Separation Between Supervisory and Monetary Agencies", in F.Bruni, ed., *Prudential Regulation, Supervision, and Monetary Policy*, Milano, Universita Bocconi.

Gurley, J. and E. Shaw (1960), *Money in the Theory of Finance*, Washington, The Brookings Institution.

* Haldane, Andrew ed. (1995), *Targeting Inflation*, Bank of England, London.

* Hanke, Steve H (1999), "Some Reflections on Currency Boards", in Blejer, Mario I., and Marko Skreb, eds. *Central Banking, Monetary Policies, and the Implications for Transition Economies, loc.cit.*, 341-366.

Hall, R E (1983), "Optimal Fiduciary Monetary Systems", JME, 12, 33-50.

Hayek, F A (1978), *Denationalization of Money — the Argument Refined*, Institute of Economic Affairs, London.

* Hetzel, Robert L (2000), "The Taylor Rule: Is it a Useful Guide to Understanding Monetary Policy?", *FRB Richmond Eco Qly*, Spring 1-33.

* Hicks, J R (1937), "Mr. Keynes and the 'Classics': A Suggested Interpretation", *Econometrica*, 5, 147-59.

Johnson, Omotunde E G et al, eds. (1998), *Payment Systems, Monetary Policy, and the Role of the Central Bank*, Washington DC, IMF.

* Keynes, J M (1936), *The General Theory of Employment, Interest and Money*, Macmillan, London.

King, R G (1983), "On the Economics of Private Money", *JME*, Vol 12, No 1.

King, Mervyn A (1996), "How Should Central Banks Reduce

Inflation? — Conceptual Issues", in FRB of Kansas City, *Achieving Price Stability*.

* King, M A (1997), "Changes in UK Monetary Policy: Rules and Discretion in Practice", JME, 39, 81-98.

* King, M A (1999), "Challenges for Monetary Policy: New and Old", *BoE Qly Bul*, 39 (4), 397-415.

King, R.G. and R. Levine (1993), "Financial Intermediation and Economic Development", in C. Mayer and X.Vives,eds., *Capital Markets and Financial Intermediation*, Cambridge, Cambridge Univ. Press.

King, R.G. and Charles Plossner (1984), "Money, Credit and Prices in a Real Business Cycle", AER, June, Vol. 74, pp. 363-380.

Kiyotaki, N (1991), "A Contribution to the Pure Theory of Money", JET, 53 (2), 215-35.

Klein, B (1974), "The Competitive Supply of Money", JMCB, Vol 6, No.4.

Kozicki, Sharon (1999), "How Useful are Taylor Rules for Monetary Policy?", *FRB Kansas City Econ Rev.*, Second Quarter, 5-33.

* Kydland, Finn and Edward Prescott (1977), "Rules rather than Discretion : The Inconsistency of Optimal Plans", JPE, 85, 473-91.

Laidler, David (1981), "Monetarism: An Interpretation and an Assessment", EJ, 91, March, 1-28. Reprinted in B. Snowdon & H R Vane, eds. *A Macroeconomics Reader*, Routledge, London and New York, 1997.

Leeper, Eric M., Christopher A Sims, and Tao Zha (1996), "What Does Monetary Policy Do?", *Brookings Papers*, 2, 1-63.

Leiderman, Leonardo, and Lars E O Svensson, eds. (1995), *Inflation Targets*, CEPR, London.

Lewis, Karen (1991), "Why Doesn't Society Minimize Central Bank Secrecy", *Economic Enquiry*, 29, pp.403-415.

Lippi, Francesco (1999), *Central Bank Independence, Targets and Credibility: Political and Economic Aspects of Delegation Arrangements for Monetary Policy*, Cheltenham, Edward Edgar.

* Lucas, R.E (1976), "Macroeconomic Policy Evaluation: A Critique", JME, Vol1 (2), 19-46.

* Lucas, R E (1972), "Expectations and the Neutrality of Money", JET, 4, 103-24.

Mankiw, Gregory N (2000), The Inexorable and Mysterious Trade Off Between Inflation and Unemployment, NBER WP, 7884, Sept.

Mayer, T (1990), *Monetarism and Macroeconomic Policy*, Aldershot: Edward Elgar.

McNees, Stephen K (1992), "A Forward-looking Monetary Policy Reaction Function: Continuity and Change", *New England Eco Rev.*, Nov-Dec 3-13.

McCallum, Bennett T (1997), "Crucial Issues Concerning Central Bank Independence", JME, 39, 99-112.

* McCallum, Bennett T (1999), "Recent Developments in Monetary Policy Analysis: The Roles of Theory and Evidence", NBER WP 7088, April.

* McKinnon, Ronald I (1973), Money and Capital in Economic Development, The Brookings Institution, Washington DC.

Meltzer, Allan H (1998), "Monetarism: The Issues and the Outcome", AEJ March, 8-31.

Miron, J.A (1986), "Financial Panics, the Seasonality of the Nominal Interest Rate, and the Founding of the Fed", AER, 76 (1), 125-40.

Mishkin, Frederic S (2000), "What Should Central Banks Do?", *FRB St Louis Rev*, 82 (6), Nov/Dec., 1-14.

Mishkin, Frederic S and Adam S Posen (1997), "Inflation Targeting: Lessons from Four Countries", *FRB NY Eco Pol Rev* 3 (Aug), 9-110.

*Mishkin, Frederic S (1995), 'Symposium on the Monetary Transmission Mechanism", JE Per, 9-4

Persson, Torsten and Guido Tabellini (1990), eds., *Macroeconomic Policy, Credibility, and Politics*, London, Harwood.

Persson, Torsten, and Guido Tabellini (1993), "Designing Institutions for Monetary Stability", *Carnegie-Rochester Conference Series on Public Policy*, 39, 53-84

Phelps, E (1967), "Phillips curves expectations of inflation and optimal unemployment over time", *Economica*, NS 34 (Aug), 254-81.

Select References — 259

Phillips, A W (1958), "The Relation Between Unemployment and the Rate of Change of Money Wage Rates in the United Kingdom, 1861-1957", *Economica* NS 25 (Nov) 283-99.

*Poole, W (1970), "Optimal Choice of Monetary Policy Instruments in a Simple Stochastic Macro Model", QJE, 84, May.

*Rogoff, Kenneth (1985), "The Optimal Degree of Commitment to an Intermediate Target", QJE 100 (4) Nov., 1169-89.

*Rogoff, Kenneth (1989),"Reputation, Coordination and Policy", in Barro, Robert, ed., *Modern Business Theory*, Cambridge, MA, Harvard Univ. Press.

Romer, C D and D H Romer (1989), "Does Monetary Policy Matter? A New Test in the Spirit of Friedman and Schwartz", NBER *Macroeconomics Annual*, 121-170.

*Romer,C D and D H Romer (1990), "New Evidence on the Monetary Transmission Mechanism", *Brookings Papers*, Vol 1, 149-98.

*Rossi, Marco (1997), *Payment Systems in the Financial Markets: Real Time Gross Settlement Systems and the Provision of Intraday Liquidity*, Houndsmill, Macmillan.

Rothschild, M and J Stiglitz (1976), "Equilibrium Unemployment as a Worker Discipline Device", AER 74, 433-44.

*Sargent, Thomas J (1998), *Central Banking in Theory and Practice*, Lionel Robbins Lectures, London, MIT.

* Sayers, R S (1957), *Central Banking After Bagehot*, Clarendon Press, Oxford.

Schaling, Eric (1995), *Institutions and Monetary Policy: Credibility, Flexibility, and Central Bank Independence*, Aldershot, Edward Elgar.

Siegel, Jeremy J (1981), "Bank Reserves and Financial Stability", JF, XXXVI, 5, Dec., 1073-1084.

* Smaghi, Lorenzo Bini and Daniel Gros (2000), *Open Issues in European Central Banking*, London, Macmillan.

Smith, Vera C (1936), *The Rationale of Central Banking*, P S King & Son, London.

* Solomon, Elinor Harris (1997), *Virtual Money*, Oxford University Press, New York and Oxford.

Spence, M (1973), "Job Market Signalling", QJE, 87, 355-74.

Spence, M (1974), *Market Signaling*, Cambridge, Mass, Harvard University Press.

* Stiglitz, Joseph (1998), "Central Banking in a Democratic Society", *de Economist-Leiden*, Vol. 146 (2), July, 199-226.

* Stiglitz, Joseph and A Weiss (1981), "Credit Rationing in Markets with Imperfect Information", AER, June 71 (3), 393-410.

Sunderrajan, V, Arne B. Petersen, and Gabriel Sensenbrenner, eds. (1997), *Central Bank Reform in the Transition Economies*, Washington, IMF.

* Svensson, Lars E O (1997), "Inflation Forecast Targeting: Implementing and Monitoring Inflation Targets", EER 41, 1111-1146.

Svensson, Lars E O (1997), "Optimal Inflation Targets, 'Conservative' Central Banks, and Linear Inflation Contracts", *AER*, 87, 98-114.

Svensson, Lars E O (1999), "Open Economy Inflation Targetting", *JIE*, 50, 155-83.

* Svensson, Lars E O (1999), Inflation Targeting as a Monetary Policy Rule", NBER WP 6790, also JME 43, 607-54.

Svensson, Lars E O (2000),"How Should Monetary Policy Be Conducted in an Era of Price Stability?", in FRB of Kansas city, *New Challenges for Monetary Policy*, Kansas. City

* Svensson, Lars E.O., and Michael Woodford (2000), Indicator Variables for Optimal Policy, European Central Bank WP 12, February.

Taylor, John B (1989), "Monetary Policy and the Stability of Macroeconomic Relationships", *JAE*, 4, 161-178.

* Taylor, John B (1993), "Discretion Versus Policy Rules in Practice", *Carnegie-Rochester Conference Series on Public Policy*, 39, 195-214.

* Taylor, John B (1995), "The Monetary Transmission Mechanism: An Empirical Framework", JEPer 9 (4), 11-26.

Taylor, John B (1996), "How Should Monetary Policy Respond to Shocks While Maintaining Long-run Price Stability — Conceptual Issues", in *Achieving Price Stability*, Fed Res Bank of

Kansas City.

* Taylor, John B, ed. (1999), *Monetary Policy Rules*, Chicago, Univ Chicago Press.

* Walsh, Carl (1998), *Monetary Theory and Policy*, Cambridge, MIT Press.

* Walsh, Carl (1995), "Optimal Contracts for Central Bankers', AER, 85, 150-67.

White, L H (1984), *Free Banking in Britain: Theory, Experience, and Debate, 1800-1845*, Cambridge University Press, Cambridge.

Woodford, Michael (1999), Optimal Monetary Policy Inertia, NBER WP 7261, Aug.

---

* These references are recommended readings.

† This part may not include all the references given within the text of the book as some references are also given at the end of most of the chapters.

Legend : AEJ = Atlantic Economic Journal; AER = American Economic Review; BoE Qly Bul = Bank of England Quarterly Bulletin; Brookings Papers = Brookings Papers on Economic Activity; EER = European Economic Review; EI = Economic Inquiry; EJ = Economic Journal; FRB represents Federal Reserve Bank and references to NY, Rich., represent New York and Richmond; JAE = Journal of Applied Econometrics; JBF= Journal of Banking and Finance; JEL = Journal of Economic Literature; JEPer = Journal of Economic Perspectives; JET = Journal of Economic Theory; JIE = Journal of International Economics; JF = Journal of Finance; JMCB = Journal of Money, Credit and Banking; JME = Journal of Monetary Economics; JPE = Journal of Political Economy; NBER WP = National Bureau of Economic Research Working Paper; OREP = Oxford Review of Economic Policy; Rev Eco St = Review of Economic Studies; QJE = Quarterly Journal of Economics.

$\mathcal{I}ndex$

Accountability of central banks
(see transparency)

Ad hoc treasury bills **45, 71, 82-83, 217**
(also see monetised deficit)

Adverse selection **73, 87, 88, 95-97**
...and moral hazard **131, 132, 235**

Ahmed, Shagil **137**

Akerlof, G.A. **97**

Alesina, A. **217**

Alesina, A. and Lawrence Summers
217

Allen, Franklin and Douglas Gale **157**

Asako, Kazumi and Helmut Wagner
137

Asset price collapse **124, 158**

Asset quality of banks (indicator) **167**

Asian crisis **159,160, 237-246**

Auctioning **63, 78-79**
...Dutch auction **78**
...Japanese auction **78**
...Vikrey auction **79**

Bagehot, Walter **22, 44, 85, 86, 90, 213**

Balance sheet channel
(see credit channel)

Bank of England **51, 155, 213, 221**

Bank for International Settlements
155, 171, 173, 174, 226

Bank rate **115-116**

Barro, R.J. **103, 104, 137**

Barro, R.J. and David Gordon **109,
213, 214**

Basle Principles **165, 175, 176, 192-
198**

Bencivenga, Valerie and Bruce Smith
138

Bernanke, B. and Mark Gertler **132**

Bespham, J.A. **65**

B.K. Bhoi **104**

Bonds, sovereign issues abroad
(see under central bank)

Bordo, M.D. **90**

Buiter, W.H. and Anne Sibert **222**

Cagan, Phillip **41, 134**

CAMELS **166-168**

Canzoneri, Matthew **223**

Capital adequacy of banks **167**

Cash reserve ratio (CRR) **121-122**

Central bank
...accountability (see transparency
practices under monetary policy)
...advisor on debt matters **64**
...banker to bank under test **87**
...as lender of last resort **85-91**
...banker to maintain government
accounts **61-62**
...for bank restructuring **91-93**
...as domestic debt manager **62-68**
...monetary and non-monetary
functions of   **212**
...need for **21-23, 235-236**
...number at the end of the 20th
century **31-37**
...as provider of technical services
91
...relationship with currency
boards **50-51**
...for issue of sovereign bonds
abroad **74-75**

Central Bank of Sri Lanka **30**

Central banking
...centralized versus decentralized
systems   **219-221**
...interest in **23-24**
...in open/semi-open economies
24-25
...in the Indian context **27-30**
...in emerging market economies
25-27
...versus free banking school **21-22**

Chandavarkar, Anand G. **115**

Chaudhuri, Soumitra **67**

Credit channel **131-132, 139**

Credit information bureau **87-88**

Crowding out **68, 70, 80-81**

Commercial banks
...as agents of central banks **61,
93-94**
...as service providers **94**

Crisis management and crisis
prevention **182-185**
(also see New international
financial architecture)

Cukierman, A. **217**

Currency
...crisis in Mexico **88**
...demand for......in theory **41-42**
...demand for......in reality **42**
...issue by service provider **45-46**
...issue and distribution **41-43**
...principles of issue **46-47**
...printing and distribution only by
central banks **43-45**

Davis, E.P. **157**

Debt management
...by central banks **62-68**
...by a separate agency **75-77**
...conflict of interest with monetary policy **68-74**

Debt sustainability **64-65**
...in the Indian context **67-68**

Deferred net settlement (DNS) system **53-54**

Deficit financing **69-70**

Demand for money exercises for monetary targeting **134-138**

Devolvement of debt **71**

Dhal, Sarat C. **104, 106**

Discount & Finance House of India (DFHI) **29**

Discretion, the case for **110-112**

Donde, Kshitija and Mridul Saggar **106**

Dual objectives of monetary policy **104, 232**
...for performing microeconomic and strategic functions **105**
...reconciliation through a policy rule **105-108**

Dynamic inconsistency **109, 213-214** (or time inconsistency)

Earnings and profitability of banks **167** (as an indicator)

Early warning signals **160-163, 186-188**

Eichengreen, Barry **183**

Eijffinger, Sylvester (eds) **217**

Eijffinger, Sylvester and Marco Hoeberichts **142**

European Central Bank **219, 220, 221, 222**

ECB model **23**
(also see centralized versus decentralized systems under central banking)

Exchange rate channel **128-129, 139**

Exchange rate targeting **102**

Fed **62, 90, 219, 220**
(also Federal banks)

Federal Bank of St. Louis **134**

Federal Bank of New York **51**

Federal Open Market Committee **220, 223, 225**

Financial autonomy of central banks **216-217**

Financial crisis
...spill-over **160, 182**
...contagion **160, 182**

Financial development **234-235**
...and growth **138**

Financial derivatives **157-158**

Foreign exchange swaps **89-90, 119, 120**

Financial stability
...asset price collapse **158**
...in the context of financial development **155-160**
...international dimensions of, **158-160, 182, 185**

...as a result of non-compliance of laws **157**

...objective **111**

...policy regime shifts **156**

...sensitivity/stress tests **168**

...transparency **157**

Financial Stability Forum **155, 172, 173, 174**

Financial Supervisory Authority (of UK) **180**

Flavin, M.A. **65**

Friedman, Benjamin and Kenneth Kuttner **137**

Friedman, Milton **22, 107, 114**

Friedman, Milton and Anna Schwartz **90, 134, 137**

Fry, Maxwell **53**

Gale, Douglas **157**

Garfinkle, M. and S. Oh **223**

Gertler, Mark **132**

Ghosh, Atish, Anne-Marie Gulde and Holger Wolf **49**

Ghosh, Saibal **179**

Goodfriend, Marvin **223**

Goodhart, Charles **86**

Goldfeld, Stephen **136**

Gordon, David **109, 213, 214**

Government securities

...auctioning of, **63, 78-79**

...development **73, 120-121**

...devolvement of, **71**

...private placement **71-72**

Greenwood, Jeremy and Bruce Smith **138**

Group of Twenty **27, 173**

Gulde, Anne-Marie **49**

Hafer, R.W. and David Wheelock **136**

Hamilton, J.D. and M.A. Flavin **65**

Hanke, Steve **49**

Hayek, Frederic von **22**

Hedging mechanisms **160-163**

Herd behavior **156, 244**

Hoeberichts, Marco **142**

Independence of central banks (also referred to as autonomy)

...accountability, dissemination, and transparency **223-226, 234**

...definition **211-212**

...financial autonomy **216-217**

...impact on inflation and economic performance **217**

...in the context of international standards and codes **226-228**

...legislation for **215**

...measurement of **217-218**

...personnel independence **216**

...theoretical basis of **213-214**

Industrial Development Bank of India **29, 181**

Industrial Reconstruction Bank of India **29**

Insurance Regulatory and Development Authority **181**

Inflation
...bias **213-214**
...relation with growth **104**
...targeting **103, 232**
...threshold rate of **103-104**

Information asymmetry
(see adverse selection)

Information systems **235**

Illiquidity versus Insolvency **86, 161**

Interest rate channel **128**

Interest rate rule **107**

Interest rate swaps **119**

International Monetary Fund **24, 29,
30, 88, 155, 170, 171, 173, 175,
176, 177, 185, 226**

International standards and codes
...Indian initiatives **177, 201-210**
...international initiatives **169-177,
198-200**
...Nawrath Group **174**
...Report on Compliance to
Standards and Codes (RoSCs)
175-176
...self assessment **176**
...Sheng Group **174**

Intra-day liquidity **58-59. 89**

Jadhav, Narendra **136**

Joshi, Himanshu and Mridul Saggar
136

Judd, John P. and J.L. Scadding **136**

Keynes, John M **127**

Khan, Mohsin and A. Senhadji **104, 138**

King, Mervyn **104**

King, R.G. and Charles Plossner **137**

King R.G. and Ross Levine **138**

Kydland, Finn and Edward Prescott
109, 213

Laffer argument **66**

Lakshmi, R. **114**

Leeper, Eric M., Christopher Sims and
Tao Zha **137**

Lender of last resort (LoLR) **85-91**
...evidence of LoLR functioning
90-91

Levine, Ross **138**

Liquidity **72, 74, 117**
...relation with regulations and
supervision **162-163, 167**

Liquidity adjustment facility in India
118, 145-146

Liquidity forecasts **163-165**

Management soundness of banks as
an indicator **167**

Market based indicators **168**

Mason, P.R. **65**

McCallum, Bennett **107**

McKinnon, Ronald **138**

Menon, K.A. **133**

Meyer, Laurence **117**

Miron, J.A. **90**

Mishkin, Frederic **126, 137**

Monetary aggregates channel **126-128**

Money multiplier **57, 127-128, 134, 147-148**

Monetary Policy
...indicators **112-113**
...instruments **115-125**
...lags in **113-114, 140-141**
...objectives **68-69, 102-105, 232-233**
...payment system **140, 149-151**
...transmission mechanism **102, 110, 125-140, 232-233**
...transparency **141-143, 234**
...uncertainties **140-141**

Monetary Policy Committee of the Bank of England **221, 222**

Money supply and output relationship **137-138**

Money supply rule **107**

Monetary targeting **102, 127, 134, 135, 137**
...limitation of **138**

Monetised deficit (direct monetisation) **70, 71** (also see ad hoc treasury bills)

Multiple equilibria **161, 243-244**

Nachane, D.M. and R. Lakshmi **114**

Narain, Aditya and Saibal Ghosh **179**

National Bank for Agriculture and Rural Development **29, 181**

National Housing Bank **181**

New International Financial Architecture **183-185**

Nominal income targeting **102**

Oh, S. **223**

Obstfeld, Maurice **243**

Open market operations **89-90, 116-121**
...structural **117**
...fine-tuning **117**

Payment system **230-231**
...services **51-54, 91**
...and monetary policy **140, 149-151**

Persson, T. and G. Tabellini **215**

Plossner, Charles **137**

Poole, William **136**

Potential Output (output gap) **106**

Prescott, Edward **109, 213**

Private placement of securities **71-72**

Radelet, Steven and Jeffrey Sachs **245**

Rakshit, Mihir **67**

Rangarajan, C. **70**

Rasche, R.H. **134**

Real Time Gross Settlement **53-54, 58-59**

Reserve Bank of India **27, 28, 29, 82, 83, 92, 176, 181, 217**

RBI Act **27, 28, 47**

Reserve Bank of New Zealand **76, 215**

Refinancing **86-87**

Rules versus/and discretion **109-110, 233**

Repos **72, 74, 89-90, 118, 119**
(also reverse repos)

Reserve money rule **107**

Ricardian equivalence **81**

Risk management in banks **161-162, 189-191**

Rogoff, Kenneth **109**

Rogoff model **214**

Roldos, Jorge **106**

Roubini, N. and Xavier, Sala-I-Martin **138**

Rules, the case for **109**

Sachs, Jeffrey **245**

Saggar, Mridul **106, 136**

Sayers, R.S. **21**

Scadding, J.L. **136**

Schwartz, Anna **90, 134, 137**

Security and Exchange Board of India (SEBI) **181**

Seignorage **43-44, 46**

Selective credit controls **124-125**

Senhadji, A. **104, 138**

Sensitivity to market risk **168**
(indicator)

Shaw, Edward **138**

Sibert, Anne **222**

Sims, Christopher **137**

Small Industries Development Bank of India (SIDBI) **181**

Smith, Bruce **138**

Smith, Vera **22**

Spaventa, Lugi **65**

Spence, M. **97**

Solvency condition of government **65-66**

Statutory liquidity ratio **63, 67, 74, 122-124**

Stiglitz, Joseph and A. Weiss **95, 97**

Summers, Lawrence **217**

Supervision
...and regulation **165-169**
...Board for **181**
...organizational arrangements **178-182**

Swinburne, Mark and Marta Castello-Branco **212**

Systems and controls **168**

Tabellini, G. **215**

Taylor, John **107**

Taylor rule **107-108, 113**

Tinbergen-Brainard tradition **111**

Tinbergen type argument **103**

Time inconsistency
(see dynamic inconsistency)

Tobin's 'q' **130-131**

Transmission channels
(see under monetary policy)

Unit Trust of India (UTI) **29**

Vasudevan A. **136, 174**

Vasudevan, A., B.K. Bhoi and S.C.
  Dhal **104**

Vasudevan, A. and K.A. Menon **133**

Wagner, Helmut **137**

Walsh, Carl **214, 215**

Wealth effect channel **129-131**

Weiss, A. **95, 97**

Wheelock, David **136**

Winkler, Bernhard **142**

Wolf, Holger **49**

World Bank **30, 155, 171, 173, 175,
  176, 177, 185, 226**

Xavier, Sala-I-Martin **138**

Zha, Tao **137**

_____

Note: The authors' names cited in the index
are only of those which occur in the
main narrative of the book.

Recent Publications from AF include....

Planning Commission Reports on
Labour and Employment

Report of the Task Force on Employment Opportunities
Report of the Steering Committee on Labour & Employment for the 10th Five Year Plan (2002-2007)
Report of the Special Group on Targeting Ten Million Employment Opportunities per Year over the 10th Plan Period

Reports of the National Commissions on Labour
1969 · 1991 · 1967

Book + CD-ROM
Report of the National Commission on Labour : 2002
Report of the National Commission on Labour : 1967
Report of the National Commission on Rural Labour : 1991

Reports on India's Power Sector

Blueprint for Power Sector Development in India
Vision 2012 — Power for All
Distribution Policy Committee Report
Report of the Expert Group on Settlement of SEB Dues
Report of the Expert Group on Restructuring of SEBs
Electricity Bill — 2001

Corruption in India
The **Roadblock** to National Prosperity
N. Vittal

EDI 52 — Economic Developments in India

A Decade of Economic Reforms in India
The Past, The Present, The Future...

Indian Agriculture in the Changing Environment 2

3rd Edition : 2002-2003
Understanding the Problems of Indian Economy
Uma Kapila

India's **Banking and Financial Sector in the New Millennium** Volume 1

Manual of SEBI Notifications & Legislations
2002 edition
Act, Rules, Regulations, Guidelines, Schemes, Reports
CD-ROM

Manual of RBI Notifications
2002 edition
Book + CD-ROM
ECM
FEMA

Academic Foundation's Monthly Bulletin on
BANKING and FINANCE 30

Set of 2 Volumes
Financial Sector Reforms & India's Economic Development
Volume Two 2
N.A. Mujumdar

India's Economy in the 21st Century
A Collection of Select Articles
New ! 2nd Revised & Enlarged Edition : 2002

Indian Economy Since Independence
Uma Kapila
FOURTEENTH EDITION

Indian Economy Documents Library
Reports
Policy Documents
Discussion Papers
CD

...Publishing To Make A Difference !

Academic Foundation
4772-73 / 23 Bharat Ram Road (23 Ansari Road), Darya Ganj, New Delhi - 110 002. INDIA
Phones : 3245001 / 02 / 03 / 04   Fax : (011) 3245005   E-mail : academic@vsnl.com   www.academicfoundation.com

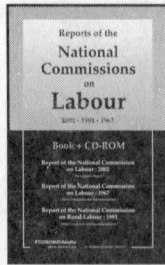

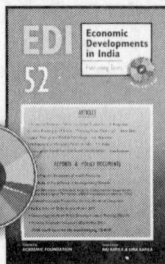

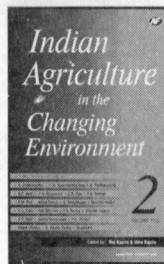

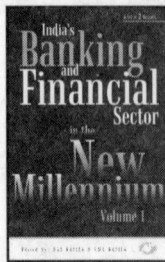

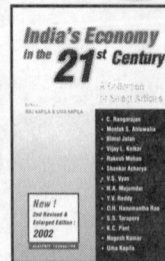